Readings in the
HISTORY OF EDUCATION

Edited by

Harry J. Siceluff

Southwest Missouri State College

McCutchan Publishing Corporation
2526 Grove Street
Berkeley, California 94704

Standard Book Number: 8211-1817-X
Library of Congress Catalog Card Number: 70-100960

PREFACE

The study of the history of education is traditionally part of the teacher's education. Sometimes it confronts the student at the outset of his professional study, but, more frequently, it serves as a kind of capstone to his education courses.

To the student, such a course may appear to be an anomaly, having no relationship to the series of "how to" courses to which he is exposed. "Why," he is likely to cry, sometimes in anguish, "must I study the history of people and events and ideas long since past? How will this make me a better teacher?" These are important questions, and they deserve careful and accurate answers.

An answer often heard is that one can neither understand the present nor predict the future without knowledge of the past. This statement is particularly relevant to the field of education, since basic educational ideas, curriculum, and methodology have developed over the centuries in a sequential manner. Much of the current controversy in education can be better understood through a knowledge of the past. For example, the turmoil brought on by recent court decisions concerning such problems as integration of public schools, transportation of parochial school pupils, practices in scripture reading and the use of required prayers, and released time for religious instruction can be avoided if the student is familiar with earlier decisions, with the attitudes of the men who framed our constitution, and with the basic ideas developed in Europe which caused these men to think as they did. Using this knowledge as a basis, the student can understand the current situation and can predict, with considerable accuracy, the direction that future decisions will take.

A second answer is that knowledge of the past is a necessity in the development of teaching as a profession. The professional teacher must be more than a highly skilled craftsman. An expert craftsman he must be indeed—skilled in the formulation of objectives, in the use of modern learning theories and teaching techniques, and in the application of new curriculum designs. His work takes on new dimensions, however, when it evolves from a knowledge of how education has taken form, of how great ideas have borne fruit in the hands of great teachers of the past, and of how certain educational patterns, developing through the centuries, shape the nature of his own work. Such knowledge is the mark of the professional.

Finally, real learning, as well as real teaching, is an exciting experience. The teacher who knows nothing of the educational past can never feel the excitement that comes from the knowledge that he stands in a long line of men and women who have devoted their lives to the welfare of mankind and particularly to the welfare of the young. The teacher who lacks such knowledge is, in fact, a mere craftsman.

This kind of excitement is rarely found by reading a typical textbook in the history of education or, for that matter, any other history textbook. Such books serve the important purpose of providing information concerning what has happened. But "whatness" provides only the bare bones of the past. These bones are clothed with flesh and blood when the student has real experience with people and events of the past.

This experience can best be achieved through the study of primary source material. It is not particularly exciting to know, for example, that the methodology of the modern elementary school evolved from the techniques developed by Pestalozzi, or that the Socratic method was one of the first attempts at inductive learning. It is exciting, however, when one reads Pestalozzi's own words as he describes his new techniques, explains their relationships to his educational goals, and recounts his struggles with the traditionalists of his own day. And who has not felt the excitement inherent in the dialogue between Socrates and young Euthydemus as the youth is forced, by Socrates' artful questioning, to think inductively?

These readings have been assembled in order to add real meaning and excitement to the plain facts of the history of education. In general, they consist of primary sources, and the few secondary sources have been chosen to serve the same purpose. As an adjunct to a typical textbook, the readings should serve to deepen and extend the student's understanding.

It should be noted that the readings encompass the history of education in the western world. The materials dealing with American education have been removed from the chronological organization and placed in a separate section. Although this section includes readings from the twentieth century, no attempt has been made to include materials dealing with modern comparative education.

H.J.S.

TABLE OF CONTENTS

THE ANCIENT WESTERN WORLD

THE RENAISSANCE AND THE REFORMATION

THE DEVELOPMENT OF REALISM AND NATIONAL EDUCATION

THE ANCIENT WESTERN WORLD

1. EARLY SPARTAN EDUCATION*

Plutarch

Plutarch (46-120) was a Boeotian Greek who spent many years in teaching and government service in Athens and Rome. He is best known for a series of short biographies of Greek and Roman leaders. The following material is taken from his Life of Lycurgus. Either a mythical or a real historical figure who lived somewhere between 900 B.C. and 600 B.C., Lycurgus is assumed to be the reformer of the constitution of Sparta, in which the Spartan military system was established. The selection gives a clear picture of Spartan education.

As for the education of youth, which he looked upon as the greatest and most glorious work of a lawgiver, he began with it at the very source, taking into consideration their conception and birth, by regulating the marriages. For he did not (as Aristotle says) desist from his attempt to bring the women under sober rules. They had, indeed, assumed great liberty and power on account of the frequent expeditions of their husbands, during which they were left sole mistresses at home, and so gained an undue deference and improper titles; but notwithstanding this he took all possible care of them. He ordered the virgins to exercise themselves in running, wrestling, and throwing quoits and darts; that their bodies being strong and vigorous, the children afterwards produced from them might be the same; and that, thus fortified by exercise, they might the better support the pangs of childbirth, and be delivered with safety.

It was not left to the father to rear what children he pleased, but he was obliged to carry the child to a place called *Lesche*, to be examined by the most ancient men of the tribe, who were assembled there. If it was strong and well proportioned, they gave orders for its education, and assigned it to one of the nine thousand shares of land; but if it was weakly and deformed, they ordered it to be thrown into the place called *Apothetae*, which is a deep cavern near the mountain Taygetus; concluding that its life could be no advantage either to itself or to the public, since nature had not given it at first any strength or goodness of constitution. . . . The Spartan children were not under tutors purchased or hired with money, nor were the parents at liberty to educate them as they pleased: but as soon as they were seven years old, Lycurgus ordered them to be enrolled in companies, where they were all kept under the same order and discipline, and had their exercises and recreations in common. He who showed the most conduct and courage amongst them, was made captain of the company. The rest kept their eyes upon him, obeyed his orders, and bore with patience the punishment he inflicted: so that their whole education was an exercise of obedience. The old men were present at their diversions, and often suggested some occasion of dispute or quarrel, that they might observe with exactness the spirit of each, and their firmness in battle.

*From *Plutarch's Lives,* extracts from the life of Lycurgus.

2

As for learning they had just what was absolutely necessary. All the rest of their education was calculated to make them subject to command, to endure labor, to fight and conquer. They added, therefore, to their discipline, as they advanced in age; cutting their hair very close, making them go barefoot, and play, for the most part, quite naked. At twelve years of age, their undergarment was taken away, and but one upper one a year allowed them. Hence they were necessarily dirty in their persons, and not indulged the great favor of baths, and oils, except on some particular days of the year. They slept in companies, on beds made of the tops of reeds, which they gathered with their own hands, without knives, and brought from the banks of the Eurotas. In winter they were permitted to add a little thistledown, as that seemed to have some warmth in it.

At this age, the most distinguished amongst them became the favorite companions of the elder; and the old men attended more constantly their places of exercise, observing their trials of strength and wit, not slightly and in a cursory manner, but as their fathers, guardians, and governors: so that there was neither time nor place, where persons were wanting to instruct and chastise them. One of the best and ablest men of the city was, moreover, appointed instructor of the youth: and he gave the command of each company to the discreetest and most spirited of those called _Irens_. An _Iren_ was one that had been two years out of the class of boys: a _Milliren_, one of the oldest lads. This _Iren_, then, a youth twenty years old, gives orders to those under his command, in their little battles; and has them to serve him at his house. He sends the oldest of them to fetch wood, and the younger to gather pot-herbs: these they steal where they can find them, either slyly getting into gardens, or else craftily and warily creeping to the common tables. But if any one be caught, he is severely flogged for negligence or want of dexterity. They steal, too, whatever victuals they possibly can, ingeniously contriving to do it when persons are asleep, or keep but indifferent watch. If they are discovered, they are punished not only with whipping, but with hunger. Indeed, their supper is but slender at all times, that, to fence against want, they may be forced to exercise their courage and address. This is the first intention of their spare diet: a subordinate one is, to make them grow tall. . . .

The boys steal with so much caution, that one of them having conveyed a young fox under his garment, suffered the creature to tear out his bowels with his teeth and claws, choosing rather to die than to be detected. Nor does this appear incredible, if we consider what their young men can endure to this day; for we have seen many of them expire under the lash at the altar of Diana Orthia.

The _Iren_, reposing himself after supper, used to order one of the boys to sing a song; to another he put some question which required a judicious answer: for example, _Who was the best man in the city?_ or, _What he thought of such an action?_ This accustomed them from their childhood to judge of the virtues, to enter into the affairs of their countrymen. For if one of them was asked, Who is a good citizen, or who an infamous one, and hesitated in his answer, he was considered a boy of slow parts, and of a soul that would not inspire to honor. The answer was likewise to have a reason assigned for it, and proof conceived in a few words. He whose account of the matter was wrong, by way of punishment, had his thumb bit by the _Iren_. The old men and magistrates often attended these little trials, to see whether the _Iren_ exercised his authority in a rational and proper manner. He was permitted, indeed, to inflict the penalties; but when the boys were gone, he was to be chastised himself, if he had punished them either with too much severity or remissness.

The adopters of favorites also shared both in the honor and disgrace of their boys: and one of them is said to have been mulcted by the magistrates, because the boy whom he had taken into his affections let some ungenerous word or cry escape him as he was fighting. This love was so honorable, and in so much esteem, that the virgins too had their lovers amongst the most virtuous matrons. A competition of affection caused no misunderstanding, but rather a mutual friendship between those that had fixed their regards upon the same youth, and a united endeavor to make him as accomplished as possible.

2. PERICLES ON ATHENIAN EDUCATION*

Thucydides

Thucydides (471-400 B.C.), a Thracian Greek, was one of the earliest Greek historians. This extract, quoted from Pericles by Thucydides, is an excellent statement of the aims of Athenian education during the Golden Age.

"If, then, we prefer to meet danger with a light heart but without laborious training, and with a courage which is gained by habit and not enforced by law, are we not greatly the gainers? Since we do not anticipate the pain, although, when the hour comes, we can be as brave as those who never allow themselves to rest; and thus, too, our city is equally admirable in peace and in war. For we are lovers of the beautiful, yet simple in our tastes, and we cultivate the mind without loss of manliness. Wealth we employ, not for talk and ostentation, but when there is real use for it. To avow poverty with us is no disgrace; the true disgrace is in doing nothing to avoid it. An Athenian citizen does not neglect the state because he takes care of his own household; and even those of us who are engaged in business have a very fair idea of politics. We alone regard a man who takes no interest in public affairs, not as a harmless, but as a useless character; and if few of us are originators, we are all sound judges of a policy. The great impediment to action is, in our opinion, not discussion, but the want of that knowledge which is gained by discussion preparatory to action. For we have a peculiar power of thinking before we act and of acting too, whereas other men are courageous from ignorance but hesitate upon reflection. And they are surely to be esteemed the bravest spirits who, having the clearest sense both of the pains and pleasures of life, do not on that account shrink from danger."

3. ATHENS AT THE PEAK OF
THE GOLDEN AGE**

A. S. Wilkins

The material below presents an excellent picture of Athens as a great cultural center during the Golden Age. Note that there were many opportunities for cultural development in addition to the schools of the period.

But above all things the Athenian of the time of Pericles was living in an atmosphere of unequalled genius and culture. He took his way past the temples where the friezes of Phidias seemed to breathe and struggle, under the shadow of the colonnades reared by the craft of Ictinus or Callicarates and glowing with the hues of Polygnotus, to the agora where, like his Aryan forefathers by the shores of the Caspian, or his Teutonic cousins in the forests of Germany, he was to take

*From the writings of Thucydides, Book II.
**From *National Education in Greece in the Fourth Century B.C.* by A. S. Wilkins, London, 1873.

his part as a free man in fixing the fortunes of his country. There he would listen, with the eagerness of one who knew that all he held most dear was trembling in the balance, to the pregnant eloquence of Pericles. Or, in later times, he would measure the sober prudence of Nicias against the boisterous turbulence of Cleon, or the daring brilliance of Alcibiades. Then, as the great Dionysia came round once more with the spring-time, and the sea was open again for traffic, and from every quarter of Hellas the strangers flocked for pleasure or business, he would take his place betimes in the theater of Dionysus, and gaze from sunrise to sunset on the successive tragedies in which Sophocles, and Euripides, and Ion of Chios, were contending for the prize of poetry. Or, at the lesser festivals, he would listen to the wonderful comedies of Euopolis, Aristophanes, or the old Cratinus, with their rollicking fun and snatches of sweetest melody, their savage attacks on personal enemies and merry jeers at well-known cowards or wantons, and, underlying all, their weighty allusions and earnest political purpose. As he passed through the market-place, or looked in at one of the wrestling schools, he may have chanced to come upon a group of men in eager conversation, or hanging with breathless interest on the words of one of their number; and he may have found himself listening to an harangue of Gorgias, or to a fragment of the unsparing dialectic of Socrates. What could books do more for a man who was receiving such an education as this? It was what the student gazed on, what he heard, what he caught by the magic of sympathy, not what he read, which was the education furnished by Athens. Not by her discipline, like Sparta and Rome, but by the unfailing charm of her gracious influence, did Athens train her children.

4. ATHENIAN EDUCATION IN THE GOLDEN AGE*

Plato

In the material below, Plato (429-348 B.C.) provides a description of Athenian education during the Golden Age. The extract is from one of the Socratic dialogues found in Plato's Protagoras.

Education and admonition commence in the first years of childhood, and last to the very end of life. Mother and nurse and father and tutor are quarrelling about the improvement of the child as soon as ever he is able to understand them: he cannot say or do anything without their setting forth to him that this is just and that is unjust; this is honourable, that is dishonourable; this is holy, that is unholy; do this and abstain from that. And if he obeys, well and good; if not, he is straightened by threats and blows, like a piece of warped wood. At a later stage they send him to teachers, and enjoin them to see to his manners even more than to his reading and music; and the teachers do as they are desired. And when the boy has learned his letters and is beginning to understand what is written, as before he understood only what was spoken, they put into his hands the works of great poets, which he reads at school; in these are contained many admonitions, and many tales, and praises, and encomia of ancient famous men, which he is required to learn by heart, in order that he may imitate or emulate them and desire to become like them. Then, again, the teachers of the lyre take similar care that their young disciple is temperate and gets into no mischief; and when they have taught him the use of the lyre, they introduce him to the poems of other excellent poets, who are the lyric poets; and these they set to music,

*From the *Protagorus* of Plato, "Teaching of Morals."

and make their harmonies and rhythms quite familiar to the children's souls, in order that they may learn to be more gentle, and harmonious, and rhythmical, and so more fitted for speech and action; for the life of man in every part has need of harmony and rhythm. Then they send them to the master of gymnastic, in order that their bodies may better minister to the virtuous mind, and that they may not be compelled through bodily weakness to play the coward in war or on any other occasion. This is what is done by those who have the means, and those who have the means are the rich; their children begin education soonest and leave off latest. When they have done with masters, the state again compels them to learn the laws, and live after the pattern which they furnish, and not after their own fancies; and just as in learning to write, the writing-master first draws lines with a style for the use of the younger beginner, and gives him the tablet and makes him follow the lines, so the city draws the laws, which were the invention of good law-givers who were of old time; these are given to the young man, in order to guide him in his conduct whether as ruler or ruled; and he who transgresses them is to be corrected, or, in other words, called to account, which is a term used not only in your country, but also in many others. Now when there is all this care about virtue private and public, why, Socrates, do you still wonder and doubt whether virtue can be taught? Cease to wonder, for the opposite would be far more surprising.

5. FAULTS OF THE SOPHISTS*

Isocrates

Isocrates (436-388 B.C.) was a Sophist who studied with Socrates, Protagoras, and Gorgias. Probably the greatest of the Greek teachers, he organized the first Athenian school of rhetoric. While he was himself a Sophist, he recognized the weaknesses of many of his colleagues. Here he criticizes these weaknesses and states his own beliefs concerning education.

If all those who undertake instruction, would speak the truth, nor make greater promises than they can perform, they would not be accused by the illiterate. Now, those who inconsiderately have dared to boast, have been the cause that those men seem to have reasoned better, who indulge their indolence, than such as study philosophy: for, first, who would not detest and despise those who pass their time in sophistic chicanery? who pretend indeed, that they seek truth, but, from the beginning of their promises, labour to speak falsities; for I think it manifest to all, that the faculty of foreknowing future things is above our nature: nay, we are so far from such prudence, that Homer, who, for his wisdom, has acquired the highest fame, has sometimes introduced gods in his poem, consulting about futurity; not that he knew the nature of their minds, but that he would show to us, that this was one of those things which are impossible for man. These men are arrived at that pitch of insolence, that they endeavor to persuade the younger, that, if they will be their disciples, they shall know what is best to be done, and thereby be made happy; and, after they have erected themselves into teachers of such sublime things, they are not ashamed to ask of them four or five minae; though, did they sell any other possession for much less than its value, they would not hesitate to grant themselves mad. But now exposing to sale all virtue and happiness (if we will believe them), they dare argue, that, as being wise men, they ought to be the preceptors of others; yet

*An oration by Isocrates.

they say indeed, that they are not indigent of money, while, to diminish its idea, they call it pitiful gold and silver; though they require a trifling gain, and only promise to make those next to immortal, who will commence their disciples. But what is the absurdest of all, is, that they are diffident of those very persons from whom they are to receive their reward, though they themselves are to teach them justice; for they make an agreement, that the money shall be deposited with those whom they never taught. Doing right in regard of their own security, but acting contrary to their own promises: for it becomes those who teach any other thing, by a cautious bargain to avoid controversy (for nothing impedes, but that those who are ingenious in other respects, may not be honest in regard of contracts); yet how can it be but absurd, that they, who pretend to teach virtue and temperance as an art, should not chiefly trust to their own disciples; for they who are just towards other men, will certainly not trespass against those, by whom they were made both good and equitable.

When therefore some of the unlearned, considering all these things, see those who profess teaching wisdom and happiness, indigent themselves of many things, requiring a small sum of their scholars, and observing contradictions in silly sentences, though they see them not in actions; professing likewise, that they know futurity, yet not capable of speaking or deliberating properly of things present; and that those are more consistent with themselves, and do more things right who follow common opinions, than those who say they are possessed of wisdom: when they see this, I say, they think such disputations mere trifles, a loss of time in idle things, and not a real improvement of the human mind.

Nor is it just to blame these men only, but those likewise who profess to teach civil science to the citizens; for they also disregard truth; and think it artful, if they draw as many as possible, by the smallness of the recompence, and the greatness of their promises, and so receive something of them: and they are so stupid, and imagine others so, that though they write orations more inaccurate than some who are unlearned speak extempore, yet they promise they will make their disciples such orators, that they shall omit nothing in the nature of things; nay, that they will teach them eloquence, like grammar; not considering the nature of each, but thinking, that on account of the excellence of their promises, they will be admired, and the study of eloquence seem of higher value; not knowing, that arts render not those famous who insolently boast of them, but those who can find out and express whatever is in them. But I would purchase willingly, at a great price, that philosophy could effect this; perhaps, then, I should not be left the farthest behind, nor have the least share of its benefits: but as the nature of the thing is not so, I would have these triflers to be silent; for I see reflections not only cast upon the faculty, but that all are accused who are conversant in the same studies. I wonder when I see those thought worthy of having scholars, who perceive not they produce a fixed art, and bound down by rules, for example of that which depends chiefly on genius. Is there any one, excepting them, who is ignorant, that, as for letters and grammar, they are unchangeable, and the same, and that we always use the same words about those things; but that the nature of eloquence is quite the contrary: for what has been said by another is not equally useful to him who speaks after; but he is the most excellent in this art, who speaks worthily indeed of his subject, but also those things which never were invented by others. The greatest difference betwixt these arts is this: it is impossible orations should be good, unless there be in them an observation of time and decorum; but there is no need of this in letters. Wherefore those who use such foreign examples, ought rather to pay than receive money, because, wanting much instruction themselves, they pretend to teach others. But if I ought not only to accuse others, but explain my own sentiments, all wise men, I believe, will agree with me, that many, studious of philosophy, have led a private life; but that some others, though they never were the scholars of sophists, were skilled both in eloquence and governing the state; for the faculty of eloquence, and all other ingenuity, is innate in men, and is the portion of such as are exercised by use and experience; though instruction renders such more knowing in art, and better qualified for life: for learning has taught them to draw, as it were from a store, what else perhaps they would but casually light on. But as for those who are of a weaker genius, it will never render them adroit pleaders, or good orators, but will make them excel themselves, and become more prudent in many things. Since I am advanced so far, I will speak more clearly of this topic; I say then, it is no difficult matter to learn those forms or orders of things, by which we know how to compose orations, if any one puts himself under the care not of such as easily vaunt themselves, but such as have the real science; but, in regard of what relates to particular things, which we must first see, and mix together, and dispose in order, and, besides, not lose opportunities, but vary the whole discourse with arguments, and conclude it in a harmonious and musical manner: these things, I say, require great care, and are the province of a manly and wise mind; and the scholar must, besides his having necessary ingenuity, perfectly instruct himself in the different kinds of orations, and be exercised in the practice: but it becomes the master to explain all these as accurately as possible, so as to omit nothing which may be taught. As for the rest, show himself such an example, that they who can imitate and express it, may be able to speak in a more beautiful and elegant manner than others. In whatever regard any thing of what I have mentioned is wanting, it must follow, that his disciples will be less perfect.

And for those sophists who have lately sprung up, and fallen into this arrogance, though numerous now, they will be forced at last to conform to my rules. Now, there remain those who were born before us, and have dared to write of arts, not to be dismissed without just reprehension; who have professed, that they would teach how we should plead under an accusation, choosing out the most odious expression of all, which their enviers ought to have done, and not they who preside over this institution; since this, as far as it can be taught, can conduce no more to the composing of law-orations than all others: yet the sophists are worse than those who grovel amidst contentions, because, while they recite such miserable orations, as did any one imitate, he must become unfit for all things, yet affirm, that virtue and temperance are taught in them; but the latter, exhorting to popular orations, and neglecting the other advantages they were possessed of, have suffered themselves to be esteemed teachers of bustling in business, and of gratifying avarice; yet they will sooner assist those who will obey the precepts of this learning, in the habit of equity than eloquence. But let no one think, that I imagine justice can be taught; for I do not think there is any such art which can teach those who are not disposed by nature, either temperance or justice; though I think the study of popular eloquence helps both to acquire and practice it. But that I may not seem to accuse other men's promises, and magnify things more than I ought, I judge I shall easily manifest to any one by the same arguments with which I have persuaded myself that these things are so.

6. THE SOCRATIC METHOD*

Xenophon

Xenophon (c.430-c.355 B.C.) was an Athenian reactionary. As a young man, he studied with Socrates, and his Memorabilia *gives us much information concerning the teaching of Socrates. The following selection gives an excellent description of the use of the Socratic method. Socrates engages in a conversation with Euthydemus, a young man who wishes to become a statesman. Note how Socrates, using questions, forces Euthydemus to clarify his own thinking.*

"Tell me, Euthydemus, have you really, as I hear, collected many of the writings of the men who are said to have been wise?" "I have indeed, Socrates," replied he, "and I am still collecting, intending to persevere until I get as many as I possibly can." "By Juno," rejoined Socrates, "I feel admiration for you, because you have not preferred acquiring treasures of silver and gold rather than of wisdom; for it is plain that you consider that silver and gold are unable to make men better, but that the thoughts of wise men enrich their possessors with virtue." Euthydemus was delighted to hear this commendation, believing that he was thought by Socrates to have sought wisdom in the right course. Socrates, observing that he was gratified with the praise, said "And in what particular art do you wish to become skilful, that you collect these writings?"

As Euthydemus continued silent, considering what reply he should make, Socrates again asked, "Do you wish to become a physician? for there are many writings of physicians." "Not I, by Jupiter," replied Euthydemus. "Do you wish to become an architect, then? for a man of knowledge is needed in that art also." "No, indeed," answered he. "Do you wish to become a good geometrician, like Theodorus?" "Nor a geometrician either," said he. "Do you wish, then, to become an astronomer?" said Socrates. As Euthydemus said "No" to this, "Do you wish, then," added Socrates, "to become a rhapsodist, for they say that you are in possession of all the poems of Homer?" "No, indeed," said he, "for I know that the rhapsodists, though eminently knowing in all the poems of Homer, are, as men, extremely foolish." "You are perhaps desirous, then," proceeded Socrates, "of attaining that talent by which men become skilled in governing states, in managing households, able to command, and qualified to benefit other men as well as themselves." "I indeed greatly desire," said he, "Socrates, to acquire that talent." "By Jupiter," returned Socrates, "you aspire to a most honorable accomplishment, and a most exalted art, for it is the art of kings, and is called the royal art. But," added he, "have you ever considered whether it is possible for a man who is not just to be eminent in that art?" "I have certainly," replied he; "and it is not possible for a man to be even a good citizen without justice." "Have you yourself, then, made yourself master of that virtue?" "I think," said he, "Socrates, that I shall be found not less just than any other man." "Are there, then, works of just men, as there are works of artisans?" "There are, doubtless," replied he. "Then," said Socrates, "as artisans are able to show their works, would not just men be able also to tell their works?" "And why should not I," asked Euthydemus, "be able to tell the works of justice; as also, indeed, those of injustice; for we may see and hear of no small number of them every day?"

"Are you willing, then," said Socrates, "that we should make a *delta* on this side, and an *alpha* on that, and then that we should put whatever seems to us to

*From *Memorabilia* by Xenophon, Book IV, Chapter II.

be a work of justice under the *delta,* and whatever seems to be a work of injustice under the *alpha?*" "If you think that we need those letters," said Euthydemus, "make them." Socrates, having made the letters as he proposed, asked, "Does falsehood then exist among mankind?" "It does, assuredly," replied he. "Under which head shall we place it?" "Under injustice, certainly." "Does deceit also exist?" "Unquestionably." "Under which head shall we place that." "Evidently under injustice." "Does mischievousness exist?" "Undoubtedly." "And the enslaving of men?" "That, too, prevails." "And shall neither of these things be placed by us under justice, Euthydemus?" "It would be strange if they should be," said he. "But," said Socrates, "if a man being chosen to lead an army, should reduce to slavery an unjust and hostile people, should we say that he committed an injustice?" "No, certainly," replied he. "Should we not rather say that he acted justly?" "Indisputably." "And if in the course of the war with them he should practice deceit?" "That also would be just," said he. "And if he should steal and carry off their property, would he not do what was just?" "Certainly," said Euthydemus; "but I thought at first that you asked these questions only with reference to our friends." "Then," said Socrates, "all that we have placed under the head of injustice, we must also place under that of justice?" "It seems so," replied Euthydemus. "Do you agree, then," continued Socrates, "that, having so placed them, we should make a new distinction, that it is just to do such things with regard to enemies, but unjust to do them with regard to friends, and that toward his friends our general should be as guileless as possible?" "By all means," replied Euthydemus. "Well, then," said Socrates, "if a general, seeing his army dispirited, should tell them, inventing a falsehood, that auxiliaries were coming, and should, by that invention, check the despondency of his troops, under which head should we place such an act of deceit?" "It appears to me," said Euthydemus, "that we must place it under justice." "And if a father, when his son requires medicine, and refuses to take it, should deceive him, and give him the medicine as ordinary food, and, by adopting such deception, should restore him to health, under which head must we place such an act of deceit?" "It appears to me that we must put it under the same head." "And if a person, when his friend was in despondency, should, through fear that he might kill himself, steal or take away his sword, or any other weapon, under which head must we place that act?" "That, assuredly, we must place under justice." "You say, then," said Socrates, "that not even toward our friends must we act on all occasions without deceit?" "We must not, indeed," said he, "for I retract what I said before, if I may be permitted to do so." "It is indeed much better that you should be permitted," said Socrates, "than that you should not place actions on the right side. But of those who deceive their friends in order to injure them (that we may not leave even this point unconsidered) which of the two is the more unjust, he who does so intentionally or he who does so involuntarily?" "Indeed, Socrates," said Euthydemus, "I no longer put confidence in the answers which I give; for all that I said before appears to me now to be quite different from what I then thought; however, let me venture to say that he who deceives intentionally is more unjust than he who deceives involuntarily." . . .

"Do you know any persons called slave-like?" "I do." "Whether for their knowledge or their ignorance?" "For their ignorance, certainly." "Is it, then, for their ignorance of working in brass that they receive this appellation?" "Not at all." "Is it for their ignorance in the art of building?" "Nor for that." "Or for their ignorance of shoemaking?" "Not on any of these accounts; for the contrary is the case, as most of those who know such trades are servile." "Is it, then, an appellation of those who are ignorant of what is honorable, and good, and just?" "It appears so to me." "It, therefore, becomes us to exert ourselves in every way to avoid being like slaves." "But, by the gods, Socrates," rejoined Euthydemus, "I firmly believed that I was pursuing that course of study by which I should, as I expected, be made fully acquainted with all that was proper to be known by a man striving after honor and virtue; but now, how dispirited must you think I feel, when I see that, with all my previous labor, I am not even able to answer about what I ought most of all to know, and am acquainted with no other course which I may pursue to become better!"

7. THE IDEAL RULER*

Plato

In The Republic, *Plato (c.428-c.348 B.C.) develops his concept of the ideal state and then describes the kind of education necessary in such a state. In Plato's system, philosophers, since they are the wisest of men, are to be the rulers of the state. In the selection below, Plato states his belief that the philosopher is the best possible ruler and then develops the necessary qualifications of such a man.*

And thus, Glaucon, after the argument has gone a weary way, the true and the false philosophers have at length appeared in view.

I do not think, he said, that the way could have been shortened.

I suppose not, I said; and yet I believe that we might have a nearer view of both of them if there were not many other questions awaiting us, which he who desires to see in what the life of the just differs from that of the unjust must consider.

And what question is next in order? he asked.

Surely, I said, there can be no doubt about that. Inasmuch as philosophers only are able to grasp the eternal and unchangeable, and those who wander in the region of the many and variable are not philosophers, I must ask you which of the two kinds should be the rulers of our State?

And how can we truly answer that question?

Ask yourself, I replied, which of the two are better able to guard the laws and institutions of our State; and let them be our guardians.

Very good.

Neither, I said, can there be any question that the guardian who is to keep anything should have eyes rather than no eyes?

There can be no question of that.

And are not those who are truly and indeed without the knowledge of the true being of each thing, and have in their souls no clear pattern, and are unable as with a painter's eye to look at the very truth and to that original to repair, and having perfect vision of the other world to order the laws about beauty, goodness, justice in this, if not already ordered, and to guard and preserve the order of them—are they not, I say, simply blind?

Assuredly, he replied, that is very much their condition.

And shall they be our guardians when there are others who, besides being their equals in experience and not inferior to them in any particular of virtue, have also the knowledge of the truth?

There can be no reason, he said, for rejecting those who have this great and pre-eminent quality, if they do not fail in any other respect.

*From Plato's *Republic*, Book VI.

Suppose then, I said, that we determine how far they can unite this and the other excellences.

By all means.

In the first place, as we began by observing, the nature of the philosopher was to be ascertained; about which, if we are agreed, then, if I am not mistaken, we shall also be agreed that such an union of qualities is possible, and that those in whom they are united, and those only, should be rulers in the State. Let us assume that philosophical minds always love knowledge of a sort which shows them the eternal nature not varying from generation and corruption.

Agreed.

And further, I said, let us admit that they are lovers of all true being; there is no part whether greater or less, or more or less honourable, which they are willing to renounce; as we said before of the lover and the man of ambition.

True.

There is another quality which they will also need if they are to be what we were saying.

What quality?

Truthfulness: they will never intentionally receive falsehood, which is their detestation, and they will love the truth.

Yes, that may be affirmed of them.

'May be,' my friend, I replied, is not the word; say rather, 'must be affirmed': for he whose nature is amorous of anything cannot help loving all that belongs or is akin to the object of his affections.

Right, he said.

And is there anything more akin to wisdom than truth?

How can there be?

Or can the same nature be a lover of wisdom and a lover of falsehood?

Never.

The true lover of learning then must from his earliest youth, as far as in him lies, desire all truth?

Assuredly.

But then again, he whose desires are strong in one direction will have them weaker in others; they will be like a stream which has been drawn off into another channel.

True.

He whose desires are drawn towards knowledge in every form will be absorbed in the pleasures of the soul, and will hardly feel bodily pleasure—I mean, if he be a true philosopher and not a sham one.

That is most certain.

Such an one is sure to be temperate and the reverse of covetous; for the motives which make another man desirous to have and to spend, are no part of his character.

Very true.

Another criterion of the philosophical nature has also to be considered.

What is that?

There should be no secret corner of meanness; for littleness is the very opposite of a soul which is ever longing after the whole of things both divine and human.

Most true, he replied.

Then how can he who has magnificence of mind and is the spectator of all time and all existence, think much of human life?

He cannot.

Or can such an one account death fearful?

No indeed.

Then the cowardly and mean nature has no part in true philosophy?

Certainly not.

Or again: can he who is harmoniously constituted, who is not covetous or mean, or a boaster, or a coward—can he, I say, ever be unjust or hard in his dealings?

Impossible.

Then you will note whether a man is just and gentle, or rude and unsociable; these are the signs which distinguish even in youth the philosophical nature from the unphilosophical.

True.

And there is another point which should be remarked.

What point?

Whether he has or has not a pleasure in learning; for no one will love that which gives him pain, and in which after much toil he makes little progress.

Certainly not.

And again, if he is forgetful and retains nothing of what he learns, will he not be an empty vessel?

That is certain.

Labouring in vain, he must end in hating himself and his fruitless occupation?

Yes.

Then the forgetful soul cannot be ranked among philosophers; a philosopher ought to have a good memory?

Certainly.

Yet again, the inharmonious and unseemly nature can only tend to disproportion?

Undoubtedly.

And do you consider truth to be akin to proportion or to disproportion?

To proportion.

Then, besides other qualities, let us seek for a well-proportioned and gracious mind, whose own nature will move spontaneously towards the true being of everything.

Certainly.

Well, and do not all these qualities go together, and are they not necessary to a soul, which is to have a full and perfect participation of being?

They are absolutely necessary, he replied.

And must not that be a blameless study which he only can pursue who has a good memory, and is quick to learn, noble, gracious, the friend of truth, justice, courage, temperance, who are his brethren?

The god of jealousy himself, he said, could find no fault with such a study.

And to these, I said, when perfected by years and education, and to these only you will entrust the State.

8. CONSTITUTIONAL REQUIREMENTS IN ATHENIAN EDUCATION*

Aristotle

The following material is taken from The Constitution of Athens *by Aristotle (384-322 B.C.). It describes the process of examination for citizenship and the period of military training and service prior to the assumption of full citizenship by the Athenian young man.*

*From *Constitution of Athens,* Aristotle.

The present state of the constitution is as follows: Citizenship is a right of children whose parents are both of them citizens. Registration as a member of a deme or township takes place when eighteen years of age are completed. Before it takes place the townsmen of the deme find a verdict on oath, firstly, whether they believe the youth to be as old as the law requires, and if the verdict is in the negative he returns to the ranks of the boys. Secondly, the jury find whether he is freeborn and legitimate. If the verdict is against him he appeals to the Heliaea, and the municipality delegate five of their body to accuse him of illegitimacy. If he is found by the jurors to have been illegally proposed for the register, the State sells him for a slave; if the judgment is given in his favor, he must be registered as one of the municipality. Those on the register are afterwards examined by the senate, and if any one is found not to be eighteen years old, a fine is imposed on the municipality by which he is registered. After approbation, they are called *epheboi,* or cadets, and the parents of all who belong to a single tribe hold a meeting and, after being sworn, choose three men of the tribe over forty years of age, whom they believe to be of stainless character and fitted for the superintendence of youth, and out of these the commons in ecclesia select one superintendent for all of each tribe, and a governor of the whole body of youths from the general body of the Athenians. These take them in charge, and after visiting with them all the temples, march down to Piraeus, where they garrison the north and south harbors, Munychia and Acte. The commons also elect two gymnastic trainers for them, and persons who teach them to fight in heavy armor, to draw the bow, to throw the javelin, and to handle artillery. Each of the ten commanders receives as pay a drachma [about twenty cents] per diem, and each of the cadets four obols [about thirteen cents]. Each commander draws the pay of the cadets of his own tribe, buys with it the necessaries of life for the whole band (for they mess together by tribes), and purveys for all their wants. The first year is spent in military exercises. The second year the commons meet in the theater and the cadets, after displaying before them their mastery in warlike evolutions, are each presented with a shield and spear, and become mounted patrols of the frontier and garrison the fortresses. They perform this service for two years, wearing the equestrian cloak and enjoying immunity from civic functions. During this period, to guard their military duties from interruption, they can be parties to no action either as defendant or plaintiff, except in suits respecting inheritances, or heiresses, or successions to hereditary priesthoods. When three years are completed they fall into the ordinary body of citizens.

9. EDUCATION OF THE ATHENIAN CITIZEN*

Aristotle

Aristotle (344-322 B.C.) was the last of the great Greek authorities on education. While he spoke of education in many of his writings, the most extended development of the subject was in his Politics, *from which the following selection is taken. Here, Aristotle states that education must be universal and that it is properly the function of the state. It should be remembered that he is speaking only of the education of an Athenian citizen.*

No one will doubt that the legislator should direct his attention above all to the education of youth, or that the neglect of education does harm to states. The citizen should be moulded to suit the form of government under which he

*From *Politics,* Aristotle.

lives. For each government has a peculiar character which originally formed and which continues to preserve it. The character of democracy creates democracy, and the character of oligarchy creates oligarchy; and always the better the character, the better the government.

Now for the exercise of any faculty or art a previous training and habituation are required; clearly therefore for the practice of virtue. And since the whole city has one end, it is manifest that education should be one and the same for all, and that it should be public, and not private,—not as at present, when every one looks after his own children separately, and gives them separate instruction of the sort which he thinks best; the training in things which are of common interest should be the same for all. Neither must we suppose that any one of the citizens belongs to himself, for they all belong to the state, and are each of them a part of the state, and the care of each part is inseparable from the care of the whole. In this particular the Lacedaemonians are to be praised, for they take the greatest pains about their children, and make education the business of the state.

That education should be regulated by law and should be an affair of state is not to be denied, but what should be the character of this public education, and how young persons should be educated, are questions which remain to be considered. For mankind are by no means agreed about the things to be taught, whether we look to virtue or the best life. Neither is it clear whether education is more concerned with intellectual or with moral virtue. The existing practice is perplexing; no one knows on what principle we should proceed—should the useful in life, or should virtue, or should the higher knowledge, be the aim of our training; all three opinions have been entertained. Again, about the means there is no agreement; for different persons, starting with different ideas about the nature of virtue, naturally disagree about the practice of it. There can be no doubt that children should be taught those useful things which are really necessary, but not all things; for occupations are divided into liberal and illiberal; and to young children should be imparted only such kinds of knowledge as will be useful to them without vulgarizing them. And any occupation, art, or science, which makes the body or soul or mind of the freeman less fit for the practice or exercise of virtue, is vulgar; wherefore we call those arts vulgar which tend to deform the body, and likewise all paid employments, for they absorb and degrade the mind. There are also some liberal arts quite proper for a freeman to acquire, but only in a certain degree, and if he attend to them too closely, in order to attain perfection in them, the same evil effects will follow. The object also which a man sets before him makes a great difference; if he does or learns anything for his own sake or for the sake of his friends, or with a view to excellence, the action will not appear illiberal; but if done for the sake of others, the very same action will be thought menial and servile. The received subjects of instruction, as I have already remarked, are partly of a liberal and partly of an illiberal character.

10. EDUCATION IN SPARTA AND ATHENS*

K. J. Freeman

Freeman, in his The Schools of Hellas, *provides a classic account of the educational practices of the Greeks. The following selection clearly indicates the differences between Spartan and Athenian education.*

The preceding chapters have sufficiently established, as it seems to me, that Hellenic education alike at Sparta and at Athens, in theory and in practice,

*From The Schools of Hellas by K. J. Freeman, London, 1907, pp. 275-79, 281-82.

aimed at producing the best possible citizen, not the best possible money-maker; it sought the good of the community, not the good of the individual. The methods and materials of education naturally differed with the conception of good citizenship held in each locality, but the ideal object was always the same.

The Spartan, with his schoolboy conception of life, believed that the whole duty of man was to be brave, to be indifferent to hardships and pain, to be a good soldier, and to be always in perfect physical condition; when his Hellenic instincts needed satisfaction, he made his military drill into a musical dance and sang songs in honour of valour. Long speaking and lengthy meditation he regarded with contempt, for he preferred deeds to words and thoughts, and the essence of a situation could always be expressed in a single sentence. This Spartan conception of citizenship fixed the aim of Spartan education. Daily hardships, endless physical training, perpetual tests of pluck and endurance, were the lot of the Spartan boy. He did not learn to read or write or count; he was trained to speak only in single words or in the shortest of sentences, for what need had a Spartan of letters or of chattering? His imagination had also to be subordinated to the national ideal: his dances, his songs, his very deities, were all military.

The Athenian's conception of the perfect citizen was much wider and much more difficult of attainment. Pluck and harmony of physical development did not satisfy him: there must be equal training of mind and imagination, without any sacrifice of bodily health. He demanded of the ideal citizen perfection of body, extensive mental activity and culture, and irreproachable taste. "We love and pursue wisdom, yet avoid bodily sloth; we love and pursue beauty, yet avoid bad taste and extravagance," proclaims Perikles in his summary of Athenian ideals. Consequently Athenian education was triple in its aims; its activities were divided between body, mind, and taste. The body of the young Athenian was symmetrically developed by the scientifically designed exercises of the palaistra. At eighteen the State imposed upon him two years of physical training at public cost. In after life he could exercise himself in the public gymnasia without any payment; there was no actual compulsion, except the perpetual imminence of military service, which, however, almost amounted to compulsion.

As to mental instruction, every boy had to learn reading, writing, arithmetic, and gain such acquaintance with the national literature as these studies involved. The other branch of primary education, playing and singing, intended to develop the musical ear and taste, was optional, but rarely neglected. The secondary education given by the Sophists, rhetors, and philosophers was only intended for the comparatively few who had wealth and leisure.

Taste and imagination were cultivated in the music and art schools, but the influences of the theater, the Akropolis, the temples and public monuments, and the dances which accompanied every festival and religious occasion, were still more potent, and were exercised upon all alike. This aesthetic aspect of education was regarded as particularly important in Hellas owing to the prevalent idea that art and music had a strong influence over character.

For the training of character was before all things the object of Hellenic education; it was this which Hellenic parents particularly demanded of the schoolmaster. So strongly did they believe that virtue could be taught, that they held the teacher responsible for any subsequent misdemeanour of his pupils. . . .

Since the main object of the schools of Hellas was to train and mould the character of the young, it would be natural to suppose that the schoolmasters and every one else who was to come into contact with the boys were chosen with immense care, special attention being given to their reputation for virtue and conduct. At Sparta this principle was certainly observed. Education was controlled by a paidonomos, selected from the citizens of the highest position and reputation, and the teaching was given, not by hired foreigners or slaves, but by the citizens themselves under his supervision. But then the teaching at Sparta dealt mostly with the manners and customs of the State, or with bodily or military exercises, known to every grown man, and the citizens had plenty of leisure. The Athenians were in a more difficult position. There were more subjects for the boy to learn, and some of them the parents might have neither the capacity nor the time to teach. Owing also to the day-school system at Athens and the peculiarities of Hellenic manners, the boys needed some one always at hand to take them to and from school and palaistra. Thus both paid teachers and attendants were needed. But it was also necessary not to let education become too expensive lest the poor should be unable to afford it. Consequently the paidagogoi came often to be the cheapest and most worthless slaves, and the schoolmasters as a class to be regarded with supreme contempt. No doubt careful parents chose excellent paidagogoi, schoolmasters, and paidotribai for their sons, and made the choice a matter of much deliberation: the teachers at the best schools were often men of position and repute. But that the class as a whole was regarded with contempt there can be little doubt. The children went into school as they would have gone into any other shop, with a sense of superiority, bringing with them their pets, leopards and cats and dogs, and playing with them during lesson-times. Idlers and loungers came into the schools and palaistrai, as they came into the market-booths, to chatter and look on, seriously interrupting the work. The schoolmasters and paidotribai at Athens were, in fact, too dependent upon their public to take a strong line, and, in spite of their power, often exercised, of inflicting corporal punishment, they seem to have been distinctly at the mercy of the pupils and their friends. The paidagogoi too, though they seem to have kept their pupils in order, were often not the right people to control a boy's conduct; they were apt to have a villainous accent, and still more villainous habits. It must be confessed that the Athenians, in their desire to make education cheap, ran a very great risk of spoiling what in their opinion was its chief object, the training of character. . . .

It was the sense of duty to the State, the resolution to promote the happiness of the whole citizen-body, which made parents willing to undergo any sacrifice in order to have their sons educated in the way which would best minister to this ideal. The bills of the masters of letters and music and of the paidotribai, and the lengthy loss of the son's services in the shop or on the farm in Attica, the break-up of family life at Sparta, must have been a sore trial to the parents and have involved many sacrifices. Yet there is no trace of grumbling. The Hellene felt that it was quite as much his duty to the State to educate her future citizens properly as it was to be ready to die in her cause, and he did both ungrudgingly. If the laws which made the teaching of letters compulsory at Athens fell into desuetude, it was only because the citizens needed no compulsion to make them do their duty. Nor had the State to pay the school bills; for every citizen, however poor, was ready to make the necessary sacrifices of personal luxuries and amusements in order to do his duty by having his children properly taught. The State only interfered to make schooling as cheap and as easy to obtain as possible.

11. OUR DEBT TO THE GREEKS*

S. H. Butcher

Our cultural and educational obligations to the Greeks are very great. Their love of freedom and knowledge, developed in a time characterized by ignorance and tyranny, has permeated all of western culture. The selection from Butcher provides a clear summary of their contributions to us.

The Greeks, before any other people of antiquity, possessed the love of knowledge for its own sake. To see things as they really are, to discern their meanings and adjust their relations, was with them an instinct and a passion. Their methods in science and philosophy might be very faulty, and their conclusions often absurd, but they had that fearlessness of intellect which is the first condition of seeing truly. Poets and philosophers alike looked with unflinching eyes on all that met them, on man and the world, on life and death. They interrogated Nature, and sought to wrest her secret from her, without misgiving and without afterthought. Greece, first smitten with the passion for truth, had the courage to put faith in reason, and in following its guidance to take no count of consequences. . . .

At the moment when Greece first comes into the main current of the world's history, we find a quickened and stirring sense of personality, and a free play of intellect and imagination. The oppressive silence with which Nature and her unexplained forces had brooded over man is broken. Not that the Greek temper is irreverent, or strips the universe of mystery. The mystery is still there and felt, and has left many undertones of sadness in the bright and heroic records of Greece; but the sense of mystery has not yet become mysticism. . . . Greek thinkers are not afraid that they may be guilty of prying into the hidden things of the gods. They hold frank companionship with thoughts that had paralysed Eastern nations into dumbness or inactivity, and in their clear gaze there is no ignoble terror. Inroads, indeed, there were at times from the East of strange gods and fanatical rites; and half-lit spaces always remained in which forms of faith or ritual, lower as well as higher than the popular creed, took shelter; but, on the whole, we are henceforth in an upper and a serener air in which man's spiritual and intellectual freedom is assured. . . .

It was the privilege of the Greeks to discover the sovereign efficacy of reason. They entered on the pursuit of knowledge with a sure and joyous instinct. Baffled and puzzled they might be, but they never grew weary of the quest. The speculative faculty which reached its height in Plato and Aristotle, was, when we make due allowance for time and circumstance, scarcely less eminent in the Ionian philosophers; and it was Ionia that gave birth to an idea, which was foreign to the East, but has become the starting-point of modern science—the idea that Nature works by fixed laws. . . . The early poet-philosophers of Ionia gave the impulse which has carried the human intellect forward across the line which separates empirical from scientific knowledge; and the Greek precocity of mind in this direction, unlike that of the Orientals, had in it the promise of uninterrupted advance in the future—of great discoveries in mathematics, geometry, experimental physics, in medicine also and physiology. . . .

Again, the Greeks set themselves to discover a rational basis for conduct. Rigorously they brought their actions to the test of reason, and that not only by the mouth of philosophers, but through their poets, historians, and orators. Thinking and doing, "the spirit of counsel and might"—clear thought and noble action—did not to the Greek mind stand opposed. . . .

Some Aspects of the Greek Genius by S. H. Butcher, London, 1891.

The East did not attempt to reconcile the claims of the state and the individual. The pliant genius of Greece first made the effort. In Greece first the idea of the public good, of the free devotion of the citizen to the state, of government in the interests of the governed, of the rights of the individual, took shape. The problem of the relation between the state and the individual was, indeed, very imperfectly solved in Greece. The demands, for instance, of the state were pitched too high, and implied a virtue almost heroic in its members. Even in Athens, where individual liberty was most regarded, certain urgent public needs were supplied mainly by the precarious method of private generosity instead of by state organisation. But though the Greeks may not have solved the political problem, they saw that there was a problem to solve, and set about it rationally; and they were the first to do so. They were gifted with a power, peculiarly Western, of delicate adjustment, of combining principles apparently opposite, of harmonising conflicting claims; they possessed a sense of measure, a flexibility, a faculty of compromise, opposed to the fatal simplicity with which Eastern politics had been stricken. Not tyranny, not anarchy, satisfied the Greek, but ordered liberty. . . .

This brief sketch may serve to indicate the qualities most distinctive of the Greek genius—the love of knowledge, the love of rational beauty, the love of freedom. In their first contact with the East—with Egypt and Assyria—during the period known as the Graeco-Phoenician period of art, the Greeks had a trying ordeal to pass through. They came out of it, as we have seen, in a characteristic fashion.

1. Their political instinct was alien to Assyrian despotism.

2. Their lay instinct rose up against Egyptian priestcraft.

3. Their instinct for beauty and reason combined rejected in both arts—in Assyrian and Egyptian alike—what was monstrous and lifeless.

4. Their instinct for knowledge, their curiosity, their cosmopolitanism, led them to adopt the foreign *technique,* and to absorb all that was fruitful in the foreigners' ideas. They borrowed from every source, but all that they borrowed they made their own. The Phoenicians, it has been said, taught the Greeks writing, but it was the Greeks who wrote. In every department the principle holds good. They stamped their genius upon each imported product, which was to them but the raw material of their art. . . . Such, briefly, is our debt to Greece. And when we speak of Greece we think first of Athens. . . .

To Greece, then, we owe the love of Science, the love of Art, the love of Freedom: not Science alone, Art alone, or Freedom alone, but these vitally correlated with one another and brought into organic union. And in this union we recognise the distinctive features of the West. The Greek genius is the European genius in its first and brightest bloom. From a vivifying contact with the Greek spirit Europe derived that new and mighty impulse which we call Progress. . . .

From Greece came that first mighty impulse whose far-off workings are felt by us to-day, and which has brought it about that progress has been accepted as the law and goal of human endeavour. Greece first took up the task of equipping man with all that fits him for civil life and promotes his secular well-being; of unfolding and expanding every inborn faculty and energy, bodily and mental; of striving restlessly after the perfection of the whole, and finding in this effort after an unattainable ideal that by which man becomes like to the gods. . . .

12. CULTURE IN ALEXANDRIA*

J. W. Draper

Hellenistic culture reached its greatest heights in the city of Alexandria, the seat of government of the Ptolemies from 304 B.C. to 30 B.C. Its cultural achievements, particularly in mathematics and science, are almost unbelievable. Draper gives a clear picture of this stimulating educational environment.

... A great state institution was founded at Alexandria. It became celebrated as the Museum. To it, as a centre, philosophers from all parts of the world converged. It is said that one time not less than fourteen thousand students were assembled there. Alexandria, in confirmation of the prophetic foresight of the great soldier who founded it, quickly became an immense metropolis, abounding in mercantile and manufacturing activity. As is ever the case with such cities, its higher classes were prodigal and dissipated, its lower only to be held in restraint by armed force. Its public amusements were such as might be expected—theatrical shows, music, horse-racing. In the solitude of such a crowd, or in the noise of such dissipation, any one could find a retreat—atheists who had been banished from Athens, devotees from the Ganges, monotheistic Jews, blasphemers from Asia Minor. . . .

The Alexandrian Museum soon assumed the character of a University. In it those great libraries were collected, the pride and boast of antiquity. Demetrius Phalareus was instructed to collect all the writings in the world. So powerfully were the exertions of himself and his successors enforced by the government that two immense libraries were procured. They contained 700,000 volumes. In this literary and scientific retreat, supported in ease and even in luxury—luxury, for allusions to sumptuous dinners have descended to our times—the philosophers spent their time in mental culture by study, or mutual improvement by debates. The king himself conferred appointments to these positions; in later times, the Roman emperors succeeded to the patronage, the government thereby binding in golden chains intellect that might otherwise have proved troublesome. . . . A botanical garden, in connection with the Museum, offered an opportunity to those who were interested in the study of the nature of plants; a zoological menagerie afforded like facilities to those interested in animals. . . . An anatomical school [was added], suitably provided with means for the dissection of the human body, this anatomical school being the basis of a medical college for the education of physicians. For the astronomers Ptolemy Euergetes placed in the Square Porch an equinoctial and a solstitial armil, the graduated limbs of these instruments being divided into degrees and sixths. There were in the observatory stone quadrants, the precursors of our mural quadrants. On the floor a meridian line was drawn for the adjustment of the instruments. There were also astrolabes and dioptras. Thus, side by side, almost in the king's palace, were noble provisions for the cultivation of exact science and for the pursuit of light literature. Under the same roof were gathered together geometers, astronomers, chemists, mechanicians, engineers. There were also poets, who ministered to the literary wants of the dissipated city—authors who could write verse, not only in correct metre, but in all kinds of fantastic forms—trees, hearts, and eggs. Here met together the literary dandy and the grim theologian. . . .

. . . The Museum made an impression upon the intellectual career of Europe so powerful and enduring that we still enjoy its results. That impression was twofold, theological and physical. The dialectical spirit and literary culture

*From *History of the Intellectual Development of Europe* by J. W. Draper, New York, 1876, Vol. I, pp. 187-92.

diffused among the Alexandrians prepared that people, beyond all others, for the reception of Christianity. . . .

But it was not alone as regards theology that Alexandria exerted a power on subsequent ages; her influence was as strongly marked in the impression it gave to science. Astronomical observatories, chemical laboratories, libraries, dissecting-houses, were not in vain. There went forth from them a spirit powerful enough to tincture all future times. Nothing like the Alexandrian Museum was ever called into existence in Greece or Rome, even in their palmiest days. It is the unique and noble memorial of the dynasty of the Ptolemies, who have thereby laid the whole human race under obligations, and vindicated their title to be regarded as a most illustrious line of kings. The Museum was, in truth, an attempt at the organization of human knowledge, both for its development and its diffusion. It was conceived and executed in a practical manner worthy of Alexander. And though, in the night through which Europe has been passing—a night full of dreams and delusions—men have not entertained a right estimate of the spirit in which that great institution was founded, and the work it accomplished, its glories being eclipsed by darker and more unworthy things, the time is approaching when its action on the course of human events will be better understood, and its influences on European civilization more clearly discerned.

Thus, then, about the beginning of the third century before Christ, in consequence of the Macedonian campaign, which had brought the Greeks into contact with the ancient civilization of Asia, a great degree of intellectual activity was manifested in Egypt. On the site of the village of Rhacotis, once held as an Egyptian post to prevent the ingress of strangers, the Macedonians erected that city which was to be the entrepot of the commerce of the East and West, and to transmit an illustrious name to the latest generations. Her long career of commercial prosperity, her commanding position as respects the material interests of the world, justified the statesmanship of her founder, and the intellectual glory which has gathered round her has given an enduring lustre to his name.

13. THE IMPORTANCE OF THE LAWS
OF THE TWELVE TABLES*

Cicero

The Laws of the Twelve Tables represent the first attempt at a legal codification by the ancient Romans. Adopted in 451 B.C. and 450 B.C., they formed the basis of Roman life for many centuries. They also were the principal materials used in the early schools in the teaching of reading and writing. Every Roman boy was required to be familiar with them. The continuing importance of the Laws is shown in the following material from Cicero (106-43 B.C.). Writing in 55 B.C., Cicero indicated the relevance of the Laws to Roman culture.

Though all the world exclaim against me, I will say what I think: that single little book of the Twelve Tables, if any one look at the fountains and sources of laws, seems to me, assuredly, to surpass the libraries of all the philosophers, both in weight of authority, and in plenitude of utility. And if our country has our love, as it ought to have in the highest degree,—our country, I say, of which the force and natural attraction is so strong, that one of the wisest of mankind preferred his Ithaca, fixed, like a little nest, among the roughest of rocks, to immortality itself,—with what affection ought we to be warmed toward such a country as ours, which, preëminently above all other countries, is the seat of

*From *De Oratore,* Cicero, Book I, Chapter XLIV.

virtue, empire, and dignity? Its spirit, customs, and discipline ought to be our first objects of study, both because our country is the parent of us all, and because as much wisdom must be thought to have been employed in framing such laws, as in establishing so vast and powerful an empire. You will receive also this pleasure and delight from the study of the law, that you will then most readily comprehend how far our ancestors excelled other nations in wisdom, if you compare our laws with those of their Lycurgus, Draco, and Solon. It is indeed incredible how undigested and almost ridiculous is all civil law, except our own; on which subject I am accustomed to say much in my daily conversation, when I am praising the wisdom of our countrymen above that of all other men, and especially of the Greeks. For these reasons have I declared, Scaevola, that the knowledge of the civil law is indispensable to those who would become accomplished orators.

14. MARCUS AURELIUS ON EDUCATION*

Marcus Aurelius

Emperor Marcus Aurelius (121-180), a Stoic philosopher, provides a good account of education given in the family. Writing at the height of the Roman Empire concerning his own childhood education, he described the practices of the earlier generations of Romans. Note the importance of the family in his description.

From my grandfather Verus [I learned] good morals and the government of my temper.

From the reputation and remembrance of my father, modesty and a manly character.

From my mother, piety and beneficence, and abstinence, not only from evil deeds, but even from evil thoughts; and further, simplicity in my way of living, far removed from the habits of the rich.

From my great-grandfather, not to have frequented public schools, and to have had good teachers at home, and to know that on such things a man should spend liberally.

From my governor, . . . I learned endurance of labour, and to want little, and to work with my own hands, and not to meddle with other people's affairs, and not to be ready to listen to slander.

From Diognetus (my tutor), not to busy myself about trifling things, and not to give credit to what was said by miracle-workers and jugglers about incantations and the driving away of daemons and such things; and not to breed quails (for fighting), nor to give myself up passionately to such things; and to endure freedom of speech; and to have become intimate with philosophy; and to have been a hearer, first of Bacchius, then of Tandasis and Marcianus; and to have written dialogues in my youth; and to have desired a plank bed and skin, and whatever else of the kind belongs to the Grecian discipline.

From Rusticus I received the impression that my character required improvement and discipline; and from him I learned not to be led astray to sophistic emulation, nor to writing on speculative matters, nor to delivering little hortatory orations, nor to showing myself off as a man who practices much discipline, or does benevolent acts in order to make a display; and to abstain from rhetoric, and poetry, and fine writing; and not to walk about in the house in my outdoor dress, nor to do other things of the kind; and to write my letters with simplicity,

*From *The Thoughts,* Marcus Aurelius Antoninus, George Long, trans., London, 1873, Chapter 1.

like the letter which Rusticus wrote from Sinuessa to my mother; and with respect to those who have offended me with words, or done me wrong, to be easily disposed to be pacified and reconciled, as soon as they have shown a readiness to be reconciled; and to read carefully, and not to be satisfied with a superficial understanding of a book; nor hastily to give my assent to those who talk overmuch; and I am indebted to him for being acquainted with the discourses of Epictetus, which he communicated to me out of his own collection.

From Apollonius I learned freedom of will and undeviating steadiness of purpose; and to look to nothing else, not even for a moment, except to reason; . . .

From Sextus, a benevolent disposition, and the example of a family governed in a fatherly manner, and the idea of living conformably to nature; . . .

From Alexander the grammarian, to refrain from fault-finding, and not in a reproachful way to chide those who uttered any barbarous or solecistic or strange-sounding expression; but dexterously to introduce the very expression which ought to have been used, and in the way of answer or giving confirmation, or joining in an inquiry about the thing itself, not about the word, or by some other fit suggestion. . . .

From my brother Severus, to love my kin, and to love truth, and to love justice; . . . and from him I received the idea of a polity in which there is the same law for all, a polity administered with regard to equal rights and equal freedom of speech, and the idea of a kingly government which respects most of all the freedom of the governed; . . .

From Maximus I learned self-government, and not to be led aside by anything; and cheerfulness in all circumstances, as well as in illness; and a just admixture in the moral character of sweetness and dignity, and to do what was set before me without complaining. . . .

In my father I observed mildness of temper, and unchangeable resolution in the things which he had determined after due deliberation; and no vainglory in those things which men call honours; and a love of labour and perseverance; and a readiness to listen to those who had anything to propose for the common weal; and undeviating firmness in giving to every man according to his deserts; and a knowledge derived from experience of the occasions for vigorous action and for remission. . . . I observed too his habit of careful inquiry in all matters of deliberation, and his persistency, and that he never stopped his investigation through being satisfied with appearances which first present themselves; and that his disposition was to keep his friends, and not to be soon tired of them, nor yet to be extravagant in his affection; and to be satisfied on all occasions, and cheerful; and to foresee things a long way off, and to provide for the smallest without display; and to check immediately popular applause and all flattery; and to be ever watchful over the things which were necessary for the administration of the empire, and to be a good manager of the expenditure, and patiently to endure the blame which he got for such conduct; and he was neither superstitious with respect to the gods, nor did he court men by gifts or by trying to please them, or by flattering the populace; but he showed sobriety in all things and firmness, and never any mean thoughts or action, nor love of novelty. . . . There was in him nothing harsh, nor implacable, nor violent, nor, as one may say, anything carried to the sweating point; but he examined all things severally, as if he had abundance of time, and without confusion, in an orderly way, vigorously and consistently. And that might be applied to him which is recorded of Socrates, that he was able both to abstain from, and to enjoy, those things which many are too weak to abstain from, and cannot enjoy without excess. But to be strong enough both to bear the one and to be sober in the other is the mark of a man who has a perfect and invincible soul, such as he showed in the illness of Maximus.

To the gods I am indebted for having good grandfathers, good parents, a good sister, good teachers, good associates, good kinsmen and friends, nearly everything good. . . .

15. RESPECT FOR EDUCATION IN THE FAMILY*

Horace

Horace (65-8 B.C.), one of the greatest of the Roman poets, lived during the Augustan Age of Rome. Although he received a sophisticated education in Athens and Rome, he recalled that the basis of his education had been given to him by his father. In his Satires, from which the material below is taken, he describes his childhood education.

And yet, if the faults and defects of my nature are moderate ones, and with their exception my life is upright (just as if one were to censure blemishes found here and there on a handsome body), if no one can truly lay to my charge avarice, meanness, or frequenting vicious haunts, if (that I may praise myself) my life is pure and innocent, and my friends love me, I owe it all to my father; he, though not rich, for his farm was a poor one, would not send me to the school of Flavius, to which the first youths of the town, the sons of the centurions, the great men there, used to go, with their bags and slates on their left arm, taking the teacher's fee on the Ides of eight months in the year; but he had the spirit to carry me, when a boy, to Rome, there to learn the liberal arts which any knight or senator would have his own sons taught. Had any one seen my dress, and the attendant servants, so far as would be observed in a populous city, he would have thought that such expense was defrayed from an old hereditary estate. He himself was ever present, a guardian incorruptible, at all my studies.

16. DISSATISFACTION WITH "MODERN" EDUCATION IN THE TIME OF TACITUS**

Tacitus

Tacitus (c.55-c.117) was a Roman historian and a prominent figure in Roman government. In this selection, he compares the old Roman educational practices with those of his own day. He clearly laments the decline of the family as an educational unit.

. . . Before I enter on the subject, let me premise a few words on the strict discipline of our ancestors, in educating and training up their children. In the first place the son of every family was the legitimate offspring of a virtuous mother. The infant, as soon as born, was not consigned to the mean dwelling of a hireling nurse, but was reared and cherished in the bosom of its mother, whose highest praise it was to take care of her household affairs, and attend to her children. It was customary likewise for each family to choose some elderly relation of approved conduct, to whose charge the children were committed. In her presence not one indecent word was uttered; nothing was done against

*From *Satires,* Horace, Book I.
**From *Dialogue Concerning Oratory,* Tacitus, chapters 28, 29, 34, 35.

propriety and good manners. The hours of study and serious employment were settled by her direction; and not only so, but even the diversions of the children were conducted with modest reserve and sanctity of manners. Thus it was that Cornelia, the mother of the Gracchi, superintended the education of her illustrious issue. It was thus that Aurelia trained up Julius Caesar; and thus Atia formed the mind of Augustus. The consequence of this regular discipline was, that the young mind, whole and sound, and unwarped by irregular passions, received the elements of the liberal arts with hearty avidity. Whatever was the peculiar bias, whether to the military art, the study of the laws, or the profession of eloquence, that engrossed the whole attention, that was imbibed thoroughly and totally.

In the present age what is our practice? The infant is committed to a Greek chambermaid, and a slave or two, chosen for the purpose, generally the worst of the whole household train, and unfit for any office of trust. From the idle tales and gross absurdities of these people, the tender and uninstructed mind is suffered to receive its earliest impressions. Throughout the house not one servant cares what he says or does in the presence of his young master; and, indeed, how should it be otherwise? since the parents themselves are so far from training their young families to virtue and modesty, that they set them the first examples of luxury and licentiousness. Thus our youth gradually acquire a confirmed habit of impudence, and a total disregard of that reverence they owe both to themselves and to others. To say truth, it seems as if a fondness for horses, actors, and gladiators, the peculiar and distinguishing folly of this our city, was impressed upon them even in the womb: and when once a passion of this contemptible sort has seized and engaged the mind, what opening is there left for the noble arts? Who talks of anything else in our houses? If we enter the schools, what other subjects of conversation do we hear among the boys? The preceptors themselves choose no other topic more frequently to entertain their hearers; for it is not by establishing a strict discipline, or by giving proofs of their genius, that this order of men gain pupils, but by fawning and flattery. Not to mention how ill instructed our youth are in the very elements of literature, sufficient pains are by no means taken in bringing them acquainted with the best authors, or in giving them a proper notion of history, together with a knowledge of men and things. The whole that seems to be considered in their education is, to find out a person for them called a rhetorician. I will presently give you some account of the introduction of this profession at Rome, and show you with what contempt it was received by our ancestors. . . .

The practice of our ancestors was agreeable to this theory. The youth who was intended for public declamation, was introduced by his father, or some near relation, with all the advantages of home discipline and a mind furnished with useful knowledge, to the most eminent orator of the time, whom thenceforth he attended upon all occasions; he listened with attention to his patron's pleadings in the tribunals of justice, and his public harangues before the people; he heard him in the warmth of argument; he noted his sudden replies; and thus, in the field of battle, if I may so express myself, he learned the first rudiments of rhetorical warfare. The advantages of this method are obvious: the young candidate gained courage, and improved his judgment; he studied in open day, amidst the heat of the conflict, where nothing weak or idle could be said with impunity; where everything absurd was instantly rebuked by the judge, exposed to ridicule by the adversary, and condemned by the whole body of advocates. In this way they imbibed at once the pure and uncorrupted streams of genuine eloquence. But though they chiefly attached themselves to one particular orator, they heard likewise all the rest of their contemporary pleaders, in many of their respective debates; and they had an opportunity of acquainting themselves with the various sentiments of the people, and of observing what pleased or disgusted them most in the several orators of the forum. Thus they were supplied with an instructor of the best and most improving kind, exhibiting, not the feigned semblance of Eloquence, but her real and lively manifestation: not a pretended, but a genuine adversary, armed in earnest for the combat; an audience, ever full and ever new, composed of foes as well as friends, and where not a single expression could fall uncensured, or unapplauded. . . .

On the other hand, our modern youth are sent to the mountebank schools of certain declaimers called rhetoricians: a set of men who made their first appearance in Rome a little before the time of Cicero. And that they were by no means approved by our ancestors plainly appears from their being enjoined, under the censorship of Crassus and Domitius, to shut up their *schools of impudence,* as Cicero expresses it. But I was going to say, our youths are sent to certain academies, where it is hard to determine whether the place, the company, or the method of instruction is most likely to infect the minds of young people, and produce a wrong turn of thought. There can be nothing to inspire respect in a place where all who enter it are of the same low degree of understanding; nor any advantage to be received from their fellow-students, where a parcel of boys and raw youths of unripe judgments harangue before each other, without the least fear or danger of criticism. And as for their exercises, they are ridiculous in their very nature. They consist of two kinds, and are either persuasive or controversial. The first, as being easier and requiring less skill, is assigned to the younger lads; the other is the task of more mature years. But, good gods! with what incredible absurdity are they composed! And this as a matter of course, for the style of the declamations must needs accord with the preposterous nature of the subjects. Thus being taught to harangue in a most pompous diction, on the rewards due to tyrannicides, on the election to be made by deflowered virgins, on the licentiousness of married women, on the ceremonies to be observed in time of pestilence, with other topics, which are daily debated in the schools, and scarce ever in the forum; when they come before the real judges . . .

17. EMPHASIS ON PUBLIC SPEAKING
IN ROMAN EDUCATION*

Cicero

By the first century B.C., the primary characteristic of higher education in Rome was the development of public speaking. Cicero (106-43 B.C.) described the attitude of Roman culture toward oratory in his De Oratore, *written in 55 B.C. Cicero was considered to be the finest orator of his day.*

. . . For when our empire over all nations was established, and after a period of peace had secured tranquillity, there was scarcely a youth ambitious of praise who did not think that he must strive, with all his endeavors, to attain the art of speaking. For a time, indeed, as being ignorant of all method, and as thinking there was no course of exercise for them, or any precepts of art, they attained what they could by the single force of genius and thought. But afterwards, having heard the Greek orators, and gained an acquaintance with Greek literature, and procured instructors, our countrymen were inflamed with an incredible passion for eloquence. The magnitude, the variety, the multitude of all

*From *De Oratore,* Cicero, Book I.

kinds of causes, excited them to such a degree, that to that learning which each had acquired by his individual study, frequent practice, which was superior to the precepts of all masters, was at once added. There were then, as there are also now, the highest inducements offered for the cultivation of this study, in regard to public favor, wealth, and dignity. The abilities of our countrymen (as we may judge from many particulars, far excelled those of the men of every other nation. For which reasons, who would not justly wonder that in the records of all ages, times, and states, so small a number of orators should be found?

But the art of eloquence is something greater, and collected from more sciences and studies, than people imagine. For who can suppose that, amid the greatest multitude of students, the utmost abundance of masters, the most eminent geniuses among men, the infinite variety of causes, the most ample rewards offered to eloquence, there is any other reason to be found for the small number of orators than the incredible magnitude and difficulty of the art? A knowledge of a vast number of things is necessary, without which volubility of words is empty and ridiculous; speech itself is to be formed, not merely by choice, but by careful construction of words; and all the emotions of the mind, which nature has given to man, must be intimately known; for all the force and art of speaking must be employed in allying or exciting the feelings of those who listen. To this must be added a certain portion of grace and wit, learning worthy of a well-bred man, and quickness and brevity in replying as well as attacking, accompanied with a refined decorum and urbanity. Besides, the whole of antiquity and a multitude of examples is to be kept in the memory; nor is the knowledge of laws in general, or of the civil law in particular, to be neglected.

18. QUINTILIAN AND THE IMPORTANCE OF PUBLIC SPEAKING*

Quintilian

Quintilian (c.35-c.95) was a Spanish-born teacher of rhetoric who lived in Rome. His Institutes of Oratory provides a complete survey of the study of rhetoric and rhetoricians. The importance of oratory in the life of the Roman citizen is apparent in the quotation below.

Preface: We are to form, then, the perfect orator, who cannot exist unless as a good man; and we require in him, therefore, not only consummate ability in speaking, but every excellence of mind. For I cannot admit that the principles of moral and honourable conduct are, as some have thought, to be left to the philosophers; since the man who can duly sustain his character as a citizen, who is qualified for the management of public and private affairs, and who can govern communities by his counsels, settle them by means of laws, and improve them by judicial enactments, can certainly be nothing else but an orator. Although I acknowledge, therefore, that I shall adopt some precepts which are contained in the writings of the philosophers, yet I shall maintain, with justice and truth, that they belong to my subject, and have a peculiar relation to the art of oratory. If we have constantly occasion to discourse of justice, fortitude, temperance, and other similar topics, so that a cause can scarce be found in which some such discussion does not occur, and if all such subjects are to be illustrated by invention and elocution, can it be doubted that, wherever power of intellect and copiousness of language are required, the art of the orator is to be there preëminently exerted? . . .

*From Institutes of Oratory, Quintilian, Preface and Book II, Chapter XVI.

Even to men, to whom speech has been denied, of how little avail is divine reason! If, therefore, we have received from the gods nothing more valuable than speech, what can we consider more deserving of cultivation and exercise? or in what can we more strongly desire to be superior to other men, than in that by which man himself is superior to other animals, especially as in no kind of exertion does labour more plentifully bring its reward? This will be so much the more evident, if we reflect from what origin, and to what extent, the art of eloquence has advanced, and how far it may still be improved. For, not to mention how beneficial it is, and how becoming in a man of virtue, to defend his friends, to direct a senate or people by his counsels, or to lead an army to whatever enterprise he may desire, is it not extremely honourable to attain, by the common understanding and words which all men use, so high a degree of esteem and glory as to appear not to speak or plead, but, as was the case with Pericles, to hurl forth lightning and thunder?

19. THE IDEAL TEACHER*

Quintilian

In his Institutes of Oratory, *Quintilian developed one of the earliest treatises on the nature of methodology and the teaching-learning act. In the selection below, he speaks of the qualifications of the teacher and of the proper relationship between teacher and student.*

As soon therefore as a boy shall have attained such proficiency in his studies, as to be able to comprehend what we have called the first precepts of the teachers of rhetoric, he must be put under the professors of that art.

Of these professors the morals must first be ascertained; a point of which I proceed to treat in this part of my work, not because I do not think that the same examination is to be made, and with the utmost care, in regard also to other teachers, (as indeed I have shown in the preceding book,) but because the very age of the pupils makes attention to the matter still more necessary. For boys are consigned to these professors when almost grown up, and continue their studies under them even after they are become men; and greater care must in consequence be adopted with regard to them, in order that the purity of the master may secure their more tender years from corruption, and his authority deter their bolder age from licentiousness. Nor is it enough that he give, in himself an example of the strictest morality, unless he regulate, also, by severity of discipline, the conduct of those who come to receive his instructions.

Let him adopt, then, above all things, the feelings of a parent towards his pupils, and consider that he succeeds to the place of those by whom the children were entrusted to him. Let him neither have vices in himself, nor tolerate them in others. Let his austerity not be stern, nor his affability too easy, lest dislike arise from the one, or contempt from the other. Let him discourse frequently on what is honourable and good, for the oftener he admonishes, the more seldom will he have to chastise. Let him not be of an angry temper, and yet not a conniver at what ought to be corrected. Let him be plain in his mode of teaching, and patient of labour, but rather diligent in exacting tasks than fond of giving them of excessive length. Let him reply readily to those who put questions to him, and question of his own accord those who do not. In commending the exercises of his pupils, let him be neither niggardly nor lavish; for the one quality begets dislike of labour, and the other self-complacency. In amending what

*From *Institutes of Oratory*, Quintilian.

requires correction, let him not be harsh, and, least of all, not reproachful; for that very circumstance, that some tutors blame as if they hated, deters many young men from their proposed course of study. Let him every day say something, and even much, which, when the pupils hear, they may carry away with them, for though he may point out to them, in their course of reading, plenty of examples for their imitation, yet *he living voice,* as it is called, feeds the mind more nutritiously, and especially the voice of the teacher, whom his pupils, if they are but rightly instructed, both love and reverence. How much more readily we imitate those whom we like can scarcely be expressed.

THE DEVELOPMENT OF CHRISTIANITY
AND THE MIDDLE AGES

20. THE EDICT OF TOLERATION*

Lactantius

Lactantius (c.260-340), a Nicomedian rhetorician, was a contemporary of Constantine the Great. A convert to Christianity, he became a tutor to the sons of Constantine. Here he writes of Galerius' Edict of Toleration, which freed the Christians from persecution and allowed them to practice their religion openly. This was to be followed, in 313, by the Edict of Milan, in which Constantine gave additional freedom to the Christians.

Among other arrangements which we are always accustomed to make for the prosperity and welfare of the Republic, we had desired formerly to bring all things into harmony with the ancient laws and public order of the Romans, and to provide that even the Christians who had left the religion of their fathers should come back to reason; since, indeed, the Christians themselves, for some reason, had followed such a caprice and had fallen into such a folly that they would not obey the institutes of antiquity, which perchance their own ancestors had first established; but at their own will and pleasure, they would thus make laws unto themselves which they should observe, and would collect various peoples in divers places in congregations. Finally, when our law had been promulgated to the effect that they should conform to the institutes of antiquity, many were subdued by the fear of danger, many even suffered death. And yet since most of them persevered in their determination, and we saw that they neither paid the reverence and awe due to the gods nor worshipped the God of the Christians, in view of our most mild clemency and the constant habit by which we are accustomed to grant indulgence to all, we thought that we ought to grant our most prompt indulgence also to these, so that they may again be Christians and may hold their conventicles, provided that they do nothing contrary to good order. But we shall tell the magistrates in another letter what they ought to do.

Wherefore, for this our indulgence, they ought to pray to their God for our safety, for that of the Republic, and for their own, that the Republic may continue uninjured on every side, and that they may be able to live securely in their homes.

This edict is published at Nicomedia on the day before the Kalends of May, in our eighth consulship and the second of Maximus.

*From *On the Death of the Persecutors*, Lactantius, chapters 34, 35.

21. CATHOLICISM PRESCRIBED IN
THE ROMAN EMPIRE*

From the *Codex Theodosianus*

The Emperor Theodosius (346-359) became a Christian in 380. Soon after, he issued the De Fide Catholica, which condemned and made subject to persecution all pagans and Arian Christians. From this point, Catholicism became, in effect, the official religion of the Roman Empire. The following selection appears in the Codex Theodosianus, *a collection of Roman laws gathered together in 480.*

We desire that all those who are under the sway of our clemency shall adhere to that religion which, according to his own testimony, coming down even to our own day, the blessed apostle Peter delivered to the Romans, namely, the doctrine which the pontiff Damasus (Bishop of Rome) and Peter, Bishop of Alexandria, a man of apostolic sanctity, accept. According to the teachings of the apostles and of the Gospel we believe in one Godhead of the Father, Son, and Holy Ghost, the blessed Trinity, alike in majesty.

We ordain that the name of Catholic Christians shall apply to all those who obey this present law. All others we judge to be mad and demented; we declare them guilty of the infamy of holding heretical doctrine; their assemblies shall not receive the name of churches. They shall first suffer the wrath of God, then the punishment in accordance with divine judgment we shall inflict.

22. EARLY CHRISTIAN EDUCATION**

A. F. Leach

The catechumenal schools of the early Christians provided necessary instruction leading to the sacrament of baptism. The students were primarily adults, since baptism frequently came late in the. life of a Christian. The following selection describes in some detail the nature of the catechumenal school.

Catechetical schools, so called, were nothing more than courses of lectures to catechumens, who, whether they were new converts or long-standing Christians, were grown-up people being prepared for baptism by catechesis, that is oral instruction, in the principles of the Christian faith. In the first three centuries of the Christian Church no one dreamt of baptizing infants. To do so would have seemed not so much profane, though it would have been that, as preposterous. Baptism was the supreme rite, the admission to the highest grade in the Christian gild, not as now the first initiation into it. Tertullian, writing in the third century on Baptism, exhorts the faithful to get over the business of marriage and founding families before they incur the awful responsibilities of baptism, a regeneration, a new birth of the soul, which was freed from all sin thereby, a "baptism of repentance." He asks, referring to the proposal made by some that children of three or four years old—no one had suggested new-born babies—should be baptized, why should the age of innocence be in a hurry to get its sins remitted? A century and a half later, when Augustine, at the age of fourteen, clamoured to be baptized, his mother told him to wait until he was older and had a deeper sense of responsibility. To be baptized was to be illuminated, and a passage in the Epistle to the Hebrews had given rise to, or perhaps rather

*From *Codex Theodosianus*.
**From *The Schools of Medieval England* by A. F. Leach, London, 1915, p. 8.

expressed, the current belief that mortal sin committed after baptism could not be forgiven. "For as touching those who once have been illuminated ... but then have fallen away it is impossible to renew them again unto repentance." The age of thirty, the traditional age at which Christ was baptized, was regarded as the normal age for baptism, but many put it off to their death-beds, and then risked being unable to receive it because through physical or mental weakness they were unable to repeat or understand the formulas.

Catechumens therefore were grown persons being informed or instructed in the mysteries of Christianity, translated by the Latin *audientes*, hearing or audience.

There are two sets of early catechetical lectures extant. The famous Didache or Teaching of the Apostles, now recognized as being a guide to catechists, is simply an exposition of the doctrines and services of the Church, a theological treatise. The Catechetical Lectures of Cyril of Alexandria, Bishop of Jerusalem, delivered in 347, are eighteen homilies or expository sermons, addressed to grown-up congregations. The title of the first is "To those to be enlightened," the *illuminandi*. The second is on the necessity for "Repentance and remission of sins," and the third expounds that "Baptism gives remission." The last thirteen go steadily through the Creed, expounding and explaining the meaning and importance of its articles. There is not a word in them to suggest that this catechist is educating the young. Chiefly he is arguing against the heathen as a missionary nowadays might in preaching to Hindoos, Brahmins, or Chinese sages.

23. THE NICENE CREED*

The Council of Nicaea, called by Constantine in 325, was attended by 225 Christian bishops. One of the results frequently attributed to the Council is the Nicene Creed, reproduced below. Most authorities believe, however, that the Creed as we know it is a revision of a statement of the Council of Nicaea which was developed at the First Council of Constantinople in 385. The Creed is still widely used in Christian liturgy.

We believe in one God, the FATHER Almighty, Maker of all things visible and invisible. And in one Lord JESUS CHRIST, the Son of God, begotten of the Father, the only-begotten; that is, of the essence of the Father, God of God, Light of Light, very God of very God, begotten, not made, being of one essence with the Father; by whom all things were made, both in heaven and on earth; who for us men, and for our salvation, came down and was incarnate and was made man; he suffered, and the third day he rose again, ascended into heaven; and he shall come to judge the living and the dead. And in the Holy Ghost. But those who say: "There was a time when he was not"; and, "He was not before he was made"; and, "He was made out of nothing," or, "He is of another substance or essence," or, "alterable"—they are condemned by the holy catholic and apostolic church.

24. PAGAN WRITINGS PROSCRIBED**

In the education of the early Christians, the works of pagan Greek and Roman writers were included. This practice was forbidden by an edict of the Fourth Council of Carthage (398). Following this edict, numerous other restrictions were prescribed. The Apostolic Constitutions, a compilation of various

*From *Canons and Creeds of the First Four Councils* by E. K. Mitchell.
**From *Great Pedagogical Essays* by F. V. N. Painter, American Book Company, 1905, pp. 151-152.

regulations adopted by the Christians before 450, states the position of the Church toward pagan writings. The loss of interest in the writings of the Greeks and Romans was to weaken Western culture until the opening of the Renaissance.

Abstain from all the heathen books. For what hast thou to do with such foreign discourses, or laws, or false prophets, which subvert the faith of the unstable? For what defect dost thou find in the law of God, that thou shouldst have recourse to those heathenish fables? For if thou hast a mind to read history, thou hast the books of the Kings; if books of wisdom or poetry, thou hast those of the Prophets, of Job, and the Proverbs, in which thou wilt find greater depth of sagacity than in all the heathen poets and sophisters, because these are the words of the Lord, the only wise God. If thou desirest something to sing, thou hast the Psalms; if the origin of things, thou hast Genesis; if laws and statutes, thou hast the glorious law of the Lord God. Do thou, therefore, utterly abstain from all strange and diabolical books. Nay, when thou readest the law, think not thyself bound to observe the additional precepts; though not all of them, yet some of them. Read those barely for the sake of history, in order to the knowledge of them, and to glorify God that he has delivered thee from such great and so many bonds. Propose to thyself to distinguish what rules were from the law of nature, and what were added afterwards, or were such additional rules as were introduced and given in the wilderness to the Israelites, after the making of the calf; for the law contains those precepts which were spoken by the Lord God before the people fell into idolatry, and made a calf like the Egyptian Apis—that is, the ten commandments. But as to those bonds which were further laid upon them after they had sinned, do not thou draw them upon thyself; for our Savior came for no other reason but that he might deliver those that were obnoxious thereto from the wrath which was reserved for them, that he might fulfil the Law and the Prophets, and that he might abrogate or change those secondary bonds which were superadded to the rest of the law. For therefore did he call to us, and say, "Come unto me, all ye that labor and are heavy laden, and I will give you rest." When, therefore, thou hast read the Law, which is agreeable to the Gospel and to the Prophets, read also the books of the Kings, that thou mayest thereby learn which of the kings were righteous, and how they were prospered by God, and how the promise of eternal life continued with them from Him; but those kings which went a-whoring from God did soon perish in their apostasy by the righteous judgment of God, and were deprived of his life, inheriting, instead of rest, eternal punishment. Wherefore by reading these books thou wilt be mightily strengthened in the faith, and edified in Christ, whose body and member thou art.

25. THE EDUCATION OF GIRLS*

St. Jerome

Saint Jerome (347-419) was one of the great leaders of the early Church. His translations became the basis for the Latin or Vulgate Bible. He was greatly interested in the education of girls and wrote various letters to Roman mothers on the subject. The material below, from one of these letters, is a definitive statement of the position of the early Church concerning the education of females.

Thus must a soul be educated which is to be a temple of God. It must learn

*From *Great Pedagogical Essays* by F. V. N. Painter, American Book Company, 1905, pp. 144-49.

to hear nothing and to say nothing but what belongs to the fear of God. It must have no understanding of unclean words, and no knowledge of the world's songs. Its tongue must be steeped while still tender in the sweetness of the Psalms. Boys with their wanton thoughts must be kept from Paula: even her maids and female attendants must be separated from worldly associates. For if they have learned some mischief they may teach more.

Get for her a set of letters made of boxwood or of ivory and called each by its proper name. Let her play with these, so that even her play may teach her something. And not only make her grasp the right order of the letters and see that she forms their names into a rhyme, but constantly disarrange their order and put the last letters in the middle and the middle ones at the beginning that she may know them all by sight as well as by sound.

Moreover, so soon as she begins to use the style upon the wax, and her hand is still faltering, either guide her soft fingers by laying your hand upon hers, or else have simple copies cut upon a tablet; so that her efforts confined within these limits may keep to the lines traced out for her and not stray outside of these. Offer prizes for good spelling and draw her onwards with little gifts such as children of her age delight in.

And let her have companions in her lessons to excite emulation in her, that she may be stimulated when she sees them praised. You must not scold her if she is slow to learn but must employ praise to excite her mind, so that she may be glad when she excels others and sorry when she is excelled by them. Above all you must take care not to make her lessons distasteful to her, lest a dislike for them conceived in childhood may continue into her maturer years. The very words which she tries bit by bit to put together and to pronounce ought not to be chance ones, but names specially fixed upon and heaped together for the purpose, those for example of the prophets or the apostles or the list of patriarchs from Adam downwards, as it is given by Matthew and Luke. In this way while her tongue will be well trained, her memory will be likewise developed.

Again, you must choose for her a master of approved years, life, and learning. A man of culture will not, I think, blush to do for a kinswoman or a high-born virgin what Aristotle did for Philip's son when, descending to the level of an usher, he consented to teach him his letters. Things must not be despised as of small account in the absence of which great results can not be achieved. The very rudiments and first beginnings of knowledge sound differently in the mouth of an educated man and of an uneducated. Accordingly you must see that the child is not led away by the silly coaxing of women to form a habit of shortening long words or of decking herself with gold and purple. Of these habits one will spoil her conversation and the other her character. She must not therefore learn as a child what afterwards she will have to unlearn.

The eloquence of the Gracchi is said to have been largely due to the way in which from their earliest years their mother spoke to them. Hortensius became an orator while still on his father's lap. Early impressions are hard to eradicate from the mind. When once wool has been dyed purple, who can restore it to its previous whiteness? An unused jar long retains the taste and smell of that with which it is first filled. Grecian history tells us that the imperious Alexander, who was lord of the whole world, could not rid himself of the tricks of manner and gait which in his childhood he had caught from his governor Leonidas. We are always ready to imitate what is evil; and faults are quickly copied where virtues appear inattainable. Paula's nurse must not be intemperate, or loose, or given to gossip. Her bearer must be respectable, and her foster-father of grave demeanor.

Let her very dress and garb remind her to Whom she is promised. Do not pierce her ears or paint her face, consecrated to Christ, with white lead or rouge. Do not hang gold or pearls about her neck or load her head with jewels, or by reddening her hair make it suggest the fires of Gehenna.

When Paula comes to be a little older and to increase like her Spouse in wisdom and stature and in favor with God and man, let her go with her parents to the temple of her true Father but let her not come out of the temple with them. Let them seek her upon the world's highway amid the crowds and the throng of their kinsfolk, and let them find her nowhere but in the shrine of the Scriptures, questioning the prophets and the apostles on the meaning of that spiritual marriage to which she is vowed. Let her imitate the retirement of Mary whom Gabriel found alone in her chamber.

And let it be her daily task to bring you the flowers which she has culled from Scripture. Let her learn by heart so many verses in the Greek, but let her be instructed in the Latin also. For, if the tender lips are not from the first shaped to this, the tongue is spoiled by a foreign accent and its native speech debased by alien elements. You must yourself be her mistress, a model on which she may form her childish conduct. Never either in you or in her father let her see what she can not imitate without sin. Remember both of you that you are the parents of a consecrated virgin, and that your example will teach her more than your precepts.

Flowers are quick to fade, and a baleful wind soon withers the violet, the lily, and the crocus. Let her never appear in public unless accompanied by you. Let her never visit a church or martyr's shrine unless with her mother. Let no young man greet her with smiles, no dandy with curled hair pay compliments to her. If our little virgin goes to keep solemn eyes and all-night vigils, let her not stir a hair's breadth from her mother's side.

She must not single out one of her maids to make her a special favorite or a confidante. What she says to one all ought to know. Let her choose for a companion not a handsome well-dressed girl, able to warble a song with liquid notes, but one pale and serious, sombrely attired and with the hue of melancholy. Let her take as her model some aged virgin of approved faith, character, and chastity, apt to instruct her by word and by example.

She ought to rise at night to recite prayers and psalms; to sing hymns in the morning; at the third, sixth, and ninth hours to take her place in the line to do battle for Christ; and, lastly, to kindle her lamp and to offer her evening sacrifice. In these occupations let her pass the day, and when night comes let it find her still engaged in them. Let reading follow prayer with her, and prayer again succeed to reading. Time will seem short when employed on tasks so many and so varied.

Let her learn, too, how to spin wool, to hold the distaff, to put the basket in her lap, to turn the spinning wheel and to shape the yarn with her thumb. Let her put away with disdain silken fabrics, Chinese fleeces, and gold brocades; the clothing which she makes for herself should keep out the cold and not expose the body which it professes to cover. Let her food be herbs and wheaten bread, with now and then one or two small fishes. And that I may not waste more time in giving precepts for the regulation of appetite, let her meals always leave her hungry and able on the moment to begin reading or chanting. I strongly disapprove—especially for those of tender years—of long and immoderate fasts in which week is added to week, and even oil and apples are forbidden as food. I have learned by experience that the ass toiling along the highway makes for an inn when it is weary.

Let her treasures be not silks or gems, but manuscripts of the Holy Scriptures; and in these let her think less of gilding, and Babylonian parchment, and arabesque patterns, than of correctness and accurate punctuation. Let her begin by learning the Psalter, and then let her gather rules of life out of the proverbs of Solomon. From the Preacher let her gain the habit of despising the world and its vanities. Let her follow the example set in Job of virtue and patience. Then let her pass on to the Gospels, never to be laid aside when once they have been taken in hand. Let her also drink in with a willing heart the Acts of the Apostles and the Epistles. As soon as she has enriched the storehouse of her mind with these treasures, let her commit to memory the prophets, the heptateuch, the books of Kings and of Chronicles, the rolls also of Ezra and Esther. When she has done all these she may safely read the Song of Songs, but not before: for, were she to read it at the beginning, she would fail to perceive that, though it is written in fleshly words, it is a marriage song of a spiritual bridal. And not understanding this she would suffer hurt from it. Cyprian's writings let her have always in her hands. The letters of Athanasius and the treatises of Hilary she may go through without fear of stumbling. Let her take pleasure in the works and wits of all in whose books a due regard for the faith is not neglected. But if she reads the works of others, let it be rather to judge them than to follow them.

You will answer, "How shall I, a woman of the world, living at Rome, surrounded by a crowd, be able to observe all these injunctions?" In that case do not undertake a burthen to which you are not equal. When you have weaned Paula as Isaac was weaned, and when you have clothed her as Samuel was clothed, send her to her grandmother and aunt; give up this most precious of gems, to be placed in Mary's chamber and to rest in the cradle where the infant Jesus cried. Let her be brought up in a monastery, let her be one amid companies of virgins, let her learn to avoid swearing, let her regard lying as sacrilege, let her be ignorant of the world, let her live the angelic life, while in the flesh let her be without the flesh, and let her suppose that all human beings are like herself.

26. USE OF THE SEVEN LIBERAL ARTS*

Rhabanus Maurus

Although the seven liberal arts were pagan in origin, they became the basis for theological education in medieval times. It was necessary that these studies be turned to theological purposes. In the selection below, Rhabanus Maurus (784-856), who was a student of Alcuin and later became the Bishop of Fulda, explains in detail how the materials in the seven liberal arts are to be used for religious education.

The first of the liberal arts is Grammar, the second Rhetoric, the third Dialectic, the fourth Arithmetic, the fifth Geometry, the sixth Music, the seventh Astronomy.

Grammar. Grammar takes its name from the written character, as the derivation of the word indicates. The definition of grammar is this: Grammar is the science which teaches us to explain the poets and historians; it is the art

*From *Education of the Clergy,* Rhabanus Maurus, F. V. N. Painter, trans.

which qualifies us to write and speak correctly. Grammar is the source and foundation of the liberal arts. It should be taught in every Christian school, since the art of writing and speaking correctly is attained through it. How could one understand the sense of the spoken word or the meaning of letters and syllables, if one had not learned this before from grammar? How could one know about metrical feet, accent, and verses, if grammar had not given one knowledge of them? How should one learn to know the articulation of discourse, the advantages of figurative language, the laws of word formation, and the correct forms of words, if one had not familiarized himself with the art of grammar?

All the forms of speech, of which secular science makes use in its writings, are found repeatedly employed in the Holy Scriptures. Every one, who reads the sacred Scriptures with care, will discover that our (biblical) authors have used derivative forms of speech in greater and more manifold abundance than would have been supposed and believed. There are in the Scriptures not only examples of all kinds of figurative expressions, but the designations of some of them by name; as allegory, riddle, parable. A knowledge of these things is proved to be necessary in relation to the interpretation of those passages of Holy Scripture which admit of a two-fold sense; an interpretation strictly literal would lead to absurdities. Everywhere we are to consider whether that, which we do not at once understand, is to be apprehended as a figurative expression in some sense. A knowledge of prosody, which is offered in grammar, is not dishonorable, since among the Jews, as Saint Jerome testifies, the Psalter resounds sometimes with iambics, sometimes with Alcaics, sometimes chooses sonorous Sapphics, and sometimes even does not disdain catalectic feet. But in Deuteronomy and Isaiah, as in Solomon and Job, as Josephus and Origen have pointed out, there are hexameters and pentameters. Hence this art, though it may be secular, has nothing unworthy in itself; it should rather be learned as thoroughly as possible.

Rhetoric. According to the statements of teachers, rhetoric is the art of using secular discourse effectively in the circumstances of daily life. From this definition rhetoric seems indeed to have reference merely to secular wisdom. Yet it is not foreign to ecclesiastical instruction. Whatever the preacher and herald of the divine law, in his instruction, brings forth in an eloquent and becoming manner; whatever in his written exposition he knows how to clothe in adequate and impressive language, he owes to his acquaintance with this art. Whoever at the proper time makes himself familiar with this art, and faithfully follows its rules in speaking and writing, needs not count it as something blameworthy. On the contrary, whoever thoroughly learns it so that he acquires the ability to proclaim God's word, performs a true work. Through rhetoric anything is proved true or false. Who would have the courage to maintain that the defenders of truth should stand weaponless in the presence of falsehood, so that those, who dare to represent false, should know how by their discourse to win the favor and sympathy of the hearers, and that, on the other hand, the friends of truth should not be able to do this; that those should know how to present falsehood briefly, clearly, and with the semblance of truth, and that the latter, on the contrary, should clothe the truth in such an exposition, that listening would become a burden, apprehension of the truth a weariness, and faith in the truth an impossibility?

Dialectic. Dialectic is the science of the understanding, which fits us for investigations and definitions, for explanations, and for distinguishing the true from the false. It is the science of sciences. It teaches how to teach others; it teaches learning itself; in it the reason marks and manifests itself according to its nature, efforts, and activities; it alone is capable of knowing; it not only will, but can lead others to knowledge; its conclusions lead us to an apprehension of our being and of our origin; through it we apprehend the origin and activity of the good, of Creator and creature; it teaches us to discover the truth and to unmask falsehood; it teaches us to draw conclusions; it shows us what is valid in argument and what is not; it teaches us to recognize what is contrary to the nature of things; it teaches us to distinguish in controversy the true, the probable, and the wholly false; by means of this science we are able to investigate everything with penetration, to determine its nature with certainty, and to discuss it with circumspection.

Therefore the clergy must understand this excellent art and constantly reflect upon its laws, in order that they may be able keenly to pierce the craftiness of errorists, and to refute their fatal fallacies.

Arithmetic. Arithmetic is the science of pure extension determinable by number; it is the science of numbers. Writers on secular science assign it, under the head of mathematics, to the first place, because it does not presuppose any of the other departments. Music, geometry, and astronomy, on the contrary, need the help of arithmetic; without it they cannot arise or exist. We should know, however, that the learned Hebrew Josephus, in his work on Antiquities, Chapter VIII of Book I, makes the statement that Abraham brought arithmetic and astronomy to the Egyptians; but that they as a people of penetrating mind, extensively developed from these germs the other sciences. The holy Fathers were right in advising those eager for knowledge to cultivate arithmetic, because in large measure it turns the mind from fleshly desires, and furthermore awakens the wish to comprehend what with God's help we can merely receive with the heart. Therefore the significance of number is not to be underestimated. Its very great value for an interpretation of many passages of Holy Scripture is manifest to all who exhibit zeal in their investigations. Not without good reason is it said in praise of God, "Thou hast ordained all things by measure, number, and weight." (Book of Wisdom XI, 21.)

But every number, through its peculiar qualities, is so definite that none of the others can be like it. They are all unequal and different. The single numbers are different; the single numbers are limited; but all are infinite.

Those with whom Plato stands in especial honor will not make bold to esteem numbers lightly, as if they were of no consequence for the knowledge of God. He teaches that God made the world out of numbers. And among us the prophet says of God, "He forms the world by number." And in the Gospel the Savior says, "The very hairs of your head are all numbered." . . . Ignorance of numbers leaves many things unintelligible that are expressed in the Holy Scripture in a derivative sense or with a mystical meaning.

Geometry. We now come to the discussion of geometry. It is an exposition of form proceeding from observation; it is also a very common means of demonstration among philosophers, who, to adduce at once the most full-toned evidence, declare that their Jupiter made use of astronomy in his works. I do not know indeed whether I should find praise or censure in this declaration of the philosophers, that Jupiter engraved upon the vault of the skies precisely what they themselves draw in the sand of the earth.

When this in a proper manner is transferred to God, the Almighty Creator, this assumption may perhaps come near the truth. If this statement seems admissible, the Holy Trinity makes use of geometry in so far as it bestows manifold forms and images upon the creatures which up to the present day it has called into being, as in its adorable omnipotence it further determines the course of the stars, as it prescribes their courses to the planets, and as it assigns to the fixed stars their unalterable position. For every excellent and well-ordered arrangement can be reduced to the special requirements of this science. . . .

This science found realization also at the building of the tabernacle and the temple; the same measuring rod, circles, spheres, hemispheres, quadrangles, and other figures were employed. The knowledge of all this brings to him, who is occupied with it, no small gain for his spiritual culture.

Music. Music is the science of time intervals as they are perceived in tones. This science is as eminent as it is useful. He who is a stranger to it is not able to fulfil the duties of an ecclesiastical officer in a suitable manner. A proper delivery in reading and a lovely rendering of the Psalms in the church are regulated by a knowledge of this science. Yet it is not only good reading and beautiful psalmody that we owe to music; through it alone do we become capable of celebrating in the most solemn manner every divine service. Music penetrates all the activities of our life, in this sense namely, that we above all carry out the commands of the Creator and bow with a pure heart to his commands; all that we speak, all that makes our hearts beat faster, is shown through the rhythm of music united with the excellence of harmony; for music is the science which teaches us agreeably to change tones in duration and pitch. When we employ ourselves with good pursuits in life, we show ourselves thereby disciples of this art; so long as we do what is wrong, we do not feel ourselves drawn to music. Even heaven and earth, as everything that happens here through the arrangement of the Most High, is nothing but music, as Pythagoras testifies that this world was created by music and can be ruled by it. Even with the Christian religion music is most intimately united; thus it is possible that to him, who does not know even a little music, many things remain closed and hidden.

Astronomy. There remains yet astronomy which, as some one has said, is a weighty means of demonstration to the pious, and to the curious a grievous torment. If we seek to investigate it with a pure heart and an ample mind, then it fills us, as the ancients said, with great love for it. For what will it not signify, that we soar in spirit to the sky, that with penetration of mind we analyze that sublime structure, that we, in part at least, fathom with the keenness of our logical faculties what mighty space has enveloped in mystery! The world itself, according to the assumption of some, is said to have the shape of a sphere, in order that in its circumference it may be able to contain the different forms of things. Thus Seneca, in agreement with the philosophers of ancient times, composed a work under the title, "The Shape of the Earth."

Astronomy, of which we now speak, teaches the laws of the stellar world. The stars can take their place or carry out their motion only in the manner established by the Creator, unless by the will of the Creator a miraculous change takes place. Thus we read that Joshua commanded the sun to stand still in Gibeon, that in the days of King Josiah the sun went backward ten degrees, and that at the death of the Lord the sun was darkened for three hours. We call such occurrences miracles, because they contradict the usual course of things, and therefore excite wonder.

That part of astronomy, which is built up on the investigation of natural phenomena in order to determine the course of the sun, of the moon, and stars, and to effect a proper reckoning of time, the Christian clergy should seek to learn with the utmost diligence, in order through the knowledge of laws brought to light and through the valid and convincing proof of the given means of evidence, to place themselves in a position, not only to determine the course of past years according to truth and reality, but also for further times to draw confident conclusions, and to fix the time of Easter and all other festivals and holy days and to announce to the congregation the proper celebration of them.

The seven liberal arts of the philosophers, which Christians should learn for their utility and advantage, we have, as I think, sufficiently discussed. We have this yet to add. When those, who are called philosophers, have in their expositions or in their writings, uttered perchance some truth, which agrees with our faith, we should not handle it timidly, but rather take it as from its unlawful possessors and apply it to our own use.

27. THE BENEDICTINE "RULE"*

Monasticism, much older than Christianity, was practiced by the early Christians. However, the medieval interest in monasticism dates from the founding in 529 of the monastery of Monte Casino in Italy by Saint Benedict. The famous "Rule" of the Benedictines was to serve as a pattern for the later medieval monastic orders.

Prologue.... we are about to found, therefore, a school for the Lord's service; in the organization of which we trust that we shall ordain nothing severe and nothing burdensome. But even if, the demands of justice dictating it, something a little irksome shall be the result, for the purpose of amending vices or preserving charity;—thou shalt not therefore, struck by fear, flee the way of salvation, which can not be entered upon except through a narrow entrance.

Concerning the weekly reader. At the tables of the brothers when they eat the reading should not fail; nor may any one at random dare to take up the book and begin to read there; but he who is about to read for the whole week shall begin his duties on Sunday. And, entering upon his office after mass and communion, he shall ask all to pray for him, that God may avert from him the spirit of elation. And this verse shall be said in the oratory three times by all, he, however, beginning it: "O Lord, open thou my lips and my mouth shall show forth thy praise." And thus, having received the benediction, he shall enter upon his duties as reader. And there shall be the greatest silence at table, so that the muttering or the voice of no one shall be heard there, except that of the reader alone. But whatever things are necessary to those eating and drinking, the brothers shall so furnish them to each other in turn, that no one shall need to ask for anything. But if, nevertheless, something is wanted, it shall rather be sought by the employment of some sign than by the voice. Nor shall any one presume there to ask questions concerning the reading or anything else; nor shall an opportunity be given: unless perhaps the prior wishes to say something, briefly, for the purpose of edifying. Moreover, the brother who reads for the week shall receive bread and wine before he begins to read, on account of the holy communion, and lest, perchance, it might be injurious for him to sustain a fast. Afterwards, moreover, he shall eat with the weekly cooks and servitors. The brothers, moreover, shall read or sing not in rotation; but the ones shall do so who will edify *their* hearers....

That after "completorium" no one shall speak. At all times the monks ought to practice silence, but most of all in the nocturnal hours. And thus at all times, whether of fasting or of eating: if it be mealtime, as soon as they have risen from the table, all shall sit together and one shall read selections or lives of the Fathers, or indeed anything that will edify the hearers. But not the Pentateuch or Kings; for, to weak intellects, it will be of no use at that hour to hear this part of Scripture; but they shall be read at other times. But if the days are fast days, when Vespers have been said, after a short interval they shall come to the reading of the selections as we have said; and four or five pages, or as much as

*From St. Benedict's "Rule," translation from E. F. Henderson's *Historical Documents of the Middle Ages,* London, 1896.

the hour permits having been read, they shall all congregate, upon the cessation
of the reading. If, by chance, any one is occupied in a task assigned to him, he
shall nevertheless approach. All therefore being gathered together, they shall say
the completing prayer; and, going out from the "completorium," there shall be
no further opportunity for any one to say anything. . . .

Concerning the daily manual labour. Idleness is the enemy of the soul. And
therefore, at fixed times, the brothers ought to be occupied in manual labour;
and again, at fixed times, in sacred reading. Therefore we believe that, according
to this disposition, both seasons ought to be arranged; so that, from Easter until
the Calends of October, going out early, from the first until the fourth hour they
shall do what labour may be necessary. Moreover, from the fourth hour until
about the sixth, they shall be free for reading. After the meal of the sixth hour,
moreover, rising from table, they shall rest in their beds with all silence; or,
perchance, he that wishes to read may so read to himself that he do not disturb
another. And the nona (the second meal) shall be gone through with more
moderately about the middle of the eighth hour; and again they shall work at
what is to be done until Vespers. But, if the exigency or poverty of the place
demands that they be occupied by themselves in picking fruits, they shall not be
dismayed: for then they are truly monks if they live by the labours of their
hands; as did also our fathers and the apostles. Let all things be done with
moderation, however, on account of the faint-hearted. From the Calends of
October, moreover, until the beginning of Lent they shall be free for reading
until the second full hour. At the second hour the tertia (morning service) shall
be held, and all shall labour at the task which is enjoined upon them until the
ninth. The first signal, moreover, of the ninth hour having been given, they shall
each one leave off his work; and be ready when the second signal strikes.
Moreover, after the refection they shall be free for their readings or for psalms.
But in the days of Lent, from dawn until the third full hour, they shall be free
for their readings; and, until the tenth full hour, they shall do the labour that is
enjoined on them. In which days of Lent they shall all receive separate books
from the library; which they shall read entirely through in order. These books
are to be given out on the first day of Lent. Above all there shall certainly be
appointed one or two elders, who shall go round the monastery at the hours in
which the brothers are engaged in reading, and see to it that no troublesome
brother chance to be found who is open to idleness and trifling, and is not intent
on his reading; being not only of no use to himself, but also stirring up others. If
such a one—may it not happen—be found, he shall be admonished once and a
second time. If he do not amend, he shall be subject under the Rule to such
punishment that the others may have fear. Nor shall brother join brother at
unsuitable hours. Moreover, on Sunday all shall engage in reading: excepting
those who are deputed to various duties. But if any one be so negligent and lazy
that he will not or can not read, some task shall be imposed upon him that he
can do; so that he be not idle. On feeble or delicate brothers such a labour or art
is to be imposed, that they shall neither be idle, nor shall they be so oppressed
by the violence of labour as to be driven to take flight. Their weakness is to be
taken into consideration by the abbot.

28. ALCUIN'S SCHOOL AT YORK*

Alcuin

The cathedral school at York, England, was one of the early medieval

*From *On the Saints of the Church at York,* Alcuin, James Rai, trans.

schools. Alcuin (735-804) was educated at York and was later master of the school. In 781 he left York to set up Charlemagne's Palace School. The following description of the work of the school at York, stated in somewhat extravagant form, gives much information concerning the curriculum.

Bide with me for a while, I pray ye, youth of York, while I proceed with poetic steps to treat of him, because here he often drenched your senses with nectar, pouring forth sweet juices from his honey-flowing bosom. Fairest Philosophy took him from his very cradle and bore him to the topmost towers of learning, opening to him the hidden things of wisdom. He was born of ancestors of sufficient note, by whose care he was soon sent to kindly school, and entered at the Minister in his early years, that his tender age might grow up with holy understanding. Nor was his parents' hope in vain; even as a boy as he grew in body so he became proficient in the understanding of books.

Then pious and wise, teacher at once and priest, he was made a colleague of Bishop Egbert, to whom he was nearly allied by right of blood. By him he is made advocate of the clergy, and at the same time is preferred as master in the city of York.

There he moistened thirsty hearts with diverse streams of teaching and the varied dews of learning, giving to these the art of the science of grammar, pouring on those the rivers of rhetoric. Some he polished on the whetstone of law, some he taught to sing together in Aeonian chant, making others play on the flute of Castaly, and run with the feet of lyric poets over the hills of Parnassus. Others the said master made to know the harmony of heaven, the labours of sun and moon, the five belts of the sky, the seven planets, the laws of the fixed stars, their rising and setting, the movements of the air, the quaking of sea and earth, the nature of men, cattle, birds and beasts, the divers kinds of numbers and various shapes. He gave certainty to the solemnity of Easter's return; above all, opening the mysteries of holy writ and disclosing the abysses of the rude and ancient law. Whatever youths he saw of conspicuous intelligence, those he joined to himself, he taught, he fed, he loved; and so the teacher had many disciples in the sacred volumes, advanced in various arts. Soon he went in triumph abroad, led by the love of wisdom, to see if he could find in other lands anything novel in books or schools; which he could bring home with him. He went also devoutly to the city of Romulus, rich in God's love, wandering far and wide through the holy places. Then returning home, he was received everywhere by kings and princes as a prince of doctors, whom great kings tried to keep that he might irrigate their lands with learning. But the master hurrying to his appointed work, returned home to his fatherland by God's ordinance. For no sooner had he been borne to his own shores, than he was compelled to take on him the pastoral care, and made high priest at the people's demand. . . .

29. INSTRUCTION IN THE PALACE SCHOOL*

Alcuin

Alcuin spent many years as a tutor to Charlemagne's sons and as the head of the Palace School. The material below provides a good example of the type of instruction carried on. Note the catechetical nature of the material. It is similar, at least in form, to many modern catechetical formulations.

*From Disputations of Pepin, the Most Noble and Royal Youth, with Albinus the Scholastic, Alcuin.

1. General questions and answers.

P. What is writing?   A. The custodian of history.

P. What is speech?   A. The interpreter of the soul.

P. What produces speech?   A. The tongue.

P. What is the tongue?   A. The whip of the air.

P. What is air?   A. The guardian of life.

P. What is life?   A. The joy of the good, the sorrow of the evil, the expectation of death.

P. What is death?   A. An inevitable event, an uncertain journey, a subject of weeping to the living, the fulfilment of wills, the thief of men.

P. What is man?   A. The slave of death, a transient traveller, a host in his dwelling.

P. What is man like?   A. Like a fruit-tree.

P. How is man placed?   A. Like a lantern exposed to the wind.

P. Where is he placed?   A. Between six walls.

P. Which are they?   A. Above, below; before, behind; right, left.

P. To how many changes is he liable?   A. To six.

P. Which are they?   A. Hunger and satiety; rest and work; waking and sleeping.

P. What is sleep?   A. The image of death.

P. What is the liberty of man?   A. Innocence.

P. What is the head?   A. The top of the body.

P. What is the body?   A. The domicile of the soul.

2. Questions of a scientific nature.

P. What is the sun?   A. The splendor of the universe, the beauty of the sky, the glory of day, the distributor of the hours.

P. What is the moon?   A. The eye of night, the dispenser of dew, the prophet of storms.

P. What are the stars?   A. The pictures of the roof of the heavens, the guides of sailors, the ornament of night.

P. What is rain?   A. The reservoir of the earth, the mother of the fruits.

P. What is fog?   A. Night in day, a labor of the eyes.

P. What is wind?   A. The disturbance of the air, the commotion of the waters, the dryness of the earth.

P. What is frost?   A. A persecutor of plants, a destroyer of leaves, a fetter of the earth.

P. What is autumn?   A. The barn of the year.

30. IMPROVEMENT OF MONASTIC EDUCATION*

Charlemagne

Charlemagne's interest in education was much greater than that of other rulers of his time. Disturbed by the illiteracy in the monasteries, he issued, in 787, proclamations to the various abbots in his jurisdiction, urging them to improve education. The following proclamation was sent to Baugulf, Abbot of Fulda.

The Proclamation of 787 A.D.

Charles, by the grace of God, King of the Franks and Lombards and Patrician of the Romans, to Abbot Baugulf and to all the congregation, also the faithful committed to you, we have directed a loving greeting by our ambassadors in the name of omnipotent God.

Be it known, therefore, to your devotion pleasing to God, that we, together with our faithful, have considered it to be useful that the bishoprics and monasteries entrusted by the favor of Christ to our control, in addition to the order of monastic life and the intercourse of holy religion, in the culture of letters also ought to be zealous in teaching those who by the gift of God are able to learn, according to the capacity of each individual, so that just as the observance of the rule imparts order and grace to honesty of morals, so also zeal in teaching and learning may do the same for sentences, so that those who desire to please God by living rightly should not neglect to please him also by speaking correctly. For it is written: "Either from thy words thou shalt be justified or from thy words thou shalt be condemned." (Matthew, xii, 37.) For although correct conduct may be better than knowledge, nevertheless knowledge precedes conduct. Therefore, each one ought to study what he desires to accomplish, so that so much the more fully the mind may know what ought to be done, as the tongue hastens in the praises of omnipotent God without the hindrances of errors. For since errors should be shunned by all men, so much the more ought they to be avoided as far as possible by those who are chosen for this very purpose alone, so that they ought to be the especial servants of truth.

For when in the years just passed letters were often written to us from several monasteries in which it was stated that the brethren who dwelt there offered up in our behalf sacred and pious prayers, we have recognized in most of these letters correct thoughts and uncouth expressions; because what pious devotion dictated faithfully to the mind, the tongue, uneducated on account of the neglect of study, was not able to express in the letter without error. Whence it happened that we began to fear lest perchance, as the skill in writing was less, so also the wisdom for understanding the Holy Scriptures might be much less than it rightly ought to be. And we all know well that, though errors of speech are dangerous, far more dangerous are errors of the understanding.

Therefore, we exhort you not only not to neglect the study of letters, but also with most humble mind, pleasing to God, to study earnestly in order that you may be able more easily and more correctly to penetrate the mysteries of the divine Scriptures. Since, moreover, images, trophes and similar figures are found in the sacred pages, no one doubts that each one in reading these will understand the spiritual sense more quickly if previously he shall have been fully instructed in the mastery of letters. Such men truly are to be chosen for this

*From the Proclamations of Charlemagne.

work as have both the will and the ability to learn and a desire to instruct others. And may this be done with a zeal as great as the earnestness with which we commend it. For we desire you to be, as it is fitting that soldiers of the church should be, devout in mind, learned in discourse, chaste in conduct and eloquent in speech, so that whosoever shall seek to see you out of reverence for God, or on account of your reputation for holy conduct, just as he is edified by your appearance, may also be instructed by your wisdom, which he has learned from your reading or singing, and may go away joyfully giving thanks to omnipotent God. Do not neglect, therefore, if you wish to have our favor, to send copies of this letter to all your suffragans and fellow-bishops and to all the monasteries. (And let no monk hold courts outside of his monastery or go to the judicial and other public assemblies. Farewell. *(Legens valeat.)*)

The Proclamation of 789 A.D.

And we also demand of your holiness that the ministers of the altar of God shall adorn their ministry by good manners, and likewise the other orders who observe a rule and the congregations of monks. We implore them to lead a just and fitting life, just as God Himself commanded in the Gospel. "Let your light so shine before men that they may see your good works and glorify your Father which is in heaven," so that by their example many may be led to serve God; and let them join and associate to themselves not only children of servile condition, but also sons of free men. And let schools be established in which boys may learn to read. Correct carefully the Psalms, the signs in writing (*notas*), the songs, the calendar, the grammar, in each monastery or bishopric, and the catholic books; because often some desire to pray to God properly, but they pray badly because of the incorrect books. And do not permit your boys to corrupt them in reading or writing. If there is need of writing the Gospel, Psalter and Missal, let men of mature age do the writing with all diligence.

31. ESTABLISHMENT OF A
CHANTRY SCHOOL*

Chantries were frequently established in medieval times, with directions that prayers were to be regularly said for the repose of the soul of some dead person. The chantry also often provided education for the boys in the community. The foundation grant below, dated 1489, is similar to earlier grants for the establishment of chantries.

To all sons of holy mother church . . . William Chamber, of Aldwincle, in the county of Northampton, health. . . .

. . . I make known to you all by these presents that I . . . have given . . . to Sir John Seliman, chaplain, for his maintenance and that of his successors . . . celebrating divine service every day at the altar of Saint Mary the Virgin in the parish church of All Saints . . . for all the souls aforesaid for ever my manor of Armeston [and other property].

That this ordinance may endure for ever I will and ordain that the chantry aforesaid shall be for ever called "The chantry of William Chamber, William Aldwincle and Elizabeth their wife," and that the chaplain for the time being shall every day . . . celebrate mass at the altar aforesaid. . . .

Moreover I will and ordain that the said chaplain for the time being shall teach and instruct, in spelling and reading, six of the poorest boys of the town of Aldwincle aforesaid, to be named by me and my wife Elizabeth while we are

*From the Foundation Grant of Aldwincle Chantry, A. F. Leach, trans.

alive, and after our death three named by the rector of Saint Peter's church in Aldwincle aforesaid, and the other three by the chaplain for the time being, freely, without demanding or taking any remuneration from their parents or friends; and the boys, when they have been so instructed and taught, shall say every night in All Saints' church in Aldwincle aforesaid, at the direction of the chaplain aforesaid, for our souls and the souls of all the faithful departed, the psalm "Out of the deep," with the prayers "Incline thine ear" and "God of the faithful."

32. CULTURAL DEVELOPMENTS IN SPAIN*

J. W. Draper

By the eleventh century, Moslem culture in Spain had reached its highest point. Far superior to the civilization in western Europe, it was to become one of the chief sources of cultural development in the Middle Ages and the early Renaissance. The great cultural and technological superiority of the Moors is clearly shown in the following selection from Draper.

Scarcely had the Arabs become firmly settled in Spain when they commenced a brilliant career. Adopting what had now become the established policy of the Commanders of the Faithful in Asia, the Emirs of Cordova distinguished themselves as patrons of learning, and set an example of refinement strongly contrasting with the condition of the native European princes. Cordova, under their administration, at its highest point of prosperity, boasted of more than two hundred thousand houses, and more than a million of inhabitants. After sunset, a man might walk through it in a straight line for ten miles by the light of the public lamps. Seven hundred years after this time there was not so much as one public lamp in London. Its streets were solidly paved. In Paris, centuries subsequently, whoever stepped over his threshold on a rainy day stepped up to his ankles in mud. Other cities, as Granada, Seville, Toledo, considered themselves as rivals of Cordova. The palaces of the khalifs were magnificently decorated. Those sovereigns might well look down with supercilious contempt on the dwellings of the rulers of Germany, France, and England, which were scarcely better than stables—chimneyless, windowless, and with a hole in the roof for the smoke to escape, like the wigwams of certain Indians. The Spanish Mohammedans had brought with them all the luxuries and prodigalities of Asia. . . . The representation of the human form was religiously forbidden . . . For this reason, the Arabs never produced artists; religion turned them from the beautiful, and made them soldiers, philosophers, and men of affairs. . . . There were, for the master himself, grand libraries. The Khalif Alhakem's was so large that the catalogue alone filled forty volumes. He had also apartments for the transcribing, binding, and ornamenting of books. A taste for caligraphy and the possession of splendidly-illustrated manuscripts seems to have anticipated in the khalifs, both of Asia and Spain, the taste for statuary and paintings among the later popes of Rome. . . .

In the midst of all this luxury, which cannot be regarded by the historian with disdain, since in the end it produced a most important result in the south of France, the Spanish khalifs, emulating the example of their Asiatic compeers, and in this strongly contrasting with the popes of Rome, were not only the patrons, but the personal cultivators of all the branches of human learning. One of them was himself the author of a work on polite literature in not less than

*From *History of the Intellectual Development of Europe* by J. W. Draper, New York, 1876.

fifty volumes; another wrote a treatise on algebra. When Zaryab the musician came from the East to Spain, the Khalif Abderrahman rode forth to meet him in honour. The College of Music in Cordova was sustained by ample government patronage, and produced many illustrious professors.

Our obligations to the Spanish Moors in the arts of life are even more marked than in the higher branches of science, perhaps only because our ancestors were better prepared to take advantage of things connected with daily affairs. They set an example of skilful agriculture, the practice of which was regulated by a code of laws. Not only did they attend to the cultivation of plants, introducing very many new ones, they likewise paid great attention to the breeding of cattle, especially the sheep and horse. To them we owe the introduction of the great products, rice, sugar, cotton, and also, as we have previously observed, nearly all the fine garden and orchard fruits, together with many less important plants, as spinach and saffron. To them Spain owes the culture of silk; they gave the Xeres and Malaga their celebrity for wine. They introduced the Egyptian system of irrigation by floodgates, wheels, and pumps. They also promoted many important branches of industry; improved the manufacture of textile fabrics, earthenware, iron, steel; the Toledo sword-blades were everywhere prized for their temper. The Arabs, on their expulsion from Spain, carried the manufacture of a kind of leather, in which they were acknowledged to excel, to Morocco, from which country the leather itself has now taken its name. They also introduced inventions of a more ominous kind—gunpowder and artillery. The cannon they used appeared to have been made of wrought iron. But perhaps they more than compensated for these evil contrivances by the introduction of the mariner's compass.

The mention of the mariner's compass might lead us correctly to infer that the Spanish Arabs were interested in commercial pursuits, a conclusion to which we should also come when we consider the revenues of some of their khalifs. That of Abderrahman III. is stated at five and a half million sterling—a vast sum if considered by its modern equivalent, and far more than could possibly be raised by taxes on the produce of the soil. It probably exceeded the entire revenue of all the sovereigns of Christendom taken together. From Barcelona and other ports an immense trade with the Levant was maintained, but it was mainly in the hands of the Jews, who, from the first invasion of Spain by Musa, had ever been the firm allies and collaborators of the Arabs. Together they had participated in the dangers of the invasion; together they had shared its boundless success; together they had held in irreverent derision, nay, even in contempt, the woman-worshippers and polytheistic savages beyond the Pyrenees —as they mirthfully called those whose long-delayed vengeance they were in the end to feel; together they were expelled. Against such Jews as lingered behind the hideous persecutions of the Inquisition were directed. But in the days of their prosperity they maintained a merchant marine of more than a thousand ships. They had factories and consuls on the Tanaïs. With Constantinople alone they maintained a great trade; it ramified from the Black Sea and East Mediterranean into the interior of Asia; it reached the ports of India and China, and extended along the African coast as far as Madagascar. Even in these commercial affairs the singular genius of the Jew and Arab shines forth. In the midst of the tenth century, when Europe was about in the same condition that Caffraria is now, enlightened Moors, like Abul Cassem, were writing treatises on the principles of trade and commerce. As on so many other occasions, on these affairs they have left their traces. The smallest weight they used in trade was the grain of barley, four of which were equal to one sweet pea, called in Arabic carat. We still use the grain as our unit of weight, and still speak of gold as being so many carats fine.

Such were the Khalifs of the West; such their splendour, their luxury, their knowledge; such some of the obligations we are under to them—obligations which Christian Europe, with singular insincerity, has ever been fain to hide. The cry against the misbeliever has long outlived the Crusades. Considering the enchanting country over which they ruled, it was not without reason that they caused to be engraven on the public seal, "The servant of the Merciful rests contented in the decrees of God." What more, indeed, could Paradise give them? But, considering also the evil end of all this happiness and pomp, this learning, liberality, and wealth, we may well appreciate the solemn truth which these monarchs, in their day of pride and power, grandly wrote in the beautiful mosaics on their palace walls, an ever-recurring warning to him who owes dominion to the sword, "There is no conqueror but God."

The khalifs of the West carried out the precepts of Ali, the fourth successor of Mohammed, in the patronage of literature. They established libraries in all their chief towns; it is said that not fewer than seventy were in existence. To every mosque was attached a public school, in which the children of the poor were taught to read and write, and instructed in the precepts of the Koran. For those in easier circumstances there were academies, usually arranged in twenty-five or thirty apartments, each calculated for accommodating four students; the academy being presided over by a rector. In Cordova, Granada, and other great cities, there were universities, frequently under the superintendence of Jews; the Mohammedan maxim being that the real learning of a man is of more public importance than any particular religious opinions he may entertain. In this they followed the example of the Asiatic khalif, Haroun Alraschid, who actually conferred the superintendence of his schools on John Masué, a Nestorian Christian. The Mohammedan liberality was in striking contrast with the intolerance of Europe. Indeed, it may be doubted whether at this time any European nation is sufficiently advanced to follow such an example. In the universities some of the professors of polite literature gave lectures on Arabic classical works; others taught rhetoric or composition, or mathematics, or astronomy. From these institutions many of the practices observed in our colleges were derived. They held Commencements, at which poems were read and orations delivered in the presence of the public. They had also, in addition to these schools of general learning, professional ones, particularly for medicine.

With a pride perhaps not altogether inexcusable, the Arabians boasted of their language as being the most perfect spoken by man.... It is not then surprising that, in the Arabian schools, great attention was paid to the study of language, and that so many celebrated grammarians were produced. By these scholars, dictionaries, similar to those now in use, were composed; their copiousness is indicated by the circumstance that one of them consisted of sixty volumes, the definition of each word being illustrated or sustained by quotations from Arab authors of acknowledged repute. They had also lexicons of Greek, Latin, Hebrew; and cyclopaedias such as the "Historical Dictionary of Sciences" of Mohammed Ibn Abdallah, of Granada.... Their poetical productions embraced all the modern minor forms—satires, odes, elegies, etc.; but they never produced any work in the higher walks of poesy, no epic, no tragedy. Perhaps this was due to their false fashion of valuing the mechanical execution of a work. They were the authors and introducers of rhyme;... this is the more interesting to us, since it was from the Provençal poetry, the direct descendant of these efforts, that European literature arose. Sonnets and romances at last displaced the grimly-orthodox productions of the wearisome and ignorant fathers of the Church.

... Many of their learned men were travellers and voyagers, constantly moving about for the acquisition or diffusion of knowledge, their acquirements being a passport to them wherever they went, and a sufficient introduction to any of the African or Asiatic courts. They were thus continually brought into contact with men of affairs, soldiers of fortune, statesmen, and became imbued with much of their practical spirit; and hence the singularly romantic character which the biographies of many of these men display, wonderful turns of prosperity, violent deaths. The scope of their literary labours offers a subject well worthy of meditation; it contrasts with the contemporary ignorance of Europe. Some wrote on chronology; some on numismatics; some, now that military eloquence had become objectless, wrote on pulpit oratory; some on agriculture and its allied branches, as the art of irrigation. Not one of the purely mathematical, or mixed, or practical sciences was omitted.

Out of a list too long for detailed quotation, I may recall a few names. Assamh, who wrote on topography and statistics, a brave soldier, who was killed in the invasion of France, A.D. 720; Avicenna, the great physician and philosopher, who died A.D. 1037; Averroes, of Cordova, the chief commentator on Aristotle, A.D. 1198. It was his intention to unite the doctrines of Aristotle with those of the Koran. To him is imputed the discovery of spots upon the sun. ... Abu Othman wrote on zoology; Alberuni, on gems—he had travelled to India to procure information; Rhazes, Al Abbas, and Al Beithar, on botany—the latter had been in all parts of the world for the purpose of obtaining specimens. Ebn Zoar, better known as Avenzoar, may be looked upon as the authority in Moorish pharmacy. Pharmacopoeias were published by the schools, improvements on the old ones of the Nestorians: to them may be traced the introduction of many Arabic words, such as syrup, julep, elixir, still used among apothecaries. A competent scholar might furnish not only an interesting, but valuable book, founded on the remaining relics of the Arab vocabulary; for, in whatever direction we may look, we meet, in the various pursuits of peace and war, of letters and of science, Saracenic vestiges. Our dictionaries tell us that such is the origin of admiral, alchemy, alcohol, algebra, chemise, cotton, and hundreds of other words. The Saracens commenced the application of chemistry, both to the theory and practice of medicine, in the explanation of the functions of the human body and in the cure of its diseases. Nor was their surgery behind their medicine. Albucasis, of Cordova, shrinks not from the performance of the most formidable operations in his own and in the obstetrical art; the actual cautery and knife are used without hesitation. He has left us ample descriptions of the surgical instruments then employed; and from him we learn that, in operations on females in which considerations of delicacy intervened, the services of properly instructed women were secured. How different was all this from the state of things in Europe: The Christian peasant, fever-stricken or overtaken by accident, hied to the nearest saint-shrine and expected a miracle; the Spanish Moor relied on the prescription or lancet of his physician, or the bandage and knife of his surgeon.

In Mathematics the Arabians acknowledged their indebtedness to two sources, Greek and Indian, but they greatly improved upon both. The Asiatic khalifs had made exertions to procure translations of Euclid, Apollonius, Archimedes, and other Greek geometers. Almainon, in a letter to the Emperor Theophilus, expressed his desire to visit Constantinople if his public duties would have permitted. He requests of him to allow Leo the mathematician to come to

Bagdad to impart to him a portion of his learning, pledging his word that he would restore him quickly and safely again. "Do not," says the high-minded khalif, "let diversity of religion or of country cause you to refuse my request. Do what friendship would concede to a friend. In return, I offer you a hundred weight of gold, a perpetual alliance, and peace." True to the instincts of his race and the traditions of his city, the Byzantine sourly and insolently refused the request, saying that "the learning which had illustrated the Roman name should never be imparted to a barbarian."

From the Hindus the Arabs learned arithmetic, especially that valuable invention termed by us the Arabic numerals, but honourably ascribed by them to its proper source, under the designation of "Indian numerals." They also entitled their treatises on the subject "Systems of Indian Arithmetic." This admirable notation by nine digits and cipher occasioned a complete revolution in arithmetical computations. As in the case of so many other things, the Arab impress is upon it; our word cipher, and its derivatives, ciphering, etc., recall the Arabic word tsaphara or ciphra, the name for the o, and meaning that which is blank or void. Mohammed Ben Musa, said to be the earliest of the Saracen authors on algebra, and who made the great improvement of substituting sines for chords in trigonometry, wrote also on this Indian system. He lived at the end of the ninth century; before the end of the tenth it was in common use among the African and Spanish mathematicians. Ebn Junis, A.D. 1008, used it in his astronomical works. From Spain it passed into Italy, its singular advantage in commercial computation causing it to be eagerly adopted in the great trading cities. We still use the word algorithm in reference to calculations. The study of algebra was intently cultivated among the Arabs, who gave it the name it bears. Ben Musa, just referred to, was the inventor of the common method of solving quadratic equations. In the application of mathematics to astronomy and physics they had long been distinguished. Almaimon had determined with considerable accuracy the obliquity of the ecliptic. He had also ascertained the size of the earth from the measurement of a degree on the shore of the Red Sea—an operation implying true ideas of its form, and in singular contrast with the doctrine of Constantinople and Rome. While the latter was asserting, in all its absurdity, the flatness of the earth, the Spanish Moors were teaching geography in their common schools from globes. In Africa, there is still preserved, with almost religious reverence, in the library at Cairo, one of brass, reputed to have belonged to the great astronomer Ptolemy. Al Idrisi made one of silver for Roger II, of Sicily; and Gerbert used one which he had brought from Cordova in the school he established at Rheims. It cost a struggle of several centuries, illustrated by some martyrdoms, before the dictum of Lactantius and Augustine could be overthrown. Among problems of interest that were solved may be mentioned the determination of the length of the year by Albategnius and Thebit Ben Corrah; and increased accuracy was given to the correction of astronomical observations by Alhazen's great discovery of atmospheric refraction. Among the astronomers, some composed tables; some wrote on the measure of time; some on the improvement of clocks, for which purpose they were the first to apply the pendulum; some on instruments, as the astrolabe. The introduction of astronomy into Christian Europe has been attributed to the translation of the works of Mohammed Fargani. In Europe, also, the Arabs were the first to build observatories; the Giralda, or tower of Seville, was erected under the superintendence of Geber, the mathematician, A.D. 1196, for that purpose. Its fate was not a little characteristic. After the expulsion of the Moors it was turned into a belfry, the Spaniards not knowing what else to do with it.

33. THE *SIC ET NON* *

Peter Abelard

Peter Abelard (1079-1142), often regarded as the founder of the University of Paris, was a famous French theologian and teacher. He wrote a book for use by his students which was called Sic et Non *(Yea and Nay). In the book, he listed many questions concerning religious beliefs and presented arguments supporting each side of the questions without reaching conclusions. Note the difference in the approach to learning in this material as compared with the catechetical approach of Alcuin.*

From the *Introduction* to *Sic et Non*

In truth, constant or frequent questioning is the first key to wisdom; and it is, indeed, to the acquiring of this (habit of) questioning with absorbing eagerness that the famous philosopher, Aristotle, the most clear-sighted of all, urges the studious when he says: "It is perhaps difficult to speak confidently in matters of this sort unless they have often been investigated. Indeed, to doubt in special cases will not be without advantage." For through doubting we come to inquiry, and through inquiry we perceive the truth. As the Truth Himself says: "Seek and ye shall find, knock and it shall be opened unto you." And He also, instructing us by His own example, about the twelfth year of His life wished to be found sitting in the midst of the doctors, asking them questions, exhibiting to us by His asking of questions the appearance of a pupil, rather than, by preaching, that of a teacher, although there is in him, nevertheless, the full and perfect wisdom of God.

Now when a number of quotations from (various) writings are introduced they spur on the reader, and allure him into seeking the truth in proportion as the authority of the writing itself is commended. . . .

In accordance, then, with these forecasts it is our pleasure to collect different sayings of the holy Fathers as we planned, just as they have come to mind, suggesting (as they do) some questioning from their apparent disagreement, in order that they may stimulate tender readers to the utmost effort in seeking the truth and may make them keener as the result of their seeking.

Types of Questions he raised for Debate

Should human faith be based on reason, or no?
Is God one, or no?
Is God a substance, or no?
Does the first Psalm refer to Christ, or no?
Is sin pleasing to God, or no?
Is God all-powerful, or no?
Can God be resisted, or no?
Has God free will, or no?
Was the first man persuaded to sin by the devil, or no?
Was Adam saved, or no?
Did all the apostles have wives except John, or no?
Are the flesh and blood of Christ in very truth and essence present in the sacrament of the altar, or no?
Do we sometimes sin unwillingly, or no?
Does God punish the same sin both here and in the future, or no?
Is it worse to sin openly than secretly, or no?

*Selections from Abelard's *Sic et Non* from *Ouvrages Inédits d'Abélard*, by V. Cousin.

34. ORDINANCES OF A MEDIEVAL GUILD*

The medieval guilds established ordinances or regulations governing their operations. The ordinances of an English guild of white-tawyers (leather dressers) are reproduced below. The date of the document is uncertain. The powers of the guild, particularly in relation to control of the craft or trade and control over apprentices and journeymen, are obviously great.

In honor of God, of our Lady, and of all Saints, and for the nurture of tranquillity and peace among the good folks the megucers, called white-tawyers, the folks of the same trade have, by assent of Richard Lacer, mayor, and of the aldermen, ordained the points under-written.

In the first place, they have ordained that they will find a wax candle, to burn before our Lady in the church of Allhallows, near London wall.

Also, that each person of the said trade shall put in the box such sum as he shall think fit, in aid of maintaining the said candle.

Also, if by chance any one of the said trade shall fall into poverty, whether through old age or because he cannot labor or work, and have nothing with which to keep himself, he shall have every week from the said box 7d. for his support, if he be a man of good repute. And after his decease, if he have a wife, a woman of good repute, she shall have weekly for her support 7d. from the said box, so long as she shall behave herself well and keep single.

And that no stranger shall work in the said trade, or keep house for the same in the city, if he be not an apprentice, or a man admitted to the franchise of the said city.

And that no one shall take the serving-man of another to work with him, during his term, unless it be with the permission of his master.

And if any one of the said trade shall have work in his house that he cannot complete, or if for want of assistance such work shall be in danger of being lost, those of the said trade shall aid him, that so the said work be not lost.

And if any one of the said trade shall depart this life, and have not wherewithal to be buried, he shall be buried at the expense of their common box. And when any one of the said trade shall die, all those of the said trade shall go to the vigil, and make offering on the morrow.

And if any serving-man shall conduct himself in any other manner than properly toward his master, and act rebelliously toward him, no one of the said trade shall set him to work, until he shall have made amends before the mayor and aldermen; and before them such misprision shall be redressed.

And that no one of the said trade shall behave himself the more thought-lessly, in the way of speaking or acting amiss, by reason of the points aforesaid; and if any one shall do to the contrary thereof, he shall not follow the said trade until he shall have reasonably made amends.

And if any one of the said trade shall do to the contrary of any point of the ordinances aforesaid, and be convicted thereof by good men of the same trade, he shall pay to the Chamber of the Gildhall of London, the first time 2s., the second time 40d., the third time half a mark, and the fourth time 10s., and shall forswear the trade.

Also,—that the good folks of the same trade shall once in the year be assembled in a certain place, convenient thereto, there to choose two men of the most loyal and befitting of the said trade, to be overseers of work and all other things touching the trade for that year; which persons shall be presented to the

*From *Memorials of London* by Henry T. Riley.

mayor and aldermen for the time being, and sworn before them diligently to inquire and make search, and loyally to present to the said mayor and aldermen such defaults as they shall find touching the said trade without sparing any one for friendship or for hatred, or in any other manner. And if any one of the said trade shall be found rebellious against the said overseers, so as not to let them properly make their search and assay, as they ought to do; or if he shall absent himself from the meeting aforesaid, without reasonable cause, after due warning by the said overseers, he shall pay to the Chamber, upon the first default, 40d.; and on the second like default, half a mark; and on the third one mark; and on the fourth, 20s., and shall forswear the trade forever.

Also, that if the overseers shall be found lax and negligent about their duty, or partial to any person for gift or for friendship, maintaining him or voluntarily permitting him to continue in his default, and shall not present him to the mayor and aldermen, as before stated, they are to incur the penalty aforesaid.

Also, that each year, at such assemblies of the good folks of the said trade, there shall be chosen overseers, as before stated. And if it be found that through laxity or negligence of the said governors such assemblies are not held, each of the said overseers is to incur the said penalty.

Also, that all skins falsely and deceitfully wrought in their trade which the said overseers shall find in the hands of any person, citizen or foreigner, within the franchise shall be forfeited to the said chamber, and the worker thereof amerced in manner aforesaid.

Also, that no one who has not been an apprentice, and has not finished his term of apprenticeship in the said trade, shall be made free of the same trade; unless it be attested by the overseers for the time being, or by four persons of the said trade, that such person is able and sufficiently skilled to be made free of the same.

Also, that no one of the said trade shall induce the servant of another to work with him in the said trade, until he has made a proper fine with his first master, at the discretion of the said overseers, or of four reputable men of the said trade. And if any one shall do to the contrary thereof, or receive the serving workman of another to work with him during his term, without leave of the trade, he is to incur the said penalty.

Also, that no one shall take for working in the said trade more than they were wont heretofore, on the pain aforesaid; that is to say, for the dyker (package of ten) of Scotch stags, half a mark; the dyker of Irish stags, half a mark; the dyker of Spanish stags, 10s., for the hundred of goat skins, 20s., the hundred of roe leather, 16s., for the hundred skins of young deer, 8s.; and for the hundred of kid skins, 8s.

35. AN OFFICIAL INDENTURE
OF APPRENTICESHIP*

Contracts or indentures for apprentices were carefully controlled, both by guilds and by legal enactments, during the Middle Ages. The following indenture, typical of such documents, was executed in Northampton, England, in 1396.

This Indenture testifies that thus it is agreed between John Hyndlee of Northampton, Brazier, on the one part, and Thomas Edward, son of Gilbert Edward of Windsor, on the other part, that the aforesaid Thomas shall place himself and serve as apprentice to the said John Hyndlee, to be subject to this

*From the *Archeological Journal,* London, 1872, Vol. XXIX, p. 184.

John Hyndlee and his assigns well and faithfully after the custom of apprentices, from the feast of All Saints next following after the present date up to the end of the seven years next succeeding shall have been fulfilled and completed, to the art called brazier's craft, practiced by the said John, during this time learning humbly.

Subject to him during the term of seven years aforesaid, the above-mentioned Thomas Edward shall keep secret all concerns of his said master John Hyndlee which ought to be concealed. He shall not do any injury to John, his master, nor see any done, but shall quickly prevent anything of the kind and shall protect his said master steadfastly from this time forth. He shall not absent himself from his aforesaid service. He shall not employ the goods and cattle of the said John, his master, without his permission. Booths, prostitutes, dies, dice, and similar games he shall not frequent, at the expense of his aforesaid master. He shall by no means commit fornication or adultery with any woman of the house and family of the said John, his master, nor shall he marry a wife, without the consent of his said master. The precepts, legal mandates, and reasonable requirements of the said John, his master, are to be faithfully observed by said Thomas; he shall diligently fulfill them, and obey the commands fully, during the whole period of his term above noted. And if the said Thomas should default from any of his agreements or from the prescribed articles, then said Thomas, according to the manner and the amount of his defection, shall make reparation to his master, John aforesaid, and shall double the term of his apprenticeship before mentioned, repeating his said service.

And the aforesaid John Hyndlee and his assigns shall direct said Thomas, his apprentice, in the above-mentioned arts in the best way said John knows and is able to do, they shall teach and instruct him. Or, if they can make him learn in no other way, let them do it by punishment. Moreover, said John shall give to the teaching and informing of said Thomas in the art called the Pewterer's craft as much as he knows how and is able to do beyond the limits of his first duties. And said John shall conceal (a hole in the deed) from said Thomas, his apprentice, none of the aforesaid arts, during the above-mentioned term.

Finally, said John and his assigns shall furnish to said Thomas everything necessary to him, his food and clothing, linen, bedding, housing, shoes, et cetera, enough to suffice him each year according as the age and stature of the said Thomas increase during the term aforesaid.

In testimony of this matter the above-mentioned parties have affixed to these Indentures their seals alternately.

Dated at Northampton, the Sunday next after the feast of Saint Luke, the apostle and evangelist, in the nineteenth year of the reign of King Richard the Second, following the Conquest.

Witnesses:—Henry Caysho, then mayor of the city of Northampton, William Wale and John Wodeward, bailiffs of the same. Richard Gosselyn, John Esex Smyth, and others.

36. REQUIRED STUDY AT THE UNIVERSITY OF PARIS*

Books studied in the medieval university had become standardized to some degree by the thirteenth century. The following books were required for the pursuit of the bachelor and master of arts degrees at the University of Paris in 1254. Note the preponderant attention to the works of Aristotle.

*From *Chartularium Universitatis Parisiensis*, Vol. I, p. 119.

I. The "Old" Logic.
    1. Introduction to the Categories of Aristotle (Isagoge), Porphyry.
    2. Categories, and On Interpretation, Aristotle.
    3. Divisions, and Topics except Bk. IV, Boethius.
II. The "New" Logic.
    1. Prior and Posterior Analytics, Aristotle.
    2. Sophistical Refutations,   "
    3. Topics,   "
III. Moral Philosophy.
    1. Ethics, 4 Bks.,   "
IV. Natural Philosophy.
    1. Physics,   "
    2. On the Heavens and the Earth, "
    3. Meteorics,   "
    4. On Animals,   "
    5. " the Soul,   "
    6. " Generation,   "
    7. " Sense and Sensible Things, "
    8. Sleep and Waking,   "
    9. Memory and Recollection,   "
    10. On Life and Death,   "
    11. " Plants,   " (?)
V. Metaphysics.
    1. Metaphysics,   "
VI. Other Books.
    1. On the Six Principles, Gilbert de la Porrée.
    2. Barbarismus (Bk. 3, Larger Grammar), Donatus.
    3. Grammar (Major and Minor), Priscian.
    4. On Causes, Costa ben Luca.
    5. On the Differences of Spirit and Soul (another translation of On Causes).

37. AN EVALUATION OF THE MEDIEVAL UNIVERSITY*

H. Rashdall

Rashdall's writings on the development of the medieval universities are definitive in nature. The following selection summarizes the work of these institutions and their influence on medieval culture.

What was the real value of the education which the mediaeval university imparted? . . .

To the modern student, no doubt, the defects of a mediaeval education lie upon the surface. The external defects of the University organization have already been incidentally noticed. In the older University system of northern Europe there is the want of selection and consequent incompetency of the teachers, and the excessive youth of the students in Arts. In the higher Faculties too we have encountered the constant effort on the part of the Doctors to evade the obligation of teaching without surrendering its emoluments, while the real teaching devolved upon half-trained Bachelors. It is, indeed, in the Student-Universities that the chairs would appear to have been most competently filled

*From *The Universities of Europe in the Middle Ages* by H. Rashdall, Oxford, 1895, Vol. II.

and their duties most efficiently discharged; in mediaeval times students were more anxious to learn than teachers were to teach. In the earlier period again there was an utter want of discipline among students who ought to have been treated as mere schoolboys. The want was partially corrected (in England) by the growth of the College system, but the improvement in this respect was balanced by the decay and degradation in the higher intellectual life of the Universities. . . . There is considerable reason to believe that in the Middle Ages a larger proportion than at the present day of the nominal students derived exceedingly little benefit from their University education. . . . In the earlier part of our period this must have been peculiarly the case, when so little exertion on the part of the student himself was required. A man was allowed year after year to sit through lectures of which he might not understand one word; later on this defect was partly remedied by the multiplication of "exercises" in College and Hall.

For the fairly competent student the main defects of a mediaeval education may be summed up by saying that it was at once too dogmatic and too disputatious. Of the superstitious adherence to Aristotle or other prescribed authority sufficient illustrations have already been given. It is, of course, a direct outcome of the intellectual vice of the age—a vice of which the human mind was by no means cured by the Renaissance or the Reformation. It lasted longest where it was most out of place. In the middle of the seventeenth century a Doctor of Medicine was compelled by the English College of Physicians to retract a proposition which he had advanced in opposition to the authority of Aristotle, under threat of imprisonment. It may seem a contradiction to allege that this education by authority was at the same time too controversial. Yet the readiness with which the student was encouraged to dispute the thesis of a prescribed opponent, and the readiness with which he would swear to teach only the system of a prescribed authority, were but opposite sides of the same fundamental defect—the same fatal indifference to facts, the facts of external nature, the facts of history, and the facts of life. Books were put in the place of things. This is a defect which was certainly not removed by the mere substitution of Classics for Philosophy. . . .

But, because it is easy enough to pick holes in the education of the past, it must not for one moment be supposed that the education either of the scholastic or of the ultra-classical period was of little value. Up to a certain point—and this is the one consolation to the educational historian—the value of education is independent either of the intrinsic value or of the practical usefulness of what is taught. . . . It was emphatically so in the Middle Ages. Kings and princes found their statesmen and men of business in the Universities—most often, no doubt, among those trained in the practical science of Law, but not invariably so. Talleyrand is said to have asserted that Theologians made the best diplomatists. It was not the wont of the practical men of the Middle Ages to disparage academic training. The rapid multiplication of Universities during the fourteenth and fifteenth centuries was largely due to a direct demand for highly educated lawyers and administrators. In a sense the academic discipline of the Middle Ages was too practical. It trained pure intellect, encouraged habits of laborious subtlety, heroic industry, and intense application, while it left uncultivated the imagination, the taste, the sense of beauty,—in a word, all the amenities and refinements of the civilized intellect. It taught men to think and to work rather than to enjoy. Most of what we understand by "culture," much of what Aristotle understood by the "noble use of leisure," was unappreciated by the mediaeval intellect. On the speculative side the Universities were (as has been said) "the school of the modern spirit": they taught men to reason and to speculate, to doubt and to inquire, to find a pleasure in the things of the intellect both for their own sake and for the sake of their applications to life. They dispelled forever the obscurantism of the Dark Ages. From a more practical point of view their greatest service to mankind was simply this, that they placed the administration of human affairs—in short the government of the world—in the hands of educated men. The actual rulers—the Kings or the aristocrats—might often be as uneducated or more uneducated than modern democracies, but they had to rule through the instrumentality of a highly educated class.

In criticizing mediaeval culture and education, attention is sometimes too much confined to the Scholastic Philosophy and Theology. The Scholastic Philosophy and Theology do, indeed, represent the highest intellectual development of the period. But they do not represent the most widely diffused or the most practically influential of mediaeval studies. Law was the leading Faculty in by far the greater number of mediaeval Universities: for a very large proportion of University students the study of Arts, in so far as they pursued it at all, took the place of a modern school rather than of a modern University. From a broad political and social point of view one of the most important results of the Universities was the creation, or at least the enormously increased power and importance, of the lawyer-class. Great as are the evils which society still owes to lawyers, the lawyer-class has always been a civilizing agency. Their power represents at least the triumph of reason and education over caprice and brute force. Lawyers have moderated or regulated despotism even when they have proved its most willing tools: just as in modern democratic communities their prominence must be looked upon as an important conservative check upon democracy.

Over the greater part of Europe the influence of the Universities meant more than this. It brought with it the increasing modification of legal and political institutions by the Roman Law, whether directly or through the Canon Law, whether by avowed adoption or by gradual and unconscious infiltration and imitation. This too was a civilizing agency, though here again an increase of civilization had often to be bought by a decline of rude, barbaric liberty. . . .

It is more directly relative to our subject to examine what have been the effects of the mediaeval Universities upon our modern educational system. The genius of the Middle Age showed itself above all in the creation of institutions. The institutions of the Middle Age are greater—they may prove more imperishable—even than its Cathedrals. The University is a distinctly mediaeval institution. By this is implied not merely that in the most altered and the most modern of the Schools so called there are customs, offices, titles, for the explanation of which we must go back to the history of the thirteenth century with its Guild movement, its Cathedral Schools, and especially its great struggle between the Chancellor of Paris and the Society of Masters. The very idea of the institution is essentially mediaeval, and it is curious to observe how largely that idea still dominates our modern schemes of education.

THE RENAISSANCE AND
THE REFORMATION

38. REGARD FOR ANCIENT WRITINGS*

Petrarch

Petrarch (1304-1374) was one of the first and greatest of the humanists. Best known for his sonnets, written in Italian, he was also a great Latinist and an avid collector of ancient manuscripts. The following letter, written in connection with the return of some of the writings of Cicero, which he had copied, illustrates the great interest in possessing the writings of the past.

Your copy of Cicero has been in my possession four years and more. There is good reason, though, for so long a delay; namely, the great scarcity of copyists who understand such work. It is a state of affairs that has resulted in an incredible loss of scholarship. Books that by their nature are a little hard to understand are no longer multiplied, and have ceased to be generally intelligible, and so have sunk into utter neglect, and in the end have perished. This age of ours consequently has let fall, bit by bit, some of the richest and sweetest fruits that the tree of knowledge has yielded; has thrown away the results of the vigils and labors of the most illustrious men of genius,—things of more value, I am almost tempted to say, than anything else in the whole world. . . .

But I must return to your Cicero. I could not do without it, and the incompetence of the copyists would not let me possess it. What was left for me but to rely upon my own resources, and press these weary fingers and this worn and ragged pen into the service? The plan that I followed was this. I want you to know it, in case you should ever have to grapple with a similar task. Not a single word did I read except as I wrote. But how is that, I hear some one say; did you write without knowing what it was that you were writing? Ah! but from the very first it was enough for me to know that it was a work of Tullius, and an extremely rare one too. And then as soon as I was fairly started, I found at every step so much sweetness and charm, and felt so strong a desire to advance, that the only difficulty which I experienced in reading and writing at the same time came from the fact that my pen could not cover the ground so rapidly as I wanted it to, whereas my expectation had been rather that it would outstrip my eyes, and that my ardor for writing would be chilled by the slowness of my reading.

So the pen held back the eye, and the eye drove on the pen, and I covered page after page, delighting in my task, and committing many and many a passage to memory as I wrote. For just in proportion as the writing is slower than the reading does the passage make a deep impression and cling to the mind.

*From one of Petrarch's letters in Robinson and Rolfe, *Petrarch*, Putnams, New York, 1898, p. 275.

39. THE DISCOVERY OF AN ANCIENT MANUSCRIPT*

Bracciolini and Bruni

Poggio Bracciolini (1380-1450) was a student of Chrysaloras and a devoted scholar of the Renaissance. A member of the Curia and at one time Apostolic Secretary, he attended the Council of Constance, which was in session in Switzerland from 1414 to 1418. While he was in Constance, he searched the monasteries in the outlying areas, looking for lost books. In the Monastery of Saint Gall, he found a copy of Quintilian's Institutes of Oratory, as well as other manuscripts. His excitement speaks for itself in his letter to Leonardo Bruni, whose reply sounds the same note of exultation.

Letter of Poggio Bracciolini

I verily believe that, if we had not come to the rescue, he [Quintilian] must speedily have perished; for it cannot be imagined that a man magnificent, polished, elegant, urbane, and witty could much longer have endured the squalor of the prison-house in which I found him, the savagery of his jailers, the forlorn filth of the place. He was indeed right sad to look upon, and ragged, like a condemned criminal, with rough beard and matted hair, protesting by his countenance and garb against the injustice of his sentence. He seemed to be stretching out his hands, calling upon the Romans, demanding to be saved from so unmerited a doom. Hard indeed it was for him to bear, that he who had preserved the lives of many by his eloquence and aid, should now find no redresser of his wrongs, no saviour from the unjust punishment awaiting him. But as it often happens, to quote Terence, that what you dare not wish for comes to you by chance, so a good fortune for him, but far more for ourselves, led us, while wasting our time in idleness at Constance, to take a fancy for visiting the place where he was held in prison. The Monastery of Saint Gallen lies at the distance of some twenty miles from that city. Thither, then, partly for the sake of amusement and partly of finding books, whereof we heard there was a large collection in the convent, we directed our steps. In the middle of a well-stocked library, too large to catalogue at present, we discovered Quintilian, safe as yet and sound, though covered with dust and filthy with neglect and age. The books, you must know, were not housed according to their worth, but were lying in a most foul and obscure dungeon at the very bottom of a tower, a place into which condemned criminals would hardly have been thrust; and I am firmly persuaded that if any one would but explore those *ergastula* of the barbarians wherein they incarcerate such men, we should meet with like good fortune in the case of many whose funeral orations have long ago been pronounced. Besides Quintilian, we exhumed the three first books, and a half of the fourth book of the *Argonautica* of (Valerius) Flaccus, and the *Commentaries* of Asconius Pedianus upon eight orations of Cicero.

When the manuscript was being copied, his friend, Lionardo Bruni, wrote to him as follows:

*Letters translated by J. A. Symonds in his *Renaissance in Italy*, London, 1888, Vol. II, pp. 135-37.

Reply of Lionardo Bruni

The republic of letters has reason to rejoice not only in the works you have discovered, but also in those you have still to find. What a glory for you it is to have brought to light by your exertions the writings of the most distinguished authors! Posterity will not forget that manuscripts which were bewailed as lost beyond the possibility of restoration, have been recovered, thanks to you. As Camillus was called the second founder of Rome, so may you receive the title of the second author of the works you have restored to the world. Through you we now possess Quintilian entire; before we only boasted the half of him, and that defective and corrupt in text. O precious acquisition! O unexpected joy! And shall I, then, in truth be able to read the whole of that Quintilian which, mutilated and deformed as it has hitherto appeared, has formed my solace? I conjure you send it me at once, that at least I may set eyes on it before I die.

40. THE COLLECTION OF AN EARLY LIBRARY*

Vespasiano

Cosimo de Medici (1389-1446), a Duke of Florence, was interested in cultural affairs and established one of the great libraries of his day. He employed Vespasiano to assemble the library. In the following material, written by Vespasiano, the enormous difficulty of collecting books in the days before the printing press is shown.

When he had finished the residence and a good part of the church, he fell to thinking how he could have the place peopled with honest men of letters; and in this way it occurred to him to found a fine library; and one day when I happened to be present in his chamber, he said to me: "In what way would you furnish this library?" I replied that as for buying the books it would be impossible, for they were not to be had. Then he said: "How is it possible then to furnish it?" I told him that it would be necessary to have the books copied. He asked in reply if I would be willing to undertake the task. I answered him, that I was willing. He told me to commence my work and he would leave everything to me; and as for the money that would be necessary he would refer the matter to Don Archangel, then prior of the monastery, who would draw bills upon the bank, which should be paid. The library was commenced at once, for it was his pleasure that it should be done with the utmost possible celerity; and as I did not lack for money I collected in a short time forty-five writers, and finished 200 volumes in twenty-two months; in which work we made use of an excellent arrangement, that of the library of Pope Nicholas, which he had given to Cosimo, in the form of a catalogue made out with his own hands. . . .

And since there were not copies of all these works in Florence, we sent to Milan, to Bologna and to other places, wherever they might be found. Cosimo lived to see the library wholly completed, and the cataloguing and arranging of the books; in all of which he took great pleasure, and the work went forward, as was his custom, with great promptness.

*From *Lives of Illustrious Men of the Fifteenth Century,* Vespasiano; from the *Life of Cosimo de' Medici,* trans. by Whitcomb in his *Literary Source Book of the Italian Renaissance,* University of Pennsylvania, 1898, p. 77.

41. THE RENAISSANCE IN ITALY*

J. R. Green

The selection below, taken from Green's Short History of the English People, *is interesting for two reasons: First, it provides a good account of the early Renaissance in Italy, when the ancient writings first became available. Secondly, it shows how the English Renaissance, with its interest in Greek language and literature and its emphasis on religion, differed from the Italian Renaissance.*

. . . The literature of the Middle Ages was dying out with the Middle Ages themselves; in letters as in life their thirst for knowledge had spent itself in the barren mazes of the scholastic philosophy, their ideal of warlike nobleness faded away before the gaudy travestie of a spurious chivalry, and the mystic enthusiasm of their devotion shrank at the touch of persecution into a narrow orthodoxy and a flat morality. The clergy, who had concentrated in themselves the intellectual effort of the older time, were ceasing to be an intellectual class at all. The monasteries were no longer seats of learning. "I found in them," said Poggio, an Italian traveller twenty years after Chaucer's death, "men given up to sensuality in abundance, but very few lovers of learning, and those of a barbarous sort, skilled more in quibbles and sophisms than in literature." The erection of colleges, which was beginning, failed to arrest the quick decline of the universities both in the numbers and learning of their students. Those at Oxford amounted to only a fifth of the scholars who had attended its lectures a century before, and "Oxford Latin" became proverbial for a jargon in which the very tradition of grammar had been lost. All literary production was nearly at an end. Historical composition lingered on indeed in compilations of extracts from past writers, such as make up the so-called works of Walsingham, in jejune monastic annals, or worthless popular compendiums. But the only trace of mental activity is to be found in the numerous treatises on alchemy and magic, on the elixir of life or the philosopher's stone, a fungous growth which most unequivocally witnesses to the progress of intellectual decay. On the other hand, while the older literary class was dying out, a glance beneath the surface shows us the stir of a new interest in knowledge among the masses of the people itself. The correspondence of the Paston family, which has been happily preserved, not only displays a fluency and vivacity as well as a grammatical correctness which would have been impossible in familiar letters a few years before, but shews country squires discussing about books and gathering libraries. The very character of the authorship of the time, its love of compendiums and abridgements of the scientific and historical knowledge of its day, its dramatic performances or mysteries, the commonplace morality of its poets, the popularity of its rimed chronicles, are additional proofs that literature was ceasing to be the possession of a purely intellectual class and was beginning to appeal to the people at large. The increased use of linen paper in place of the costlier parchment helped in the popularization of letters. In no former age had finer copies of books been produced; in none had so many been transcribed. This increased demand for their production caused the processes of copying and illuminating manuscripts to be transferred from the scriptoria of the religious houses into the hands of

*From *Short History of the English People,* by J. R. Green, London, 1888, pp. 294-95.

trade-guilds, like the Guild of Saint John at Bruges, or the Brothers of the Pen at Brussels. It was, in fact, this increase of demand for books, pamphlets, or fly-sheets, especially of a grammatical or religious character, in the middle of the fifteenth century that brought about the introduction of printing. We meet with it first in rude sheets simply struck off from wooden blocks, "block-books" as they are now called, and later on in works printed from separate and moveable types. Originating at Maintz with the three famous printers, Gutenberg, Fust, and Schoeffer, the new process travelled southward to Strasburg, crossed the Alps to Venice, where it lent itself through the Aldi to the spread of Greek literature in Europe, and then floated down the Rhine to the towns of Flanders. It was probably at the press of Colard Mansion, in a little room over the porch of Saint Donat's at Bruges, that Caxton learnt the art which he was the first to introduce into England.

42. THE CURRICULUM OF A
RENAISSANCE SCHOOL*

W. H. Woodward

The College de Guyenne, established in Bordeaux in 1534, is a typical example of the Renaissance school. Its curriculum is similar to those developed in Italy, Germany, and England. The school consisted of ten classes and could be followed by two additional years in the university at Bordeaux. The outline of the curriculum is followed by a commentary by Woodward.

Tenth, or Lowest Class. Entered at six or seven. Boys known as "Alphabetarii" or "Abecedarii."
> Textbooks: the *Alphabetum;* the Pater Noster, the Seven Penitential Psalms, and the Ave Maria; and the *Libellus Puerulorum.*
> Tests for promotion: ability to read the above, to decline and to conjugate, and to write legibly.

Ninth Class. This was the largest in the school, indicating that many boys learned the above privately and entered the school at seven or eight.
> Textbooks: Reading and writing in both French and Latin, for both fluency and speed.
> . Latin accidence of both noun and verb.
> The *disticha de moribus* of Cato, with French parallel translation; and Cordier's *Exempla partium orationis,* a small handbook of grammar.

Eighth Class. Age eight or nine.
> Textbooks: Selection of Cicero's *Letters,* selected scenes from Terence, and the *Colloquia* of Cordier.

Seventh Class. Age nine or ten.
> Textbooks: Selections from *Letters* of Cicero continued; the Latin Grammar of Despantere, written in Latin hexameters.
> Much emphasis on style and composition. French the language of instruction for the Latin.

Sixth Class. Age ten or eleven.
> Cicero's *Letters* the standard prose text. Much memorization for form, and much explanation of construction.

*From *Disciplina et Ratio Docendi,* Vinet, in *Studies in Education During the Age of the Renaissance,* Cambridge, 1906, Chapter VIII.

Fifth Class. Age eleven or twelve.

Cicero's *Letters* still the standard prose text, with emphasis as above. Also one play of Terence, and one book of the *Epistolae* of Ovid. Rules of prosody now learned.

Fourth Class. Age twelve or thirteen.

Pupils now study for first time an oration of Cicero and study with it a manual of rhetoric, such as the *De Copia* of Erasmus. Chief poetical work read in this class the *Tristia* of Ovid.

Much grammatical questioning; frequent exercises in composition; dictation of simple materials for writing Latin verse.

Greek begun in this class. Grammar begun.

Third Class. Age thirteen or fourteen.

The *Epistolae Familiares* or *Ad Atticum* of Cicero, and one other oration; the *Metamorphoses* of Ovid.

Much emphasis on rhetoric, syntax, verse composition, and Latin composition in prose and verse.

Greek continued. Grammar of Theodore Gaza.

Second Class. Age fourteen or fifteen.

Cicero's orations, selected; or readings from Vergil, Ovid, or Lucan.

Roman history now studied.

Much learning by heart; prose and verse composition; and emphasis on rhetoric.

Latin declamation now first undertaken.

Greek continued. Grammar and reading.

Arithmetic begun.

First Class. Age fifteen or sixteen.

The art of oratory, from Cicero or Quintilian.

Speeches of Cicero, in illustration.

History from Livy, Seneca, Justin, Eubropius, and P. Mela.

Poetry read from Vergil, Lucan, Persius, Juvenal, Horace, and Ovid.

Composition in prose and verse, and declamation.

Greek continued. Readings in Demosthenes and Homer.

Arithmetic extended to simple proportion, and square and cube root.

Faculte des Arts. First year. Age sixteen or seventeen.

Aristotelian Logic, from Latin version.

The *Isagoge* of Porphyry.

Greek continued.

The *Mathematicorum Breviarium* of Psellus, a dry compendium of arithmetic, music, geometry, and astronomy.

Faculte des Arts. Second year. Age seventeen or eighteen.

Aristotle's *Physica,* the *De Caelo,* and other commonly read scientific works. A study of natural philosophy, though based on ancient learning. No observation or independent thought.

Greek and mathematics continued, as above, with Proclus *de Sphaera* added.

Woodward comments on Vinet's curriculum as follows:

We have interesting light upon general methods of class instruction as pursued in the school. The retention of the mediaeval disputation, in the rational form of mutual questioning under the control of the form (class) master, was a safeguard against the prevalent fault of lecturing or dictating to the class which Erasmus so frequently ridiculed as the practice of the unskilled teacher or of the pedant parading his erudition. The construing lesson lasted as a rule for one hour, and was followed by such disputation: the pupils asked questions of each other, propounded difficulties, discussed the matter of the text and the notes given by the master. This exercise occupied half an hour. On Saturdays, in place of a set lesson at midday, disputations were arranged in which form was pitted against form. Six pupils from each brought up as many compositions in prose or in verse which had been worked in advance. These were written out in large text hand, and pinned to a screen or on the wall of the class-room: Below each line of the script was left a clear space for interlinear correction and criticism. Thus the opposers could make careful examination of each exercise, detect errors and propound improvements. This disputation lasts an hour.

Although French, as has been shown, was regularly employed for an instrument of Latin construing and composition, it was not allowed to be used in school or play-ground except by the juniors: . . . Elder boys were required to use Latin in addressing little boys, and only when not understood were they to repeat their words in French. The words of the statute of the University of Paris as revised in 1599 show that to the very end of the century the same principle was upheld in the authoritative seat of French learning. . . .

The school hours were from 8-10, 12-1, 3-5, with an extra hour twice weekly in the case of pupils reading Greek and mathematics. Sunday was, apart from one exercise for the upper forms, a whole holiday, as were certain Saints' days. On some important vigils, about fifty during the year, a half holiday was allowed. Mass was attended daily by the entire school. The school year began in September, and continued till the beginning of August.

43. STURM'S CURRICULUM AT STRASSBURG*

In 1537, Johann Sturm (1507-1589) reorganized the municipal school in Strassburg along humanistic lines. It was to become probably the greatest of the Renaissance schools. Note that it flourished after the Reformation in Germany. Note also the similarity of its curriculum to that of the College de Guyenne. The school was called the Gymnasium, a term still applied to German secondary schools.

1. *Tenth Class—Entered at the age of 7.*
   Purpose to lay a good foundation.
   Form and correct pronunciation of alphabet.
   Beginnings of Latin reading, writing, and spelling.
   Learn declensions and conjugations in Latin.
   German Catechism to be committed to memory.
2. *Ninth Class—Age 8 to 9.*
   More thorough grounding in Latin declensions and conjugations.
   Many Latin words to be learned, especially names of common objects, as much like Roman children did as possible.
   Much reading of simple Latin and memorizing of words and phrases. Inflection of all nouns and verbs.
3. *Eighth Class—Age 9 to 10.*
   Special care that the boys do not forget what has been learned in earlier classes.

*Extracts from *Plan, Classical Letters,* and *Examinations,* Sturm.

Thorough grounding in each of the eight parts of speech.

Each declension and conjugation to be fully mastered.

To read Sturm's *Letters of Cicero,* with constant reference to grammatical construction, and certain Latin dialogues.

Written exercises in style to replace oral drill.

4. *Seventh Class—Age 10 to 11.*

Rules of Latin syntax, based on Cicero, to be well ground in.

Subjects to be assigned for exercises in style.

German Catechism to be translated into Classical Latin.

Learn the scale and intervals in music.

Read two dialogues in Sturm's printed collection, the second book of *Letters of Cicero,* the precepts of Cato, the Catechism in Latin, and the "Sunday Sermons."

Written exercises in style.

5. *Sixth Class—Age 11 to 12.*

Read Cicero's longer *Letters;* also the *Andria* of Terence, and selections from Aesop, Bishop Ambrose, Martial, and Horace.

Written exercises to secure greater elegance in style.

Saturday and Sunday to be given to the shorter Latin catechism of Luther, and the reading of some letters of the Hieronymians.

Greek to be commenced in this class.

In music emphasis on time.

Boys now to be proficient in grammar, and to have a store of Latin words for every-day objects.

6. *Fifth Class—Age 12 to 13.*

Enlarge Latin vocabulary to words for unknown objects.

Meter in Latin poetry to be studied, with scanning.

Mythology to be learned.

Read Cicero's *Cato* and *Laelis,* and the *Eclogues* of Vergil.

Boys to complete their encyclopedias of Latin words.

Style to be still more thoroughly cultivated. Verse writing to be begun.

Examples of eloquence for translation, and then re-translated into Latin.

Greek to be continued; vocabulary to be enlarged; simple reading.

Pauline epistles to be read.

Now to be well grounded in Greek and Latin Grammar.

7. *Fourth Class—Age 13 to 14.*

Much drill on what has been so far learned.

"Diligent practice" to be continued on style.

Read sixth oration against Verres, second book of Cicero's *Letters to Friends,* part of *Adelphi* of Terence, and the epistles and satires of Horace in Latin; in Greek, the "Book of Examples."

Much drill on Greek grammar.

Pauline epistles to be read.

8. *Third Class—Age 14 to 15.*

Range of previous studies to be enlarged.

Rhetoric to be begun.

Read third book of Cicero's *Letters to Friends,* the *Menippus* of Lucian, and the sixth book of Vergil's *Aeneid* in Latin; in Greek, the first book of the *Iliad* or the *Odyssey,* and the best efforts of Demosthenes to be carefully studied.

Select orations in Greek to be translated into Latin, and vice versa.

Change *Odes* of Pindar and Horace into different meter.

Comedies of Terence and Plautus to be acted.

9. Second Class—Age 15 to 16.
Literal interpretation of Greek poets and orators.
Connection between oratorical and poetic usage.
Striking passages to be copied into books for learning.
Similar work with Latin authors, with comparisons.
Daily exercises in style very important.
Rhetoric to be studied now from a text, and applied to orations of Demosthenes and Cicero.
Logic to be introduced in this class.
On Sundays, the Epistles of Saint Paul to the Romans to be learned by heart.
Acting of plays to continue, being extended to include those of Aristophanes, Euripides, or Sophocles.
Read the second *Philippic* of Demosthenes, Cicero's pleas in behalf of Roscius Amerinus and Caius Rabirius, and the first book of the *Iliad.*
Elementary work in mathematics.

10. *First Class—Age 16 to 17.*
Logic and rhetoric to be extended, and applied to Cicero and Demosthenes.
Readings from Vergil, Homer, Thucydides, and Sallust.
Much translation and re-translation, writing in prose and poetry, and declamation. Dramatic representations every week.
Epistles of Saint Paul to be expounded, after the manner of the old rhetoricians.
In geometry, first book of Euclid studied.
Some very elementary instruction in astronomy.

44. THE CURRICULUM AT ETON*

H. C. Maxwell-Lyte

Eton College, actually a secondary school, was established in England in 1440 by Henry IV. It was to become the prototype of the great English public schools. By 1560, as is evident below, it had become a typical Renaissance school, although attention was also given to religion, sports, and manners.

CURRICULUM OF ETON IN 1560
LOWER OR USHER'S SCHOOL

First Form

The *Disticha de Moribus* of Dionysius Cato.
The *Exercitation Linguae Latinae* of John Lewis Vives.

Second Form

Terence.
Lucian's *Dialogues* (in Latin).
Aesop's *Fables* (in Latin).

*From *History of Eton College,* by H. C. Maxwell-Lyte, London, 1899, p. 149.

Third Form

Terence.
Aesop's *Fables* (in Latin).
Selections by Sturmius from Cicero's *Epistles*.

UPPER OR MASTER'S SCHOOL

Fourth Form

Terence.
Ovid's *Tristia*.
Epigrams of Martial, Catullus, and Sir Thomas More.

Fifth Form

Ovid's *Metamorphoses*.
Horace.
Cicero's *Epistles*.
Valerius Maximus.
Lucius Florus.
Justin.
Epitome Troporum of Susenbrotus.

Sixth and Seventh Forms

Caesar's *Commentaries*.
Cicero *de Officiis* and *de Amicitia*.
Vergil.
Lucan.
Greek Grammar.

The lower boys had to decline and conjugate words, and their seniors had to repeat rules of grammar, for the illustration of which short phrases, called 'Vulgaria' were composed and committed to memory. Some sort of Latin composition, however brief, was a necessary portion of the daily work of every Eton scholar. In the lower forms it was confined to the literal translation of an English sentence or passage, while in the Fifth Form it consisted of a theme on a subject set by the school-master. The boys in the Sixth and Seventh Forms wrote verses.

45. WYCLIFFE'S ATTEMPT AT REFORMATION*

The Lutheran Reformation was the culmination of years of incipient revolt in many areas of Europe. John Wycliffe (1320-1384), for example, spoke out strongly against what he believed to be the evils of Catholicism. After his death, his followers assembled a series of statements which attacked the Church and particularly Pope Urban VI. Note the similarity to Luther's theses, which were not to be promulgated until a hundred and thirty years later.

Furste, that this pope Urban tho sixte beres not strength of Seint Petur in erthe, but thai affermen hym to be the son of Anticriste, and that no verrey pope was isth tho tyme of Silvester (I) pope.

*From *Select English Works of John Wycliffe,* by Thomas Arnold, Oxford, 1870, Vol. II, pp. 457-58.

Here Cristen men seyne pleynly, that whatever pope or other preste, in maner of lyvynge or techynge or lawis-makynge, contrarius Crist, is verrey Anticrist, adversary of Jesus Crist, and of his apostlis, ande of alle Cristen pepul. . . .

Tho secund tyme, See ye Cristen pepl, tho willeful poverte of Jesus Crist, how he hade nought by worldly lordschipe one howse where he mygt reste his heved, but lyved by temporale almes of Mary Mawdeleyne ande other holy wymmen, as tho gospel sais. Ande see ye wisely, whether oure popis, makyng stronge palayces with pore mennes lyvelodis, with al ther glorie of richesses and jewelis, acordem with this poreness of Crist.

Tho thrid tyme, See, yee Cristen pepul, tho charitabul lyif of Crist, ande like whether oure popis contrarien hym. Where he was moste bisye in spirituale occupacione, these popis bene moste bisy in delynge of beneficis to him that moste muck brynggen or worldly favour. . . .

Where Criste mekely travelid with grete penaunce upon his fete to preche tho gospel, these popes, more then emperoures, resten in palaycis chargid with pretious in ther feete and in al ther stynkynge carione, ande prechen not tho gospel to Cristen men, but crien ever aftur glorye and riches, and make newe lawes for to magnify ther worldly state, that Crist and his apostlis durste never do.

Where Crist gafe his precious blode and lyif for to make pes and charite, these popis maken ande mayntenys werre thoroweout Cristendame, for to hold ther worldly state, moste contrarie ageyne Crist and his apostlis, ande herto spenden tho almes of kyngis, and appressen Cristen rewenes by newe subsidies.

And, that is werst, thai senden indulgenciis, foundid as thai faynen on Cristis charite and his dethe, to sle alle men contrarie to theire lustis. Certis this semes contrarious to Crist and his lovers. Seynt Robert Grosthede (Bishop of Lincoln) sais that this court is cause, welle, and begynnynge of destruccione of Cristen-dame, and loser of al tho worlde. Ande trewly, if thai be thus contrary to Crist in lyvynge and techyng, as ther open dedis and tho world ciren, thai ben cursid heretikis, manquellars bodily and gostly, Anticrist, and Sathanas transfigurid into aungelis (of) ligt. Ande, as this worthi clerk Grosthede proves, ande certis no man is verrey pope but in als myche as he sewis Crist; and in so myche Cristen men wole do aftur hym, ande no more, for alle bulles and censuris, for no creature of God.

46. THE THESES OF MARTIN LUTHER*

Martin Luther

In 1517, Martin Luther nailed his ninety-five theses to the door of the cathedral in Wittenberg, and the German Reformation, to Luther's surprise, was underway. The theses, not intended by Luther to be definitive, were submitted as proper subjects for discussion in church councils. Some of the more important theses are given below.

In the desire and with the purpose of elucidating the truth, a disputation will be held on the underwritten propositions at Wittenberg, under the presidency of

*From *Deutsche Geschichte in Zeitalter der Reformation*, Ranke, trans. by Wace and Buchheim, Vol. IV, p. 83.

the Reverend Martin Luther, Monk of the Order of Saint Augustine, Master of Arts and Sacred Theology, and ordinary Reader of the same in that place. He therefore asks those who cannot be present and discuss the subject with us orally, to do so by letter in their absence, In the name of our Lord Jesus Christ. Amen. . . .

5. The Pope has neither the will nor the power to remit any penalties, except those which he has imposed by his own authority, or by that of the canons.

6. The Pope has no power to remit any guilt, except by declaring and warranting it to have been remitted by God; or at most by remitting cases reserved for himself; in which cases, if his power were despised, guilt would certainly remain.

13. The dying pay all penalties by death, and are already dead to the canon laws, and are by right relieved from them.

20. Therefore the Pope, when he speaks of the plenary remission of all penalties, does not mean really of all, but only of those imposed by himself.

21. Thus those preachers of indulgences are in error who say that, by the indulgences of the Pope, a man is loosed and saved from all punishment.

22. For in fact he remits to souls in purgatory no penalty which they would have had to pay in this life according to the canons.

23. If any entire remission of all penalties can be granted to any one, it is certain that it is granted to none but the most perfect, that is to very few.

24. Hence, the greater part of the people must needs be deceived by this indiscriminate and high-sounding promise of release from penalties.

25. Such power as the Pope has over purgatory in general, such has every bishop in his own diocese, and every curate in his own parish, in particular.

88. Again; what greater good could the Church receive than if the Pope, instead of once, as he does now, were to bestow these remissions and participations a hundred times a day on any one of the faithful?

89. Since it is the salvation of souls, rather than money, that the Pope seeks by his pardons, why does he suspend the letters and pardons granted long ago, since they were equally efficacious?

91. If then pardons were preached according to the spirit and mind of the Pope, all these questions would be resolved with ease; nay, would not exist.

94. Christians should be exhorted to strive to follow Christ, their head, through pains, deaths, and hells.

95. And thus trust to enter heaven through many tribulations, rather than in the security of peace.

47. LUTHER'S CONCERN FOR EDUCATION*

Martin Luther

Martin Luther believed strongly in education, particularly as it related to the understanding of the Bible. Following the success of the German Reformation, he was dismayed by the danger of the collapse of education, which had been the province of the Catholic Church. As a result, he sent many letters to municipal

*From Letter to the Mayors and Aldermen of all Cities of Germany in Behalf of Christian Schools, 1524, by Martin Luther; trans. in Barnard's American Journal of Education, Vol. IV, pp. 429-30, 437-38.

authorities, urging them to provide adequate education. The letter below, addressed to mayors and aldermen of German cities, is typical.

To the Mayors and Councilmen of all the Towns of Germany:

Grace and peace from God the Father, and our Lord Jesus Christ. Beloved rulers, wise and sagacious men, . . . I would have you freely, cheerfully and in a spirit of love, give me your attention; since, doubtless, if ye obey me herein, ye obey not me, but Christ, and whoever does not follow my precepts, despises Christ, and not me. Wherefore I beseech you all, beloved rulers and friends, for the sake of God and of poor neglected youth, do not count this a small matter, as some do, who, in their blindness, overlook the wiles of the adversary. For it is a great and solemn duty that is laid upon us, a duty of immense moment to Christ and to the world, to give aid and council to the young. And in so doing we likewise promote our own best interests. And remember, that the silent, hidden and malicious assaults of the devil can be withstood only by manly Christian effort. Beloved rulers, if we find it necessary to expend such large sums, as we do yearly, upon artillery, roads, bridges, dykes, and a thousand other things of the sort, in order that a city may be assured of continued order, peace, and tranquillity, ought we not to expend on the poor suffering youth therein, at least enough to provide them with a schoolmaster or two? God, the Almighty, has, in very deed, visited us Germans with the small rain of his grace, and vouchsafed to us a right golden harvest. For we have now among us many excellent and learned young men, richly furnished with knowledge, both of the languages and of the arts, who could do great good, if we would only set them to the task of teaching our little folks. Do we not see before our very eyes, that a boy may now be so thoroughly drilled in three years, that, at fifteen or eighteen, he shall know more than hitherto all the high schools and cloisters put together have ever been able to impart? Yea, what other thing have the high schools and cloisters ever achieved, but to make asses and blockheads? Twenty, forty years would they teach you, and after all you would know nothing of Latin, or of German either; and then, too, there is their shameful profligacy, by which how many ingenuous youths have been led astray! But, now that God has so richly favored us, in giving us such a number of persons competent to teach these young folks, and to mould their powers in the best manner, truly it behooves us not to throw his grace to the wind, and not to suffer him to knock at our door in vain. . . .

"This may be so," you reply; "but, though we ought to have schools, and must have them, still what will it profit us to have Latin, Greek, Hebrew, and your other liberal arts taught in them? Will not German suffice to teach us all of the Bible and the Word of God that is essential to salvation?" Alas, I fear me, that we Germans must ever be and continue to be mere brutes and wild beasts, as our neighbors with such good reason style us. . . . Surely, were there no other good to be got from the languages, the bare thought that they are a noble and a glorious gift from God, wherewith he has visited and enriched us, almost beyond all other nations, this thought, I say, ought to be a powerful motive, yea, an allurement to cultivate them. . . . For the prince of darkness is shrewd enough to know that, where the languages flourish, there his power will soon be so rent and torn that he cannot readily repair it. But now, since he cannot keep them from expanding into a vigorous growth, and from bearing fruit, he is at work, devising how he may render them dwarfed and sickly, if so be that they may decay and die of themselves. . . .

. . . For, as the light of the sun dispels the shadows of the night, so do the languages render useless all the glosses of the Fathers. Since now, it becomes Christians to regard the Scriptures as the one only book, which is all their own, and since it is a sin and a shame for us not to be familiar with our own book, nor with the language and the word of our God;—so it is a still greater sin and shame, for us not to learn the languages, especially now that God is bringing to us and freely offering us learned men, and suitable books, and everything which we need for this purpose, and is, so to speak, urging us to the task, so desirous is he to have his book open to us. O, how joyful would those beloved Fathers have been, if they could have come to the knowledge of the Scriptures, and have learned the languages so easily as we now may do it. . . .

But, you say, "we can not bring all our children up to be students; we can not spare them; we need them at home to work for us." I answer, "I do not ask for the establishment of such schools, as we have had hitherto, where our young men have spent twenty or thirty years over Donatus or Alexander, and yet have not learned anything at all. We have now another world, and things are done after a different pattern. And I ask no more than this, namely, that boys shall attend upon such schools as I have in view, an hour or two a day, and none the less; spend the rest of their time at home, or in learning some trade, or doing whatever else you will; thus both these matters will be cared for together, while they are young and opportunities are favorable. For else, they would haply spend tenfold this time in gunning and ball-playing. So, too, your little girls may easily find time enough to go to school an hour a day, and yet do all their household duties; for they now devote more than that to overmuch play, dancing, and sleep.

It is very plain that all we need, is a cordial and earnest determination to train up our youth aright, and by this means furnish the world with wise and efficient men. For the devil is better pleased with coarse blockheads and with folks who are useful to nobody; because where such characters abound, then things do not go on prosperously here on the earth.

Hence, there is great need, not for the sake of the young alone, but also for the welfare and stability of all our institutions, temporal and spiritual alike, that we should begin at once, and in good earnest, to attend to this matter. . . .

Wherefore, dearly beloved rulers, bend yourselves to the work which God so strictly enjoins upon you, which your office involves, which our youth stand so much in need of, and which neither the world nor the spirit can afford to do without. We have lain, alas, too long in the darkness of corruption and death; too long have we been German beasts. Let us now act as becomes reasonable beings, so that God may mark our gratitude for the good things he has given us, and that other lands may see that we, too, are men; nay, more, that we are men who can either learn somewhat from them, or impart somewhat to them: so, through us, the world shall be made better. I have done my part; and with longing have I desired to bring aid and counsel to this German land. . . .

48. LUTHER ON COMPULSORY SCHOOL ATTENDANCE*

Martin Luther

In 1530, Martin Luther, still disturbed by the weakness of German education,

*From *Sermon on the Duty of Sending Children to School* by Martin Luther; trans. in Barnard's *American Journal of Education,* Vol. IV.

prepared a sermon which he ordered to be read in all Lutheran churches. In the sermon, a part of which follows, he urged compulsory attendance, not only for religious purposes, but also for the welfare of the state.

I hold it to be incumbent on those in authority to command their subjects to keep their children at school; for it is, beyond doubt, their duty to insure the permanency of the above-named offices and positions, so that preachers, jurists, curates, scribes, physicians, schoolmasters, and the like may not fail from among us; for we cannot do without them. If they have the right to command their subjects, the able-bodied among them, in time of war, to handle musket and pike, to mount the walls, or to do whatever else the exigency may require; with how much the more reason ought they to compel the people to keep their children at school, inasmuch as here upon earth the most terrible of contests, wherein there is never a truce, is ever going on, and that with the devil himself, who is lying in wait, by stealth and unawares, if so be that he may drain city and kingdom, and empty quite out of them all the brave and good, even until he has removed the kernel utterly, and naught shall be left but a mere shell, full of idle mischief-makers, to be mere puppets in his hands to do his pleasure. Then will your city or your country suffer a true famine, and, without the smoke of conflict, will be silently destroyed from within, and that without warning. Even the Turk manages in another way; for he takes every third child throughout his empire, and trains him to some calling perforce. How much more, then, ought our rulers to put at least some children to school; not that I would have a boy taken away from his parents, only that he should be educated, for his own good and the general welfare, to some calling that shall yield him abundant fruits of his industry. Wherefore, let magistrates lay these things to heart, and let them keep a vigilant look-out; and, wherever they see a promising lad, have him pledged at school.

49. MELANCHTHON'S SCHOOL PLAN*

Melanchthon

In 1527, the Elector of Saxony, probably responding to Luther's exhortations, appointed a commission to study and report to him concerning the educational needs of the country. The commission was headed by Philip Melanchthon (1497-1560), the real scholar of the German Reformation. The chief purpose of the school plan was to provide adequate religious training. Note, however, that Melanchthon was a Latinist, true to the traditions of the Renaissance.

School Plan

Preachers also should exhort the people of their charge to send their children to school, so that they may be trained up to teach sound doctrine in the church, and to serve the state in a wise and able manner. Some imagine that it is enough for a teacher to understand German. But this is a misguided fancy. For he, who is to teach others, must have great practice and special aptitude; to gain this, he must have studied much, and from his youth up. . . .

*From *Book of Visitations,* Melancthon; trans. in Barnard's *American Journal of Education,* Vol. IV.

... In our day there are many abuses in children's schools. And it is that these abuses may be corrected, and that the young may have good instruction, that we have prepared this plan. In the first place, the teachers must be careful to teach the children Latin only, not German, nor Greek, nor Hebrew, as some have heretofore done, burdening the poor children with such a multiplicity of pursuits, that are not only unproductive, but positively injurious. Such schoolmasters, we plainly see, do not think of the improvement of the children at all, but undertake so many languages solely to increase their own reputation. In the second place, teachers should not burden the children with too many books, but should rather avoid a needless variety. Thirdly, it is indispensable that the children be classified into distinct groups.

The First Group. The first group shall consist of those children who are learning to read. With these the following method is to be adopted: They are first to be taught the child's manual, containing the alphabet, the creed, the Lord's prayer, and other prayers. When they have learned this, Donatus and Cato may both be given them; Donatus for a reading-book, and Cato they may explain after the following manner: the schoolmaster must give them the explanation of a verse or two, and then in a few hours call upon them to repeat what he has thus said; and in this way they will learn a great number of Latin words, and lay up a full store of phrases to use in speech. In this they should be exercised until they can read well. Neither do we consider it time lost, if the feebler children, who are not especially quick-witted, should read Cato and Donatus not once only, but a second time. With this they should be taught to write, and be required to show their writing to the schoolmaster every day. Another mode of enlarging their knowledge of Latin words is to give them every afternoon some words to commit to memory, as has been the custom in schools hitherto. These children must likewise be kept at music, and be made to sing with the others, as we shall show, God willing, further on.

The Second Group. The second group consists of children who have learned to read, and are now ready to go into grammar. With these the following regulations should be observed: The first hour after noon every day all the children, large and small, should be practiced in music. Then the schoolmaster must interpret to the second group the fables of Aesop. After vespers, he should explain to them the Paedology of Mosellanus; and, when this is finished, he should select from the Colloquies of Erasmus some that may conduce to their improvement and discipline. This should be repeated on the next evening also. When the children are about to go home for the night, some short sentence may be given them, taken perhaps from a poet, which they are to repeat the next morning, such as, "*Amicus certus in re incerta cerniture.*"–A true friend becomes manifest in adversity. Or "*Fortuna, quem nimium foret, stultum facit.*"–Fortune, if she fondles a man too much, makes him a fool. Or this from Ovid: "*Vulgus amicitias utilitate probat.*"–The rabble value friendships by the profit they yield.

In the morning the children are again to explain Aesop's fables. With this the teacher should decline some nouns or verbs, many or few, easy or difficult, according to the progress of the children, and then ask them the rules and the reasons for such inflection. And at the same time when they shall have learned the rules of construction, they should be required to *construe*, (parse,) as it is called; this is a very useful exercise, and yet there are not many who employ it. After the children have thus learned Aesop, Terence is to be given to them; and this they must commit to memory, for they will now be older, and able to work harder. Still the master must be cautious, lest he overtask them. Next after

Terence, the children may take hold of such of the comedies of Plautus as are harmless in their tendency, as the *Aulularia,* the *Trinummus,* the *Pseudolus,* etc.

The hour before mid-day must be invariably and exclusively devoted to instruction in grammar: first etymology, then syntax, and lastly prosody. And when the teacher has gone thus far through with the grammar, he should begin it again, and so on continually, that the children may understand it to perfection. For if there is negligence here, there is neither certainty nor stability in whatever is learned beside. And the children should learn by heart and repeat all the rules, so that they may be driven and forced, as it were, to learn the grammar well.

If such labor is irksome to the schoolmaster, as we often see, then we should dismiss him, and get another in his place,—one who will not shrink from the duty of keeping his pupils constantly in the grammar. For no greater injury can befall learning and the arts, than for youth to grow up in ignorance of grammar. . . .

The Third Group. Now, when these children have been well trained in grammar, those among them who have made the greatest proficiency should be taken out, and formed into a third group. The hour after mid-day they, together with the rest, are to devote to music. After this the teacher is to give an explanation of Vergil. When he has finished this, he may take up Ovid's Metamorphoses, and the latter part of the afternoon Cicero's "Offices," or "Letters to Friends." In the morning, Vergil may be reviewed, and the teacher, to keep up practice in the grammar, may call for constructions and inflections, and point out the prominent figures of speech.

The hour before mid-day, grammar should still be kept up, that the scholars may be thoroughly versed therein. And when they are perfectly familiar with etymology and syntax, then prosody (*metrica*) should be opened to them, so that they can thereby become accustomed to make verses. For this exercise is a very great help toward understanding the writings of others; and it likewise gives the boys a rich fund of words, and renders them accomplished in many ways. In course of time, after they have been sufficiently practiced in the grammar, this same hour is to be given to logic and rhetoric. The boys in the second and third groups are to be required every week to write compositions, either in the form of letters or of verses. They should also be rigidly confined to Latin conversation, and to this end the teachers themselves must, as far as possible, speak nothing but Latin with the boys; thus they will acquire the practice by use, and the more rapidly for the incentives held out to them.

50. WÜRTEMBERG'S PLAN FOR EDUCATION*

Karl von Raumer

When the chiefs of state in the Lutheran countries assumed the powers formerly held by the Church, it was natural that state educational systems would develop. Wurtemberg was the first state to develop such a system. The School Code, *first issued in 1559, became a model after which other German school systems were patterned. The* Code *provided a number of schools, beginning on*

*From an article by Karl von Raumer; trans. in Barnard's *American Journal of Education,* Vol. VI, pp. 426-34.

the elementary level and continuing through the university. This system at least contemplates universal education. Note that the effects of the Renaissance upon the curriculum continue unabated.

1. Teutsch (German) Schools

Beginning school. Boys and girls separate. Instruction in reading and writing German, religion, and music. Such schools to be set up in every little village and hamlet. Teachers in such schools to be relieved from beadle and mass services in the churches. These schools free, and for the masses.

2. Latin Schools

A fully equipped school to have six classes, but many had less. These known as private schools. They were divided into six classes, as follows:

First or Lowest Class. (9 to 11 years of age.) Pupils in this class learned to pronounce and read Latin and began building up a vocabulary. Readings from Cato.

Second Class. (10 to 12 years of age.) Cato continued. Declensions and conjugations. Grammar studied. Vocabulary enlarged. Translation from the Latin catechism. Much drill on phrases. Music taught.

Third Class. (11 to 13 years of age.) Much drill on phrases. Reading of fables and dialogues. Letters of Cicero begun. Readings from Terence for elegance and purity. Syntax begun. Music continued.

At close of this year might be transferred to the Cloister Schools (3).

Fourth Class. (12 to 14 years of age.) Cicero's "Letters to his Friends"; his treatises on "Friendship" and "Old Age"; and Terence to be read. Syntax finished; prosody begun.

Music continued.

Greek grammar begun, with readings from the smaller Greek catechism of Brentius.

Fifth Class. (13 to 15 years of age.) All previous work to be perfected. In this class read Cicero's "Familiar Letters" and his "Offices." Also Ovid's *de Tristibus,* and the Gospels in Greek and Latin. Much attention to prosody and to exercises in style. Music continued.

Sixth Class. (14 to 16 years of age.) Cicero's "Speeches," Sallust, and the *Aeneid* of Vergil to be read. Much attention to the elegancies of the Latin tongue, and to pure poetical diction. Successful imitation of the idiom and phraseology of Cicero the aim.

In Greek to complete the grammar, and to read Xenophon's *Cyropaedia* and the larger catechism of Brentius.

Music, especially sacred, to be practiced, and the recitations of the day to be begun by singing either the *Veni sancte Spiritus* or the *Veni Creator Spiritus.*

Conversation, both in and out of school, to be in Latin.

Logic and Rhetoric to be read in this class.

3. The Lower Cloister or Grammar Schools

Could be entered after completing the Third Class, at 12 to 14 years of age. Designed for selected boys, who were to be trained for the service of the Church.

Course of study paralleled the three upper classes of the Latin Schools, but with much more emphasis on theological doctrine.

4. The Higher Cloister Schools

Entered at 15 to 16 years of age, to prepare for the University, which was usually entered at about 16 or 17.

Read Cicero and Vergil. Continued emphasis on style and purity and elegance of diction. Phrase book constructed.

Continue Greek grammar, and read Demosthenes.

Continue music, and study musical theory.

Continue Logic and Rhetoric.

Begin Arithmetic and Astronomy.

Disputations fortnightly on questions of grammar, logic, rhetoric, or the sphere.

Strict discipline, and emphasis on theology.

5. The State University at Tübingen

Studies: Greek, Hebrew, Latin, Logic, Rhetoric, Mathematics, and Theology.

51. SCHOOL REORGANIZATION UNDER HENRY VIII*

In 1541, Henry VIII reformed the cathedral school at Canterbury in agreement with the principles of the English Reformation. Aside from emphasis upon Anglican religious beliefs, it was a replication of the earlier Renaissance schools. Note the continuing emphasis on the study of Latin.

Henry VIII by the grace of God, King of England, France and Ireland, Defender of the Faith, and on earth supreme head of the Church of England and Ireland, to all the sons of holy mother church to whose notice this present writing shall come, greeting. . . .

1. The whole number of those who shall be maintained in the cathedral and metropolitical church of Christ at Canterbury

First we decree and ordain that there shall be for ever in the said church a Dean, 12 Canons, 6 Preachers, 12 Minor Canons, a deacon, a sub-deacon, 12 lay-clerks, a master of the choristers, 10 choristers, two Informators of boys in grammar, of whom one shall be the teacher and the other the under-teacher, 50 boys to be taught grammar, 12 poor to be maintained at the expense of the church, 2 vergers (wand-bearers), 2 sextons (sub-sacrists), 4 servants in the church to ring the bells and arrange other things, two door-keepers who shall be also barabers, a maniciple, a butler and an under-butler, a cook and an under-cook; who shall to the number aforesaid each in his rank sedulously serve in the same church according to our statutes and ordinances.

26. The Choristers and their [Master] number

We decree and ordain that in our church aforesaid there shall be at the election or nomination of the Dean, or in his absence the Sub-dean, and Chapter, ten choristers, boys of tender age with clear voices and fit for singing, to serve the choir, minister and sing. For their instruction and education, as well in good behaviour as in skill in singing, we will that besides the twelve clerks before-named one shall be elected by the Dean [etc.] and Chapter, of good character, upright life and skilled in singing and playing the organ, to diligently employ

*From the Parker manuscript, Corpus Christi College, Cambridge, trans. by A. F. Leach.

himself in teaching the boys, playing the organ at the proper time, and singing divine service. And if he shall be found negligent or idle in teaching he shall after three warnings be deposed from office. And he shall be bound by oath faithfully to discharge his office.

27. The Grammar Boys and their Teachers

That piety and good letters may in our church aforesaid for ever blossom, grow and flower and in their time bear fruit for the glory of God and the advantage and adornment of the commonwealth, we decree and ordain that there shall always be in our cathedral church of Canterbury, elected and nominated by the Dean or in his absence the Sub-dean and Chapter, 50 boys, poor and destitute of the help of their friends, to be maintained out of the possessions of the church, and of native genius as far as may be and apt to learn: whom however we shall not be admitted as poor boys of our church before they have learnt to read and write and are moderately learned in the first rudiments of grammar, in the judgment of the Dean or in his absence the Sub-dean and the Head Master;

And we will that these boys shall be maintained at the expense of our church until they have obtained a moderate knowledge of Latin grammar and have learnt to speak and to write Latin. The period of four years shall be given to this, or if it shall so seem good to the Dean or in his absence the Sub-dean, and the Head Master, at most five years and not more.

33. The celebration of Divine Service

...We will further that both teachers of grammar shall be present in choir on feast-days clothed in garments befitting the choir; one of them having the seat in choir next above the minor canons, the other next after the minor canons.

Moreover we will that the grammar boys who are maintained at the expense of the church shall be present in choir on feast-days, in a proper habit, and diligently do whatever duty is imposed on them by the Precentor; unless they have been otherwise directed by the Head Master. And these boys too we will shall on every day in the year when the sacred mysteries are performed at High Mass be present at the elevation of the body of the Lord, and stay there till the singing of the Agnus Dei is done; and meanwhile, two and two, meditate and say the Psalms "Have mercy on me, O Lord," and "God, have mercy upon us," and "O Lord Jesu Christ," "Out of the deep I cried," with the prayer "Absolve, we beseech thee."

38. Alms and students

The usual qualities which are found in an architect and other overseers of works in pressing on their work, namely, industry and diligence, ought also to be found in pedagogues and teachers of the tender youth, that they may as it were enter into a friendly conspiracy and contention between themselves to imbue thoroughly the scholars committed to their trust with piety and good letters; and not to study their own advantage or indulge their own love of ease so much as to look to their proficiency and the public benefit, so that they may be seen to do their duty fairly in everything. And this they will be able to do much more successfully if they endeavor sedulously to follow the order we have prescribed.

The whole number of the scholars shall be divided into five or six ranks or classes. The Under Master shall teach the three lower, and the Head Master the three upper classes.

The Course of Study

No one shall be admitted into the school who cannot read readily, or who does not know by heart in the vernacular the Lord's Prayer, the Angelic Salutation, the Apostles' Creed and the Ten Commandments. Those who are wholly ignorant of grammar shall learn the accidents of nouns and verbs, as it were out of class. When they have learnt these they shall be taken into the First Class.

In the First Class they shall learn thoroughly by heart the rudiments in English; they shall learn to put together the parts of speech; and to turn a short phrase of English into Latin; and gradually to approach other easy constructions.

In the Second Class they shall learn a little higher; they shall know the genders of nouns and the inflections of verbs written in Latin; they shall run through Cato's verses, Aesop's Fables, and some familiar Colloquies.

In the Third Class they shall endeavor to make right varyings on the nouns and anomalous verbs, so that no noun or verb may be found anywhere which they do not know how to inflect in every detail. In this form too they shall make Terence's Comedies, Mantuanus' Eclogues, and other things of that sort thoroughly familiar to them.

These classes the Under Master shall take diligent care of, instilling and inculcating the lesser rudiments into his pupils so as to make them fit and prepared to receive higher instruction.

The Under Master shall come into school at 6 A.M., and immediately after saying the prayers to God which we have prescribed, shall make his scholars daily say by heart one of the eight parts of speech until they are ready in each. Nor shall he omit on any other day to dictate to his pupils an English sentence, and that a short one, which he shall teach them to turn exactly into Latin, and to write it carefully in their parchment note-books.

In short, in anything to be done in the school the Under Master shall be subject to and shall obey the Head Master; and shall consult him on the method and plan of teaching; so that they may both agree in their great zeal for the profit of the scholars. Both too shall endeavour to teach their pupils to speak openly, finely and distinctly, keeping due decorum both with their body and their mouth.

In the Fourth Form the boys shall be taught to know the Latin syntax readily; and shall be practiced in the stories of poets, and familiar letters of learned men and the like.

In the Fifth Form they shall commit to memory the Figures of Latin Oratory and the rules for making verses; and at the same time shall be practiced in making verses and polishing themes; then they shall be versed in translating the chastest Poets and the best Historians.

Lastly, in the Sixth Form they shall be instructed in the formulas of "Copiousness of Words and Things" written by Erasmus; and learn to make varyings of speech in every mood, so that they may acquire the faculty of speaking Latin, as far as is possible for boys. Meanwhile they shall taste Horace, Cicero, and other authors of that class. Meanwhile they shall compete with one another in declamations so that they may leave well learned in the school of argument.

These classes principally the Head Master shall try to polish in Latin.

He shall come into school by 7 o'clock to perform his duty of teaching thoroughly. He too every other day shall make some English sentence into Latin and teach the flock committed to him to change it into many forms. Moreover let him understand that he has charge of the whole school.

So every week he ought to visit the whole flock, once, twice, or three times, and diligently test the abilities of the scholars and ascertain their progress in learning. If he shall prove any of them, after testing them in every way, to be slow and wholly strangers to the Muses, he shall faithfully warn their friends not to let them, being wholly unfit for letters, waste their time in vain and fill the places of others. But those he shall find to be fit and industrious he shall, at least three times a year, call up to the higher forms, namely from the first to the second, from the second to the third, and so on as each shall be thought fit. This shall be done in the presence of and after consultation with the Under Master in the case of those who are entrusted to his care.

Moreover at 6 P.M. the scholars shall return to school, and until 7 P.M. shall do their repetition and render to their fellow-pupils who have become ripe in learning, several masters also being present, whatever they have learnt through the day.

When leave to play is given they shall play and sport together, lest, wandering about here and there, they incur some loss of character, and wanting to do other things their minds gradually become estranged from learning. And they shall not practice any games which are not of a gentlemanly appearance and free of all lowness.

Lastly, whatever they are doing in earnest or in play they shall never use any language but Latin or Greek.

52. A CALVINIST SCHOOL*

The College de la Rive, actually a secondary school, was established in Geneva by the Geneva Constitution in 1559. The school, organized under the direction of John Calvin, shows the influence of the Renaissance and the Italian humanists. Note that the school had seven classes.

Class VII. In this class the pupils will learn the letters, and write them to form syllables, using a Latin-French reading book. Reading French, and afterwards Latin from a French-Latin Catechism. Drawing, and writing letters of the alphabet.

Class VI. Declensions and conjugations are begun; these occupy the first half year. Parts of speech learnt in French and Latin; more practice in hand-writing. Easy Latin sentences learnt orally, and repeated as practice in conversation.

Class V. Parts of speech finished: elements of syntax: the *Eclogues* of Vergil read: first steps in written Latin composition: Latin and French employed side by side.

Class IV. Latin syntax continued. Cicero's *Letters* begun; composition exercises are based on these. Prosody, with reading of Ovid in illustration. Greek begun; declension and conjugation; elementary construing.

Class III. Greek Grammar systematically learnt, with comparison of the two languages. Cicero,—*Letters, De Amicitia, De Senectute,*—these treatises to be turned into Greek. The *Aeneid*, Caesar, and Isocrates read.

Class II. Chief stress laid upon reading:—Livy, Xenophon, Polybius, Herodian and Homer. Logic begun:—propositions, syllogism; to be illustrated from Cicero's orations. Once a week the Gospel narrative in Greek.

Class I. Logic systematically taught from approved compendium (such as Melanchthon's); the elements of rhetoric in connection with it, and elocution. The whole doctrine of rhetoric illustrated from Cicero's speeches, and from Demosthenes (the Olynthiacs and Philippics). Homer and Vergil also analysed for

*From *Studies in Education during the Renaissance,* W. H. Woodward, Cambridge, 1906, pp. 159-60.

rhetorical purposes. Two original "declamationes" are prepared monthly. Once a week an Epistle of Saint Paul or other apostle is read in Greek.

The choice of authors and the place of logic deserve attention, not less than the acceptance of the vernacular in junior classes.

**THE DEVELOPMENT OF REALISM
AND NATIONAL EDUCATION**

53. MILTON'S CURRICULAR PLAN*

John Milton

John Milton (1608-1674) is best known for his poetic writings. However, he had some interest in education. In his Tractate on Education, *he took the typical position of the humanistic realist, basing his curriculum on the study of the ancient writers and directing the study toward realistic purposes. Like John Locke, he was interested in education only for the upper class male. The selection below is taken from the* Tractate.

For their Studies, First they should begin with the chief and necessary rules of some good Grammar, either that now us'd (Lily's), or any better. . . . Next to make them expert in the usefullest points of Grammar, . . . some easie and delightful Book of Education would be read to them; whereof the Greeks have store, as *Cebes, Plutarch*, and other Socratic discourses. But in Latin we have none of classic authority extant, except the two or three first Books of *Quintilian,* and some select pieces elsewhere. . . . At the same time, some other hour of the day, might be taught to them the rules of Arithmetick, and soon after the Elements of Geometry even playing, as the old manner was. After evening repast, till bed-time their thoughts will be best taken up in the easie grounds of Religion, and the story of the Scriptures.

The next step (13 to 16) would be to the Authors of *Agriculture, Cato, Varro,* and *Columella,* for the matter is most easie, and if the language be difficult, so much the better, it is not a difficulty above their years. And here will be an occasion of inciting and inabling them hereafter to improve the tillage of their Country, to recover the bad Soil, and to remedy the waste that is made of good; for this was one of *Hercules* praises. Ere half these Authors be read they cannot chuse but be masters of any ordinary prose. So that it will be then seasonable for them to learn in any modern Author, the use of Globes, and all the Maps; first with the old names, and then with the new: or they might be then capable to read any compendious method of natural Philosophy. And at the same time might be entering the Greek tongue, after the same manner as was before prescrib'd in the Latin; whereby the difficulties of Grammar being soon overcome, all the Historical Physiology of *Aristotle* and *Theophrastus* are open before them, and as I may say, under contribution. The like access will be to *Vitruvius,* to *Seneca's* natural questions, to *Mela, Celsus, Pliny,* or *Solinus.* And having thus past the principles of *Arithmetick, Geometry, Astronomy* and *Geography* with a general campact of Physicks, they may descend in *Mathematicks* to the instrumental science of *Trigonometry,* and from thence to Fortification, Architecture, Enginry, or Navigation. And in Natural Philosophy they may proceed leisurely from the History of Meteors, Minerals, plants and

*From *Tractate on Education* by John Milton, London, 1673.

living Creatures as far as Anatomy (Aristotle). Then also in course might be read to them out of some not tedious Writer the Institution of Physic; that they may know the tempers, the humours, the seasons, and how to manage a crudity: which he can wisely and timely do, is not only a great Physitian to himself, and to his friends, but also at some time or other, save an Army by this frugal and expenseless means only; and not let the healthy and stout bodies of young men rot away under him for want of this discipline; which is a great pity, and no less a shame to the Commander. To set forward all these proceedings in Nature and Mathematicks, what hinders, but that they may procure, as oft as shal be needful, the helpful experiences of Hunters, Fowlers, Fishermen, Shepherds, Gardeners, Apothecaries; and in other sciences, Architects, Engineers, Mariners, Anatomists; who doubtless would be ready some for reward, and some to favour such a hopeful Seminary. And this will give them such a real tincture of natural knowledge, as they shall never forget, but daily augment with delight. Then also those poets which are now counted most hard, will be both facil and pleasant, *Orpheus, Hesiod, Theocritus, Aratus, Nicander, Oppian, Dionysius,* and in Latin *Lucretius, Manilius,* and the rural part of *Vergil.*

By this time (15 or 16) . . . they may with some judgment contemplate upon moral good and evil. Then will be requir'd a special reinforcement of constant and sound endoctrinating to set them right and firm, instructing them more amply in the knowledge of Vertue and the hatred of Vice; while their young and pliant affections are led through all the moral works of *Plato, Xenophon, Cicero, Plutarch, Laertius,* and those *Locrian* remnents; but still to be reduct in their nightward studies wherewith they close the dayes work, under the determinate sentence of *David* or *Solomon,* or the Evange(l)s and Apostolic Scriptures. Being perfect in the knowledge of personal duty, they may then begin the study of Economics. And either now, or before this, they may have easily learnt at any odd hour the *Italian Tongue.* And soon after, but with wariness and good antidote, it would be wholesome enough to let them taste some choice Comedies, Greek, Latin, or *Italian:* Those Tragedies also that treat of Household matters, as *Trachiniae, Alcestis,* and the like. The next remove must be to the study of *Politicks*; to know the beginning, end, and reason of Political Societies; that they may not in a dangerous fit of the Common-wealth be such poor, shaken, and uncertain Reeds, of such a tottering Conscience, as many of our great Counsellers have lately shewn themselves, but stedfast pillars of the State.

After this they are to dive into the grounds of Law, and legal Justice; deliver'd first, and with best warrant by *Moses,* and as far as humane prudence can be trusted, in those extoll'd remains of Grecian Law-givers. *Licurgus, Solon, Zaleucus, Charondas,* and thence to all the Roman *Edicts* and Tables with their *Justinian;* and so down to the *Saxon* and common Laws of *England,* and the Statutes. Sundayes also and every evening may be now understandingly spent in the highest matters of *Theology,* and Church History ancient and modern: and ere this time the Hebrew Tongue at a set hour might have been gain'd, that the Scriptures may be now read in their own original; whereto it would be no impossibility to add the *Chaldey,* and the *Syrian* Dialect. When all these employments are well conquer'd, then will the choice Histories, *Heroic Poems,* and *Attic* Tragedies of stateliest and most regal argument, with all the famous Political Orations offer themselves; which if they were not only read; But some of them got by memory, and solemly pronunc't with right accent, and grace, as might be taught, would endue them even with the spirit and vigor of *Demosthenes* or *Cicero, Euripides,* or *Sophocles.*

And now lastly will be the time to read with them those organic arts which inable men to discourse and write perspicuously, elegantly, and according to the fitted stile of lofty, mean, or lowly. Logic therefore so much as is useful, is to be refer'd to this due place with all her well coucht Heads and Topics, untill it be time to open her contracted palm into a gracefull and ornate Rhetorick taught out of the rule of *Plato, Aristotle, Phalareus, Cicero, Hermogones, Longinus.* To which Poetry would be made subsequent, or indeed rather precedent, as being suttle and fine, but more simple, sensuous and passionate. I mean not here the prosody of verse, which they could not but have hit on before among the rudiments of Grammar; but that sublime Art which in *Aristotles Poetics,* in *Horace,* and the *Italian* Commentaries of *Castelvetro, Tasso, Mazzoni,* and others, teaches what the laws are of a true Epic Poem, what of a *Dramatic,* what of a *Lyric,* what Decomum is, which is the grand master-piece to observe. This would make them soon perceive what despicable creatures our comm(on) Rimers and Playwriters be, and shew them, what religious, what glorious and magnificent use might be made of Poetry both in divine and humane things. From hence and not till now will be the right season of forming them to be able Writers and Composers in every excellent matter, when they shall be thus fraught with an universal insight into things. Or whether they be to speak in Parliament or Counsel, honour and attention would be waiting on their lips. There would then also appear in Pulpits other Visages, other gestures, and stuff otherwise wrought then what we now sit under, oft times to as great a trial of our patience as any other that they preach to us. These are the Studies wherin our noble and our gentle youth ought to bestow their time in a disciplinary way from twelve to one and twenty; unless they rely more upon their ancestors dead, then upon themselves living.

54. MONTAIGNE'S CONTEMPT FOR HUMANISM*

M. S. de Montaigne

The social realists turned away from humanistic education because they felt that it failed to provide the training necessary for a "man of affairs." Michel de Montaigne (1533-1592), in his essay On Pedantry, *ridiculed the humanistic education of his day. The following material is typical of the attitude of the social realist.*

If a man passe by, crie out to our people; *Oh, what a wise man goeth yonder!* And of another: *Oh what a good man is yonder!* He will not faile to cast his eyes and respect toward the former. A third crier were needful, to say, *Oh what blocke-heads are those!* We are ever readie to aske, *Hath he any skill in the Greeke and Latine tongue? can he write well? doth hee write in prose or verse?* But whether hee be growne better or wiser, which should be the chiefest of his drift, that is never spoken of, we should rather enquire who is better wise, than who is more wise. We labour, and toyle, and plod to fill the memorie, and leave both understanding and conscience emptie. Even as birds flutter and skip from field to field to pecke up corne, or any graine, and without tasting the same, carrie it in their bils, therewith to feed their little ones; so doe our pedants gleane and picke learning from bookes, and never lodge it further than their lips, only to degorge and cast it to the wind.

*From *Essays,* essay on the "Education of Children," by Montaigne, Book I, 1580.

55. MONTAIGNE'S PRACTICAL EDUCATION*

M. S. de Montaigne

In his essay on the Education of Children, *Montaigne turned from ridiculing the humanists and presented his own conception of the type of education necessary for the man of affairs. Note the insistence upon the practical aspects of education and the importance given to the development of good judgment.*

A friend of mine then, having read the preceding chapter, the other day told me, that I should a little longer have insisted upon the education of children. . . . But, in truth, all I understand as to that particular is only this, that the greatest and most important difficulty of human science is the education of children. . . .

For a boy of quality, then, who pretends to letters not upon account of profit, nor so much for outward ornament, as for his own proper and peculiar use, and to furnish and enrich himself within, having rather a desire to go out an accomplished cavalier and a fine gentleman, than a mere scholar and a learned man; for such a one, I say, I would also have his friends solicitous to find him out a tutor, who has rather a well-made than a well-filled head; seeking, indeed, both if such a person can be found, but rather to prefer his manners and his judgment before mere learning, and that this man should exercise his charge after a new method.

'T is the custom of schoolmasters to be eternally thundering in their pupils' ears, as they were pouring into a funnel, whilst their business is only to repeat what others have said before: now I would have a tutor to correct this error, and that at the very first, he should, according to the capacity he has to deal with, put it to the test, permitting his pupil to taste and relish things, and of himself to choose and discern them, sometimes opening the way to him, and sometimes leaving him to break the ice himself; that is, I would not have him alone invent and speak, but that he should also hear his pupil speak in turn. Let him make him examine and thoroughly sift every thing he reads, and lodge nothing in his fancy upon simple authority and trust. Aristotle's principles will then be no more principles to him than those of Epicurus and the Stoics: let this diversity of opinions be propounded to and laid before him, he will himself choose, if he is able; if not, he will remain in doubt. For if he embraces the opinions of Xenephon and Plato by his own reason, they will no more be theirs, but become his own. Who follows another follows nothing, finds nothing, nay, is inquisitive after nothing. Let him, at least, know what he knows. It will be necessary that he imbibe their knowledge, not that he be corrupted by their precepts; and no matter if he forget where he had his learning, provided he know how to apply it to his own use. Truth and reason are common to every one, and are no more his who spake them first, than his who speaks them after. . . . To know by rote is no knowledge, and signifies no more but only to retain what one has entrusted to one's memory. That which a man rightly knows and understands, he is free dispenser of at his own full liberty, without any regard to the author from whom he had it, or fumbling over the leaves of his book. A mere bookish learning is both troublesome and ungraceful; and though it may serve for some kind of ornament, there is yet no foundation for any superstructure to be built upon it. . . .

They begin to teach us to live when we have almost done living. The boy we would breed has a great deal less time to spare; he owes but the first fifteen or

*From *Essays,* essay on the "Education of Children," 1580, by Montaigne, Book I.

sixteen years of his life to education; the remainder is due to action: let us therefore employ that short time in necessary instruction. Away with logical subtleties, they are abuses, things by which our lives can never be amended: take the plain philosophical discourses, learn first how rightly to choose, and then rightly to apply them; they are more easy to understand than one of Boccaccio's novels; a child from nurse is much more capable of them than of learning to read and write. Philosophy has discourses equally proper for childhood as for the decrepit age of man. . . .

I would not have this pupil of ours imprisoned and made a slave to his book; nor would I have him given up to the morosity and melancholic humor of a sour, ill-natured pedant. I would not have his spirit cowed and subdued by applying him to the rack and tormenting him, as some do, fourteen or fifteen hours a day, and so make a pack-horse of him. . . . I would have his outward fashion and mein, and the disposition of his limbs, formed at the same time as his mind. 'T is not a soul, 't is not a body that we are training up, but a man, and we ought not to divide him. And, as Plato says, we are not to fashion one without the other, but make them draw together like two horses hitched to a coach. . . .

With such a one, after fifteen or sixteen years' study, compare one of our college (secondary school) Latinists, who has thrown away so much time in learning nothing but to speak. The world is nothing but babble; and I hardly ever yet saw that man who did not rather prate too much, than speak too little; and yet half our age is embezzled this way. We are kept four or five years to learn words only, and to tack them together into clauses, as many more to form them into long discourse, divided into four or five parts; and other five years at least to learn succinctly to mix and interweave them after a subtle and intricate manner. Let us leave all this to those who make a profession of it. . . . We do not pretend to breed a grammarian or a logician, but a gentleman; let us leave them to throw away their time at their own fancy: our business lies elsewhere. . . .

No doubt but Greek and Latin are very great ornaments, and of very great use, but we buy them too dear: Not that fine speaking is not a very good and commendable quality; but not so excellent and so necessary as some would make it; and I am scandalized that our whole life should be spent in nothing else. I would first understand my own language, and that of my neighbors with whom most of my business and conversation lies. . . .

To return to my subject, there is nothing like alluring the appetite and affections; otherwise you make nothing but so many asses laden with books, and by dint of your lash, you give them their pocketful of learning to keep; whereas, to do well, you should not only lodge it with them, but make them espouse it.

56. LOCKE AS A SOCIAL REALIST*

John Locke

John Locke (1632-1704) is best known for his work in political theory. However, he was deeply interested in education and wrote Some Thoughts on Education, *from which the following selection is taken. As a typical social realist, Locke was interested only in the education of the young gentleman, who was to be trained to undertake the responsibilities of a man of affairs. Note Locke's interest in tutorial education.*

*From *Some Thoughts Concerning Education* by John Locke, London, 1693.

As the Father's Example must teach the Child Respect for his Tutor, so the Tutor's Example must lead the Child into those Actions he would have him do. His Practice must by no means cross his Precepts, unless he intend to set him wrong. It will be to no Purpose for the Tutor to talk of the Restraint of the Passions whilst any of his own are let loose; and he will in vain endeavour to reform any Vice or Indecency in his Pupil, which he allows in himself. Ill Patterns are sure to be follow'd more than good Rules; . . .

In all the whole Business of Education, there is nothing like to be less hearken'd to, or harder to be well observ'd, than what I am now going to say; and that is, that Children should, from their first beginning to talk, have some *discreet, sober,* nay, *wise* Person about them, whose Care it should be to fashion them aright, and keep them from all Ill, especially the infection of bad company. I think this province requires great *Sobriety, Temperance, Tenderness, Diligence,* and *Discretion;* Qualities hardly to be found united in Persons that are to be had for ordinary Salaries, nor easily to be found any where. . . .

The Consideration of Charge ought not to deter those who are able. The great Difficulty will be where to find a *proper* Person: For those of small Age, Parts, and Vertue, are unfit for this Employment, and those that have greater, will hardly be got to undertake such a Charge. You must therefore look out early, and enquire every where; for the World has People of all Sorts. . . .

. . . one fit to educate and form the Mind of a young Gentleman is not every where to be found, and more than ordinary Care is to be taken in the Choice of him, or else you may fail of your End.

The Character of a sober Man and a Scholar is, as I have above observ'd, what every one expects in a Tutor. This generally is thought enough, and is all that Parents commonly look for: But when such an one has Empty'd out into his Pupil all the Latin and Logick he has brought from the University, will that Furniture make him a fine Gentleman? Or can it be expected, that he should be better bred, better skill'd in the World, better principled in the Grounds and Foundations of true Virtue and Generosity, than his young *Tutor* is?

To form a young Gentleman as he should be, 't is fit his *Governor* should himself be well-bred, understanding the Ways of Carriage and Measures of Civility in all the Variety of Persons, Times, and Places; and keep his Pupil, as much as his Age requires, constantly to the Observation of them. This is an Art not to be learnt nor taught by Books. Nothing can give it but good Company and Observation join'd together. The Taylor may make his Clothes modish, and the Dancing-master give Fashion to his Motions; yet neither of these, tho' they set off well, make a well-bred Gentleman: No, tho' he have Learning, to boot, which, if not well manag'd, makes him more impertinent and intolerable in Conversation. Breeding is that which sets a Gloss upon all his other good Qualities, and renders them useful to him, in procuring him the Esteem and Good-will of all that he comes near. Without good Breeding his other Accomplishments make him pass but for proud, conceited, vain, or foolish.

Courage in an ill-bred Man has the Air and escape not the Opinion of Brutality: Learning becomes Pedantry; Wit, Buffoonry Plainness, Rusticity; good Nature, Fawning. And there cannot be a good Quality in him, which Want of Breeding will not warp and disfigure to his Disadvantage.

Besides being well-bred, the *Tutor* should know the World well; the Ways, the Humours, the Follies, the Cheats, the Faults of the Age he is fallen into, and particularly of the Country he lives in. These he should be able to shew to his Pupil, as he finds him capable; teach him skill in Men, and their Manners; pull off the Mask which their several Callings and Pretences cover them with, and make his pupil discern what lies at the Bottom under such Appearances. . . . that when he comes to launch into the Deep himself, he may not be like one at Sea without a Line, Compass, or Sea-Chart; but may have some Notice before-hand of the Rocks and Shoals, the Currents and Quick-sands, and know a little how to steer, that he sink not before he get Experience. . . .

A great Part of the Learning now in Fashion in the Schools of *Europe,* and that goes ordinarily into the Round of Education, a Gentleman may in a good Measure be unfurnish'd with, without any great Disparagement to himself or Prejudice to his Affairs. But Prudence and good breeding are in all the Stations and Occurrences of Life necessary; and most young Men suffer in want of them, and come rawer and more awkward into the World than they should, for this very Reason, because these Qualities, which are of all other the most necessary to be taught, and stand most in need of the Assistance and Help of a Teacher, are generally neglected and thought but a slight or no Part of a *Tutor's* Business. Latin and Learning make all the Noise; and the main Stress is laid upon his Proficiency in Things a great Part whereof belong not to a Gentleman's Calling; which is to have the Knowledge of a Man of Business, a Carriage suitable to his Rank, and be eminent and useful in his Country, according to his Station. . . .

The great Work of a *Governor,* is to fashion the Carriage, and form the Mind; to settle in his Pupil good Habits and the Principles of Virtue and Wisdom; to give him by little and little a View of Mankind, and to work him into a Love and Imitation of what is excellent and praise-worthy; and, in the Prosecution of it, to give him Vigour, Activity, and Industry. The Studies which he sets him upon, are but as it were the Exercises of his Faculties, and Employment of his Time, to keep him from Sauntering and Idleness, to teach him Application, and accustom him to take Pains, and to give him some little Taste of what his own Industry must perfect. For who expects, that under a *Tutor* a young Gentleman should be an accomplish'd Critick, Orator, or Logician? go to the Bottom of Metaphysicks, natural Philosophy, or Mathematicks? or be a Master in History or Chronology? though something of each of these is to be taught him: But it is only to open the Door, that he may look in, and as it were begin an acquaintance, but not to dwell there: And a Governor would be much blam'd that should keep his Pupil too long, and lead him too far in most of them. But of good Breeding, Knowledge of the World, Virtue, Industry, and a Love of Reputation, he cannot have too much: And if he have these, he will not long want what he needs or desires of the other.

. . . We learn not to live, but to dispute; and our Education fits us rather for the University than the World. But 't is no wonder if those who make the Fashion suit it to what they have, and not to what their Pupils want. The Fashion being once establish'd, who can think it strange, that in this, as well as in all other Things, it should prevail? . . . Reason, if consulted with, would advise, that their Children's Time should be spent in acquiring what might be useful to them when they come to be Men, rather than to have their heads stuff'd with a deal of Trash, a great Part whereof they usually never do ('t is certain they never need to) think on again as long as they live; and so much of it as does stick by them they are only the worse for. This is so well known, that I appeal to Parents themselves, who have been at Cost to have their young Heirs taught it, whether it be not ridiculous for their Sons to have any Tincture of that Sort of Learning, when they come abroad into the World? whether any Appearance of it would not lessen and disgrace them in Company? And that certainly must be an admirable Acquisition, and Deserves well to make a Part in Education, which Men are asham'd of where they are most concern'd to shew their Parts and Breeding.

57. THE METHODOLOGY OF COMENIUS*

Johann Comenius

Johann Comenius (1592-1670) was a native of Moravia. Educated in Germany, he returned to his native land, where he became a bishop in the Moravian church. Driven from Bohemia by religious persecution, he spent most of his life writing and teaching in various countries of Europe. A prolific writer on education and the author of widely used textbooks, Comenius was deeply interested in methodology and has been referred to as the founder of modern methodology in education. By the use of proper methods, he believed, it was possible to teach all things to all people and do it "quickly, pleasantly, and thoroughly." In his The Great Didactic, he developed his system of methodology. The title-page from that book, reproduced below, indicates clearly his faith in methodology as the solution to the problems of education.

(First English edition, from the original Latin edition. Edited by M.W. Keatinge. London, 1896)

THE GREAT DIDACTIC

Setting forth

The Whole Art of Teaching all Things to all Men

or

A certain Inducement to found such Schools in all
the Parishes, Towns, and Villages of every
Christian Kingdom, that the entire
Youth of both Sexes, none
being excepted, shall

QUICKLY, PLEASANTLY, & THOROUGHLY

Become learned in the Sciences, pure in Morals,
trained to Piety, and in this manner
instructed in all things necessary
for the present and for
the future life,

in which, with respect to everything that is suggested,

ITS FUNDAMENTAL PRINCIPLES are set forth from the essential
nature of the matter,
ITS TRUTH is proved by examples from the several
mechanical arts,
ITS ORDER is clearly set forth in years, months, days, and
hours, and, finally,
AN EASY AND SURE METHOD is shown, by which it can
be pleasantly brought into existence.

*Title page of Comenius's *Great Didactic*.

58. AN EARLY PROGRAM OF
VISUAL EDUCATION*

Johann Comenius

In 1658, Comenius published his Orbis Sensualium Pictus *(The World of Sense Objects Pictured), a reader for beginning students of Latin. It is an interesting example of an attempt at visual education, since he develops relationships between words and pictures. The illustrations below are from American translations of the work.*

Orbis Senfualium Pictus.

A World of Things Obvious to the Senfes Drawn in Pictures.

Invitation.   I.   *Invitatia.*

The Mafter and the Boy.

M. **C**ome Boy, learn to be wife.
P. What doth this mean, to be wife?
M. To underftand rightly,

Magifter & Puer.

M. **V**Eni Puer, difce fapere.
P. Quid hoc eft, Sapere?
M. Omnia, quæ neceffaria, recte

	Cornix cornicatur, *a'a'*	A a
The Crow crieth.	
	Agnus balat, *b ê ê ê*	B b
The Lamb blaiteth.	
	Cicada ftridet, *ci ci*	C c
The Grafhopper chirpeth.	
	Upupa dicit, *du du*	D d
The Whooppoo faith.	
	Infans ejulat, *ê ê ê*	E e
The Infant crieth.	
	Ventus flat, *fi fi*	F f
The Wind bloweth.	
	Anfer gingrit, *ga ga*	G g
The Goofe gagleth.	
	Os halat, *ba'h ha'h*	H h
The mouth breatheth out.	
	Mus mintrit, *i i i*	I i
The Moufe chirpeth.	
	Anas tetrinnit, *kha kha*	K k
The Duck quaketh.	
	Lupus ululat, *lu ulu*	L l
The Wolf howleth.	
	Urfus murmurat, *mum mum*	M m
The Bear grumbleth.	

Felis

*From Comenius's *Orbis Pictus.*

A *School*, 1.
is a Shop in which
Young Wits are fashion'd
to vertue, and it is
distinguished into *Forms*.
    The *Master*, 2.
sitteth in a *Chair*, 3.
the *Scholars*, 4.
in *Forms*, 5.
he teacheth, they learn.
    Some things
are writ down before them
with *Chalk* on a *Table*, 6.
    Some sit
at a Table, and write, 7.
he mendeth their Faults, 8.
    Some stand and rehearse
things committed to
memory, 9.
    Some talk together, 10.
and behave themselves
wantonly and carelessly;
these are chastised
with a *Ferrula*, 11.
and a *Rod*, 12.

Schola, 1.
est Officina, in quâ
Novelli Animi formantur
ad virtutem, &
distinguitur in *Classes*.
    Praeceptor, 2.
sedet in *Cathedrâ*, 3.
Discipuli, 4.
in *Subselliis*, 5.
ille docet, hi discunt.
    Quaedam
praescribuntur illis
Cretâ in *Tabellâ*, 6.
    Quidam sedent
ad Mensam, & scribunt, 7.
ipse corrigit Mendas, 8.
    Quidam stant, & reci-
tant mandata
memoriae, 9.
    Quidam confabulantur,
10. ac gerunt se
petulantes, & negligentes;
hi castigantur
Ferulâ (baculô), 11.
& *Virgâ*, 12.

59. EMPHASIS ON SCIENCE AND MATHEMATICS*

Robert Green

By the beginning of the 18th century, mathematical and scientific studies had begun to receive great attention on the college level, although they existed along with typical classical studies. In 1707, Robert Green, a fellow of Clare College at Cambridge, published A Scheme of Study. *While he gave much attention to Latin and Greek language and literature, ancient history, and theology, he also placed great emphasis on mathematics and science, as the studies listed below indicate.*

FIRST YEAR

Second half.
1. Chronology and Geography, with study of maps.

SECOND YEAR

First half.
1. Logick—*Burgerdicius, Locke.*
2. Geometry, Elements of—*Euclid, Sturmius.*

Second half.
1. Arithmetic.
2. Algebra.
3. Corpuscular Philosophy—*Cartes, Varenius, Boyle.*

THIRD YEAR

First half.
1. Experimental Philosophy, and Chemistry of Minerals, Plants, and Animals —*Philosophical Transactions, Boyle.*
2. Anatomy of
   (*a*) Animals—*Keil, Gibson, Harvey,* etc.
   (*b*) Plants and Vegetables—*Grew, Philosophical Transactions.*
   (*c*) Minerals—*Hook's Micrograph, Lowenhock.*

Second half.
1. Opticks, Dioptricks, Caloptricks, Colours, Iris—*Newton, Cartes, Kepler,* etc.
2. Conick Sections, and the Nature of Curves—*Newton, Wallis,* etc.

FOURTH YEAR

First half.
1. Mechanical Philosophy, Staticks, Hydrostaticks, Flux and Reflux, Percussion, Gravitation, etc.—*Marriot, Hugens, Boyle, Newton, Wallis,* etc.
2. Fluxions (Calculus), Infinite Series, Arithmetick of Infinites—*Wallis, Newton,* etc.

Second half.
1. Astronomy, Spherical, Hypothetical, Practical, and Physical—*Mercator, Flamstead, Newton, Kepler,* etc.
2. Logarithms and Trigonometry—*Sturmius, Briggs, Newton,* etc.

*From *A Scheme of Study*, Robert Green, in *Scholae Academicae* by Christopher Wordsworth, Cambridge, 1877, Appendix IV.

60. THE BASIS FOR FRENCH
NATIONAL EDUCATION*

la Chalotais

Louis René de Caradeuc de la Chalotais (1701-1785) was a French statesman of the pre-revolutionary period. In 1763, he published his Essay on National Education, *which heavily influenced the development of state controlled education in France and other countries. The extracts below show his distrust of education by the Church and his insistence on the education of the common people. Note his belief in following the order of nature, an idea developed by Comenius.*

TEACHERS AND PURPOSE

I do not presume to exclude ecclesiastics, but I protest against the exclusion of laymen. I dare claim for the nation an education which depends only on the State, because it belongs essentially to the State; because every State has an inalienable and indefeasible right to instruct its members; because, finally, the children of the State ought to be educated by the members of the State.

It is certain that in the education which was given at Sparta, the prime purpose was to train Spartans. It is thus that in every State the purpose should be to enkindle the spirit of citizenship; and, in our case, to train Frenchmen, and in order to make Frenchmen, to labor to make men of them.

MORAL AND POLITICAL IDEAS

The greatest vice of education, and perhaps the most inevitable, while it shall be entrusted to persons who have renounced the world, is the absolute lack of instruction on the moral and political virtues. Our education does not affect our habits, like that of the ancients. After having endured all the fatigues and irksomeness of the college, the young find themselves in the need of learning in what consist the duties common to all men. They have learned no principle for judging actions, evils, opinions, customs. They have everything to learn on matters that are so important. They are inspired with a devotion which is but an imitation of religion, and with practices which take the place of virtue, and are but the shadow of it.

NATURAL INSTRUCTION

I wish nothing to be taught children except facts which are attested by the eyes, at the age of seven as at the age of thirty.

The principles for instructing children should be those by which nature herself instructs them. Nature is the best of teachers.

Every method which begins with abstract ideas is not made for children.

Let children see many objects; let there be a variety of such, and let them be shown under many aspects and on various occasions. The memory and the imagination of children cannot be overcharged with useful facts and ideas of which they can make use in the course of their lives.

Most young men know neither the world which they inhabit, the earth which nourishes them, the men who supply their needs, the animals which serve them,

*From *Essai d'éducation nationale* by La Chalotais; extracts taken from Compayré.

nor the workmen and citizens whom they employ. They have not even any desire for this kind of knowledge. No advantage is taken of their natural curiosity for the purpose of increasing it. They know how to admire neither the wonders of nature nor the prodigies of the arts.

Education, according to La Chalotais, should be divided into two periods—the first from five to ten years, and the second from ten to seventeen. For these two periods he would have studies, as follows:

STUDIES

First period. The exercises proposed for the first period are as follows: learning to read, write, and draw; dancing and music, which ought to enter into the education of persons above the commonalty; historical narratives and the lives of illustrious men of every country, of every age, and of every profession; geography, mathematical and physical recreations; the fables of La Fontaine, which, whatever may be said of them, ought not to be removed from the hands of children, but all of which they should be made to learn by heart; and besides this, walks, excursions, merriment, and recreations; I do not propose even the studies except as amusements.

Second period. The course of study for the second period should consist of French and Latin literature, or the humanities; a continuation of history, geography, mathematics, and natural history; criticism, logic, and metaphysics; the art of invention; and ethics. He would also add "the English language for science, and the German for war."

TEXTBOOKS

I would have composed for the use of the child histories of every nation, of every century, and particularly of the later centuries, which should be written with greater detail, and which should be read before those of the more remote centuries. I would have written the lives of illustrious men of all classes, conditions, and professions, of celebrated heroes, scholars, women, and children.

La Chalotais put great dependence on elementary books, which might, he thought, be composed within two years, if the king would encourage the publication of them, and if the Academies would put them up for completion.

These books would be the best instruction which the masters could give, and would take the place of every method. Whatever course we may take, we cannot dispense with new books. These books, once made, would make trained teachers unnecessary, and there would then be no longer any occasion for discussion as to their qualities, whether they should be priests, or married, or single. All would be good, provided they were religious, moral, and knew how to read; they would soon train themselves while training their pupils.

THE STATE AND EDUCATION

It is the State, it is the larger part of the nation, that must be kept principally in view in education; for twenty millions of men ought to be held in greater consideration than one million, and the *peasantry, who are not yet a class* in France, as they are in Sweden, *ought not to be neglected in a system of instruction.* Education is equally solicitous that letters should be cultivated, and that the fields should be plowed; that all the sciences and the useful arts should be perfected; that justice should be administered and that religion should be taught; that there should be instructed and competent generals, magistrates, and ecclesiastics, and skillful artists and citizens, all in fit proportion. It is for the government to make each citizen so pleased with his condition that he may not be forced to withdraw from it.

We do not fear to assert, in general, that in the condition in which Europe now is, the people that are the most enlightened will always have the advantage over those who are less so.

61. ROUSSEAU'S IDEAS ON EDUCATION*

Jean-Jacques Rousseau

In 1762, Jean-Jacques Rousseau (1712-1778) published his Emile, *one of the great landmarks in the history of education. In this work, Rousseau insisted that learning must come through experience and not through memorization, that education should be adapted to the unfolding capacities of the child, and that the natural interests and activities of children should be the basis of education. The extracts given below, from* Emile, *give some indication of the content of this important treatise.*

The Preface.

The book was originally written for a thoughtful mother. Even if the thoughts contained in it are of no value in themselves, they ought to serve to awaken valuable thoughts in others. Every body writes and cries out against the usual methods of instruction, but no one suggests a better one. The knowledge of our century serves much more for destroying than for building up.

Childhood is not understood. The most judicious, in their teaching, confine themselves to that which it is necessary for a man to know; without considering what children are fit to learn. They are always seeking for a man in the child, without ever thinking what the child is before it becomes a man.

My system is nature's course of development. This term will be mistaken by many of my readers. They will take my book to be, not a work upon education, but the dreams of a visionary. I do not see as others do; but can I give myself others' eyes? I can not change my views; I can only suspect them. It has been often said to me, Propose only what can be accomplished. This means, propose something which is done now; or, at least, something good, of such a kind that it will come into agreement with prevalent evils. Such a collocation would destroy the good without healing the bad. I would rather adhere entirely to what is already received than to try any half measures.

The Three Teachers of Men.

We come weak into the world, and need strength; bare of every thing, and need assistance. All which we have not at our birth, and have when we grow up, we acquire by education. This education we receive either from nature, from man, or from things. The inner development of our powers and organs is the education of nature; the use which we are taught to make of this development, is education by man; and what we learn by our own experience of the circumstances which have an influence over us, the education by things.

The natural man is complete within himself; his is the numerical unity; an absolute whole; which has relations only with itself, or with its like. The man of society is only a fraction, which depends on its denominator, and whose value is determined by its relations to the whole; to the social body. Those modes of education are best for society, which are most efficient in perverting man from

*From *Émile* by Jean-Jacques Rousseau; trans. in Barnard's *American Journal of Education,* Vol. V.

nature; in robbing him of his absolute existence, in giving him the relative one, such that after it he will feel and act only as a member of society.

This opposition between education for a citizen and for a man, corresponds with the opposition between public education together, and private education in the family. The former existed in Sparta; but exists no longer, for there is no longer any fatherland, or any citizens.

Thus, there remains for us only private education, or that of nature. But what would the man educated only for himself become afterward, among others? To know this, it is necessary to know the completely educated man; and also the natural man. This book is intended to assist in gaining such knowledge.

What now is necessary to be done to educate the natural man? Much, no doubt; chiefly in order to hinder any thing from being done.

The child should be educated for the common human vocation, not for any special situation; he must merely live, in good or evil, as life should bring them; and should learn more by experience than by teaching. Considering the instability of human affairs, and the restless, rebellious spirit of the present century, which is overturning every thing, no more unnatural method of education could be devised than that which deals with a child as if he were never to leave home, or the companionship of his own friends. As soon as the unhappy pupil has gone a step away, he is lost.

Handling Children properly.

Ever since children have been instructed, no other means have been invented of managing them, but emulation, energy, jealousy, covetousness, and debased fear; those easily-excited, most dangerous and soul-destroying passions. At every injudicious lesson, you plant a vice deep within the heart. Foolish teachers think they have done wonders, when they have made the children bad, in order to communicate to them the idea of goodness. Then they say gravely, "Such is human nature." Such is your discipline, rather.

Let children be children. If we choose to reverse the order of things, we shall get premature and flavorless fruits, which soon decay; we shall have young doctors and old children. We might as well expect children to be five feet high, as to have judgment in their tenth year.

Education Negative to the Twelfth Year.

The usual education is such as if children leaped, at one bound, from the mother's breast to the age of reason. An entirely opposite method is the necessary one; an entirely negative one; which does not teach virtue and truth, but seek to preserve the heart from vices, and the understanding from error. If you can bring your pupil to his twelfth year healthy and strong, even if he could not distinguish his right hand from his left, the eyes of his understanding would open to your first lesson in reason; for he would have no prejudices, habits, or any thing to stand in the way of the efficacy of your efforts. He would soon become, under your hands, the wisest of men; and although you began with doing nothing, you would have accomplished a wonder of education.

Do the opposite of what is usual and you will almost always do right.

From the efforts to make the child not a child, but a doctor, come the multiplied fault-findings, flatteries, threats, and reasonings of fathers and teachers. Be reasonable enough not to reason with your pupil. Make him practice his body, his limbs, his senses, his faculties; but keep his soul as inactive as possible; let the character of childhood ripen in the child. By such delay you gain time to learn the gradually developing character of your pupil, before you undertake to guide it, and make precipitate mistakes.

Émile's Character at the Age of Twelve.

His exterior indicates self-possession and ease; he speaks with simplicity, and does not talk unnecessarily. His ideas are confined and clear; he knows nothing by rote, but much by experience. If he does not read so well in books, he reads better in the book of nature; he has less memory than power of judgment; he speaks but one language, but understands what he says. If he does not speak so well as others, he is much more capable of doing. He knows nothing of routine, custom, or habit; and what he did yesterday does not indicate what he will do to-day. Neither authority nor example impose upon him; he does and says only what seems good to him. He knows nothing of study, speech, or manners; but his language corresponds with his ideas, and his behavior arises from his wishes.

He has few moral ideas, but they are such as correspond to his age. Speak to him of duty or obedience, he does not know what you mean; order him, he does not understand you; but say to him, if you will do this to please me, I will sometime do something to please you, and he will instantly exert himself to comply with your wish; for nothing will please him more than to add to his legitimate influence over you, which he holds inviolable.

If he needs help himself, he makes use of the first that comes to hand, whether it be a king or a servant; for all men are alike to his sight. He shows to him whom he asks, that he does not consider any one bound to grant his request. He is simple and laconic in his expressions, and neither servile nor arrogant. Grant his request, and he does not thank you, but feels that he is your debtor; refuse it, and he does not complain nor urge you, but lets the matter drop.

Lively, active, he undertakes nothing too great for his powers, but which he has tried and understands. He has an observing and intelligent eye; and asks no useless questions about what he sees, but examines it himself. As his imagination is yet inactive, and nothing has been done to stimulate it, he sees only what really exists, does not overestimate danger, and is always cool.

Business and play are the same to him, his play is his business; he finds no difference between them. Among city children, there is none more dextrous than he, and all are weaker; he is equal to country children in strength, and surpasses them in dexterity. He is fit to lead his companions, by his talent and experience, without any other authority, without wishing to command; he is at the head of the rest, and they obey him without knowing it.

He is a mature child, and has lived a child's life; his happiness has not been exchanged for his education. If he dies young, his death is to be mourned, but not his life.

Ordinary men would not understand a boy so trained; they would see in him nothing but a scapegrace. A teacher could make no parade with him, could ask him no show questions; and those are the chief of the education of the day.

Émile in his Fifteenth Year.

Being obliged to learn by means of himself, he uses his own understanding, not that of other men; and yields nothing to authority. For most of our errors come less from ourselves than from others. By this continual practice, his mind has acquired a strength like that which is given to the body by labor and hardship. For the same reason his powers develop themselves only in proportion to his growth. He remembers only what has commended itself to his understanding. Thus he has little knowledge, but no half knowledge. He knows that his knowledge is not great; his mind is open, decided, and, if not instructed, at least capable of instruction. Of all that he does he knows the use, and of all he believes, the reason. He proceeds slowly, but thoroughly. He possesses only natural knowledge; none of history; and none of mathematics and ethics. He knows little of generalizing and forming abstractions; he observes properties common to many bodies, without reasoning upon the existence of these properties. What is strange to him he values only by its relations to himself, but this valuation is sufficient and certain. What is most useful to him he values most, and cares nothing for opinion.

Émile is laborious, moderate, patient, persevering, and courageous. His fancy, not heated in any way, never magnifies danger; he can endure sorrow with fortitude, for he has not been trained to oppose himself to fate. What death is, he does not rightly know, but, being accustomed to submit without resistance to the laws of necessity, he will die, when he must, without sighing and without pretense. Nature does not require more of us, in that moment, so abhorred by all. To live free, to set the heart as little as possible upon human things, is the surest means of learning to die.

Émile is destitute of the social virtues. He acts without respect to others; and it is right in his eyes that others should have no regard to him. He makes no demands upon others, he thinks himself under no obligation to any one. Standing alone in society, he counts only upon himself, and is capable of more than others at his age. He has no errors or vices, except such as are unavoidable. His body is healthy, his members are disciplined, his understanding correct and without prejudices, his heart free and without passions. Self-esteem, first and most natural of all the passions, has scarcely awakened in him. Without destroying the peace of any one, he has lived as peacefully, happily, and freely as nature will permit. Do you find that the child, thus educated to his fifteenth year, has wasted his earliest years?

Émile, a Natural Man.

Émile now for the first time appears upon the theater of the world; or rather he stands behind the scenes, sees the players dress and undress themselves; and by what coarse means the spectators are deceived. It will elevate him to see how the human race makes sport of itself. Educated in entire freedom, he will sorrow over the misery of kings, those slaves of all those who obey them; false wise men, in the chains of their vain honors; rich fools, the martyrs to their own luxury. He will be in danger of thinking himself wise, and all others fools; and only mortifying experience can protect him from such vanity.

I shall be thought a visionary, and Émile a phantasy, because he is so different from ordinary youths. It is overlooked that he is a natural man, but that other youths are brought up according to the notions of men.

Others, at Émile's age, are already philosophers and theologians; while he does not know yet what philosophy is, and even has not yet heard God spoken of.

I am no visionary; my pedagogy is based upon experience; since without regard to rank, nation, &c., I have found what is proper to all men, and have educated Emile according to that; not as a savage for the woods, but as a man who will have to maintain himself independent in the whirlpool of society.

Religious Instruction.

We are brought up in close connection with the natural world; and for the abstract, the purely intellectual, we have scarcely any comprehension. God withdraws our senses from themselves; the word mind has a meaning only for the philosophers. Monotheism has come, by a process of generalization, from material polytheism.

In his fifteenth year, Émile does not yet know that he has a soul; and perhaps he will find it out too early in his eighteenth.

A child, it is said, must be brought up in the religion of his father; and he must be taught that this alone is true; and that others are absurd. But if the power of this instruction extends only so far as the country in which it is given, and depends only upon authority, for which Émile has been taught to have no regard, what then? In what religion shall we educate him? To this there is only the simple answer, in none; we will only put him in a condition to choose for himself, that to which the best use of his own reason may bring him.

The Approaching Revolutions in Society.

Your education of men should be adapted to what they are in themselves; not to any thing external. By training him exclusively for one condition, you make him unfit for any other, and unfortunate, if his situation should ever change. How ridiculous is a great lord who has become a beggar, and who holds in his misery to the prejudices of his birth; how contemptible the rich man become poor, who feels himself completely degraded!

You acquiesce in the social order of the present, without considering that this order is subject to unavoidable changes; and that it is impossible for you to foresee or to prevent the revolution which may come upon your children. The great will become small, the rich poor, the monarch a subject. We are approaching a crisis; the century of revolutions. It is impossible that the great monarchies of Europe can last long. And who can say what shall then happen to you? What men have made, men can destroy; only the character given by nature is indestructible; and nature makes neither princes, nor rich men, nor great lords. What will the satrap do in his debasement, who has been educated only for his high position? What will the farmer-general do, in his poverty, who lives only upon his money? Happy will he be, then, who shall understand how to leave the condition which has left him, and to remain a man in spite of fate.

62. CONDORCET'S PLAN FOR FRENCH NATIONAL EDUCATION*

Marquis de Condorcet

Marie Jean Caritat, Marquis de Condorcet (1743-1794), was a French mathematician and philosopher. The French revolutionary government was interested in developing an educational system which would insure the preservation of liberty and equality. Condorcet submitted such a plan to the French Legislative Assembly. A synopsis of this bill is given below. It is one of the early attempts to develop an educational system dedicated to the preservation of democracy.

The plan instituted five grades of schools, in which the instruction was to be progressive: (1) *Primary Schools;* (2) *Secondary Schools;* (3) *Institutes;* (4) *Lyceums;* (5) a *National Society of Arts and Sciences.*

The *Primary School* receives children at the age of six years. Every village containing over four hundred inhabitants must be provided with one. Tuition will

*From *Histoire d'Instruction Publique* by Professor Vallet de Viriville; trans. in Barnard's *American Journal of Education,* Vol. XXII.

be given in the rules of arithmetic, the first elements of morality, the rudimentary knowledge of natural science and economy, essential either to agriculture, arts, or commerce, according to the rural or manufacturing occupations of the population. Religion will be taught in the churches by the respective ministers of their different creeds. A small collection of books will be furnished to each school for the use of the children.

In *Secondary Schools,* the tuition comprehends grammar; the history and geography of France, and the neighboring countries; drawing; the principles of the mechanical arts; some instruction in moral and social science, with the explanation of the chief laws and regulations of agreements and contracts; the elements of mathematics, natural philosophy, natural history applied to the arts, manufactures, and commerce. Every secondary school will have a library, some models of machinery, and some philosophical instruments. There will be one at least in every district, or a school for every four thousand inhabitants.

Institutes. The studies are divided into four classes, 1. Mathematical and physical sciences. 2. Moral and political science. 3. Application of the sciences to the arts. 4. Literature and the fine arts. Every institute is furnished with a library and a collection of machines and scientific instruments, with a botanic, and agricultural garden; these three collections are public. There will be at least one institute in each department.

Lyceums. The same plan and arrangements as in the Institutes, but on a grander scale, in the extent and profundity of the studies. There should be nine lyceums in France, distributed in different parts of its territory.

National Society of Arts and Sciences. It was actually the Institute enlarged and connected by a close and direct link to instruction and practical science. Its duty was to direct, oversee, simplify, and increase general education. This supervision and directorship was to transmit from the highest to the lowest, from grade to grade, to the inferior ranks of the hierarchy. The law recognized beside these establishments, five societies to encourage the progress of science, letters, and arts, but with limited range.

Ways and Means. Instruction in all its degrees outlined was to be gratuitous, and the appropriations necessary for this purpose were estimated at twenty-nine millions of francs. From this sum a periodical allowance of one million three hundred thousand francs was to be devoted to the *Élèves de la patrie.* Condorcet ranks under this term, those penniless children who distinguish themselves, at the beginning, or at any point whatever in their studies, and to whom the state furnished aid in the form of a stipend, in order to permit them to pursue, sheltered from need, the degrees of scientific apprenticeship remaining to be overcome.

63. ELEMENTARY EDUCATION BEFORE PESTALOZZI*

Adolph Diesterweg

Adolph Diesterweg (1790-1860) was an ardent disciple of Pestalozzi and brought Pestalozzian techniques into the Prussian schools. Speaking at the celebration of the one-hundredth anniversary of the birth of Pestalozzi, he described the educational practices prior to the development of Pestalozzian schools. That improvement was needed is obvious.

*From an address by Adolph Diesterweg; trans. in Barnard's *American Journal of Education,* Vol. IV.

Our present system of common or public schools—that is schools which are open to all children under certain regulations—date from the discovery of printing, in 1436, when books began to be furnished so cheaply that the poor could buy them. Especially after Martin Luther had translated the Bible into German, and the desire to possess and understand that invaluable book became universal, did there also become universal the desire to know how to read. Men sought to learn, not only for the sake of reading the Scriptures, but also to be able to read and sing the Psalms, and to learn the Catechism. For this purpose schools for children were established, which were essentially reading schools. Reading was the first and principal study; next came singing, and then memorizing texts, songs, and the Catechism. At first the ministers taught; but afterward the duty was turned over to the inferior church officers,—the choristers and sextons. Their duties as choristers and sextons were paramount, and as schoolmasters only secondary. The children paid a small monthly fee; no more being thought necessary, since the schoolmaster derived a salary from the church.

Nobody either made or knew how to make great pretensions to educational skill. If the teacher communicated to his scholars the acquirements above mentioned, and kept them in order, he gave satisfaction; and no one thought any thing about separate institutions for school children. There were no school books distinctively so called; the children learned their lessons in the Bible or the Psalter, and read either in the Old or the New Testament.

Each child read by himself; the simultaneous method was not known. One after another stepped up to the table where the master sat. He pointed out one letter at a time, and named it; the child named it after him; he drilled him in recognizing and remembering each. Then they took letter by letter of the words, and by getting acquainted with them in this way, the child gradually learned to read. This was a difficult method for him; a very difficult one. Years usually passed before any facility had been acquired; many did not learn in four years. It was imitative and purely mechanical labor on both sides. To understand what was read was seldom thought of. The syllables were pronounced with equal force, and the reading was without grace or expression.

Where it was possible, but unnaturally and mechanically, learning by heart was practiced. The children drawled out texts of Scripture, Psalms, and the contents of the Catechism from the beginning to end; short questions and long answers alike, all in the same monotonous manner. Anybody with delicate ears who heard the sound once, would remember it all his life long. There are people yet living, who were taught in that unintelligent way, who can corroborate these statements. Of the actual contents of the words whose sounds they had thus barely committed to memory by little and little, the children knew absolutely almost nothing. They learned superficially and understood superficially. Nothing really passed into their minds; at least nothing during their school years.

The instruction in singing was no better. The master sang to them the psalm-tunes over and over, until they could sing them, or rather screech them, after him.

Such was the condition of instruction in our schools during the sixteenth, seventeenth, and two-thirds of the eighteenth centuries; confined to one or two studies, and those taught in the most imperfect and mechanical way.

It was natural that youth endowed, when healthy, with an ever increasing capacity for pleasure in living, should feel the utmost reluctance at attending school. To be employed daily, for three or four hours, or more, in this mechanical toil, was no light task; and it therefore became necessary to force the children to sit still, and study their lessons. During all that time, especially in the seventeenth century, during the fearful Thirty Years' War, and subsequently, as the age was sunk in barbarism, the children of course entered the schools ignorant and untrained. "As the old ones sung, so twittered the young." Stern severity and cruel punishments were the order of the day; and by them the children were kept in order. Parents governed children, too young to attend, by threats of the schoolmaster and the school; and when they went, it was with fear and trembling. The rod, the cane, the raw-hide, were necessary apparatus in each school. The punishments of the teacher exceeded those of a prison. Kneeling on peas, sitting on the shame-bench, standing in the pillory, wearing an ass-cap, standing before the school door in the open street with a label on the back or breast, and other similar devices, were the remedies which the rude men of the age devised. To name a single example of a boy whom all have heard of, of high gifts, and of reputable family,—Dr. Martin Luther reckoned up fifteen or sixteen times that he was whipped upon the back in one forenoon. The learning and training corresponds; the one was strictly a mechanical process; the other, only bodily punishment. What wonder that from such schools there came forth a rude generation; that men and women looked back all their lives to the school as to a dungeon, and to the teacher as a taskmaster, and jailer; that the schoolmaster was of a small repute; that understrappers were selected for school duty and school discipline; that dark, cold kennels were used for schoolrooms; that the schoolmaster's place, especially in the country, was assigned him amongst the servants and the like.

This could not last; it has not, thank God! When and by what efforts of admirable men the change took place, I shall relate a little later on.

64. PESTALOZZI'S CONCEPT OF GOOD EDUCATION*

J. H. Pestalozzi

In 1799, Johann Heinrich Pestalozzi (1746-1827) opened his school in Burgdorf. The institution was supported by a Society of Friends of Education, and, in 1800, Pestalozzi prepared a formal report concerning his school to the Society. The early part of the report, which provides a clear statement of his method, is reproduced below.

I am trying to psychologize the instruction of mankind; I am trying to bring it into harmony with the nature of my mind, with that of my circumstances and my relations to others. I start from no positive form of teaching, as such, but simply ask myself:—

"What would you do, if you wished to give a single child all the knowledge and practical skill he needs, so that by wise care of his best opportunities he might reach inner content?"

I think to gain this end the human race needs exactly the same thing as the single child.

I think, further, the poor man's child needs a greater refinement in the methods of instruction than the rich man's child.

Nature, indeed, does much for the human race, but we have strayed away from her path. The poor man is thrust away from her bosom, and the rich destroy themselves both by rioting and by lounging on her overflowing breast.

The picture is severe. But ever since I have been able to see I have seen it so; and it is from this view that the impulse arises within me, not merely to plaster

*From *The Method*, a report by Pestalozzi, Aix-la-Chapelle, 1828.

over the evils in schools which are enervating the people of Europe, but to cure them at their root.

But this can never be done without subordinating all forms of instruction to those eternal laws by which the human mind is raised from physical impressions on the senses to clear ideas.

I have tried to simplify the elements of all human knowledge according to these laws, and to put them into a series of typical examples that shall result in spreading a wide knowledge of Nature, general clearness of the most important ideas in the mind, and vigorous exercises of the chief bodily powers, even among the lowest classes.

I know what I am undertaking; but neither the difficulties in the way, nor my own limitations in skill and insight, shall hinder me from giving my mite for a purpose which Europe needs so much. And, gentlemen, in laying before you the results of those labors on which my life has been spent, I beg of you but one thing. It is this:—Separate those of my assertions that may be doubtful from those that are indisputable. I wish to found my conclusions entirely upon complete convictions, or at least upon perfectly recognized premises.

The most essential point from which I start is this:—

Sense-impression of Nature is the only true foundation of human instruction, because it is the only true foundation of human knowledge.

All that follows is the result of this sense-impression, and the process of abstraction from it. Hence in every case where this is imperfect, the result also will be neither certain, safe, nor positive; and in any case, where the sense-impression is inaccurate, deception and error follow.

I start from this point and ask:—"What does Nature itself do in order to present the world truly to me, so far as it affects me? That is—By what means does she bring the sense-impressions of the most important things around me to a perfection that contents me?" And I find,—She does this through my surroundings, my wants and my relations to others.

Through my surroundings she determines the kinds of sense-impressions I receive. Through my wants she stimulates my activities. Through my relations to others she widens my observation and raises it to insight and forethought. Through my surroundings, my wants, my relations to others, she lays the foundations of my knowledge, my work, and my right-doing.

And now I ask myself:—"What general method of the Art of Teaching has the experience of ages put into the hands of humanity to strengthen this influence of Nature in developing intelligence, energy, and virtue in our race?" And I find these methods are speech, the arts of drawing, writing, reckoning, and measuring.

And when I trace back all these elements of the human Art to their origin, I find it in the common basis of our mind, by means of which our understanding combines those impressions which the senses have received from Nature, and represents them as wholes, that is, as concepts.

And when I ask again:—What are the unmistakable consequences of thus rudely despising these laws, I cannot conceal from myself the physical atrophy, one-sidedness, warped judgment, superficiality, and presumptuous vanity that characterize the masses in this generation, are the necessary consequences of despising these laws, and of the isolated, unpsychological, baseless, unorganized, unconnected teaching, which our poor race has received in our lower schools.

Then the problem I have to solve is this:—How to bring the elements of every art into harmony with the very nature of my mind, by following the psychological mechanical laws by which my mind rises from physical sense-impressions to clear ideas.

Nature has two principal and general means of directing human activity towards the cultivation of the arts, and these should be employed, if not before, at least side by side with any particular means. They are singing, and the sense of the beautiful.

With song the mother lulls her babe to sleep; but here, as in every thing else, we do not follow the law of Nature. Before the child is a year old, the mother's song ceases; by that time she is, as a rule, no longer a mother to the weaned child. For him, as for all others, she is only a distracted, over-burdened woman. Alas! that it is so. Why has not the art of ages taught us to join the nursery lullabies to a series of national songs, that should rise in the cottages of the people from the gentle cradle song to the sublime hymn of praise? But I cannot fill this gap. I can only point it out.

It is the same with the sense of the beautiful. All Nature is full of grand and lively sights, but Europe has done nothing to awaken in the poor a sense for these beauties, or to arrange them in such a way as to produce a series of impressions, capable of developing this sense. The sun rises for us in vain; in vain for us he sets. In vain for us do wood and meadow, mountain and valley spread forth their innumerable charms. They are nothing to us.

Here, again, I can do nothing; but if ever popular education should cease to be the barbarous absurdity it now is, and put itself into harmony with the real needs of our nature, this want will be supplied.

I leave these means of directing the Art generally, and turn to the forms by which special means of education, speaking, reading, drawing, and writing should be taught.

65. A PESTALOZZIAN SCHOOL IN OPERATION*

John Griscom

By the early part of the nineteenth century, Pestalozzi's school had become well known and was widely imitated. Many American teachers went to Europe to observe the school in operation. John Griscom, who operated a private school in New York City, visited Europe in 1818 and, a year later, published A Year In Europe, *in which he described his visit to Pestalozzi's school in Yverdon. Griscom's book, which influenced American schools, provides a clear picture of the Pestalozzian school in operation. The extract below is taken from* A Year In Europe.

Breakfast finished, our first and chief concern here was to visit the celebrated Institute of Pestalozzi. This establishment occupies a large castle the use of which was granted to Pestalozzi by the Canton of Berne, when the town of Yverdon was included in that Canton, and the government of the Pays de Vaud, to which it now belongs, continues the grant. On entering the castle, we were invited into a private room. I gave my letters to the person in attendance, who took them immediately to the chief. The good old man soon came in, seized me warmly by the hand, and seeing my hat on my head, he pointed to it in a sort of ecstacy, with his eyes almost filled with tears. I hardly knew how to interpret this emotion, and asked him if he wished me to take it off. He answered very earnestly, "No, no, no; keep it on; you are right." He seemed very glad to see us, and as he speaks French very imperfectly, and with an indistinct accent, he said he would call Monsieur Greaves to talk with us. This gentleman soon came and

*From *A Year in Europe* by John Griscom, New York, Vol. I.

entered immediately into a detail of the institution, its principles, its spirit, its arrangement, etc. He is an Englishman, and as I found upon inquiry, brother to the lady I had seen at Lausanne. He has been some weeks with Pestalozzi, for the purpose of understanding his system thoroughly, in order to aid a sister in England in the education of her children. He enters warmly into its concern, and will be useful in making it better known. He explained to us very clearly the leading ideas and views of human nature which induced Pestalozzi to become an instructor of youth. . . .

His school consists at present of about 90 boys,—German, Prussian, French, Swiss, Italian, Spanish, and English. It is divided into four principal classes, according to the attainments of the pupils. These classes are subdivided into others. There are seven schoolrooms in the castle, and twelve teachers or professors. . . .

We spent most of the day in the different schoolrooms witnessing the exercises of the scholars. Very few books are used, as it is expected the children can read well before they come there. But to describe the modes of teaching, so as to render them clearly intelligible, would require much more time and space than I can possibly allot to it, were I ever so competent to make it known. We saw the exercises of arithmetic, writing, drawing, mathematics, lessons in music and gymnastics, something of geography, French, Latin, and German. To teach a school, in the way practiced here, without book, and almost entirely by verbal instruction, is extremely laborious. The teacher must be constantly with the child, always talking, questioning, explaining, and repeating. The pupils, however, by this process, are brought into very close intimacy with the instructor. Their capacities, all their faculties and propensities, become laid open to his observation. This gives him an advantage which can not possibly be gained in the ordinary way in which schools are generally taught. The children look well, appear very contented, and apparently live in great harmony one with another; which, considering the diversity of national character and temper here collected, can be attributed only to the spirit of love and affection which sways the breast of the principal of the institution, and extends its benign influence throughout all the departments.

The success of this mode of instruction greatly depends upon the personal qualifications of those who undertake to conduct it. There is nothing of mechanism in it, as in the Lancastrian plan; no laying down of precise rules for managing classes, etc. It is all mind and feeling. Its arrangements must always depend on the ages, talents, and tempers of the scholars, and require on the part of the teachers the most diligent and faithful attention. Above all, it requires that the teacher should consider himself as the father and bosom friend of his pupils, and to be animated with the most affectionate desires for their good. Pestalozzi himself is all this. His heart glows with such a spirit that the good old man can hardly refrain from bestowing kisses on all with whom he is concerned. He holds out his hands to his pupils on every occasion, and they love him as a child loves its mother. His plan of teaching is just fit for the domestic fireside, with a father or mother in the center, and a circle of happy children around them. He is aware of this, and wishes to extend the knowledge of his plan to every parent. Pestalozzi is 72 years of age. It is quite unfortunate for the progress of his system on the continent, that he pays so little attention to exteriors, regarding dress, furniture, etc., as of no moment whatever, provided the mind and heart be right.

66. NATIONALISTIC EDUCATION
IN PRUSSIA*

In 1763, Frederick, King of Prussia, issued his General Regulations for
Elementary Schools and Teachers in Prussia. *The school code became the basis
for state controlled education in Prussia. It is an excellent example of nationalistic control over education. The extracts below show the general nature of the
system.*

GENERAL REGULATIONS OF ELEMENTARY SCHOOLS AND TEACHERS
August 12, 1763

We Frederick, *by the grace of God, King,* etc.:
Whereas, to our great displeasure, we have perceived that schools and the
instruction of youth in the country have come to be greatly neglected, and that
by the inexperience of many sacristans (*custos*) and schoolmasters, the young
people grow up in stupidity and ignorance, it is our well-considered and serious
pleasure, that instruction in the country, throughout all our provinces, should be
placed on a better footing, and be better organized than heretofore. For, as we
earnestly strive for the true welfare of our country, and of all classes of people;
now that quiet and general peace have been restored, we find it necessary and
wholesome to have a good foundation laid in the schools by a rational and
Christian education of the young for the fear of God, and other useful ends.
Therefore, by the power of our own highest motive, of our care and paternal
disposition for the best good of all our subjects, we command hereby, all
governors, consistories and other collegiates of our country; that they shall, on
their part, contribute all they can, with affection and zeal, to maintain the
following GENERAL SCHOOL REGULATIONS, and in future to arrange all
things in accordance with the law to the end that ignorance, so injurious and
unbecoming to Christianity, may be prevented and lessened, and the coming time
may train and educate in the schools more enlightened and virtuous subjects.
School attendance age. First, it is our pleasure that all our subjects, parents,
guardians or masters, whose duty it is to educate the young, shall send their
children to school, and those confided to their care, boys and girls, if not sooner,
certainly when they reach the age of five years; and shall continue regularly to
do so, and require them to go to school until they are thirteen or fourteen years
old, and know not only what is necessary of Christianity, fluent reading and
writing, but can give answer in everything which they learn from the schools
book, prescribed and approved by our consistory.
Apprentices to be taught. Masters to whom children in Prussia, by custom are
bound to render work for certain years, are seriously advised not to withdraw
such children from school until they can read well, and have laid a good
foundation in Christian knowledge; also made a beginning in writing, and can
present a certificate from the minister and schoolmaster to this effect to the
school-visitors. Parents and guardians ought much more to consider it their
bounden duty that their children and wards receive sufficient instruction in the
necessary branches.
Leaving certificates. If children, by their own aptitude or by the care of the

*From *General-Land-Schul Reglement* by King Frederick the Great; trans. in
Barnard's *American Journal of Education,* Vol. XXII.

teacher are sufficiently advanced in the common studies before they attain their thirteenth or fourteenth year, even then the parents or guardians are not at liberty to retain them at home, but can do so only when the superintendents or inspectors, after a notice from the minister and a testimonial of the school-master, that the pupil has acquired a sufficient knowledge, have issued a regular dismissal based on the above testimonial. Still such children must attend the Repetition School, not only on Sundays, at the minister's, but also on weekdays at the schoolmaster's.

Attendance required. As in many towns, parents do not send their children to school in summer, on the plea that they have to guard the cattle; our magistrates and judges in the districts containing towns and communes, shall see that a special shepherd is engaged, rather than allow the children to be kept from school. . . .

School hours. In order to regulate definitely the summer and winter schools, we decree that winter schools must be held on all the six days of the week, from 8 to 11 o'clock in the forenoon, and from 1 to 4 o'clock in the afternoon, except Wednesday and Saturday afternoons. The winter school must be con-tinued from Michaelmas to the Easter-days. But the summer schools shall be open only in the forenoon or, if necessary by the location of the place, during three hours every weekday, when the ministers can best decide at what hour to commence. No vacations are to be given, not even during harvest time; the schools shall be kept in the prescribed manner, with this distinction, that in summer each lesson is to be of half an hour's duration, and in winter of a full hour.

Sunday instruction. On Sundays, beside the lesson of the Catechism or repetition school by the minister given in the Church, the schoolmaster shall give in the school a recapitulary lesson to the unmarried people of the township. They shall there practice reading and writing. Reading should be from the New Testament or some other edifying book, and as an exercise in writing, the young people should write some passages, or the Epistle, or Gospel of the day. In towns where the schoolmaster is not likewise sexton, and not obliged to travel through the parish with the clergyman, he shall be bound to sing with the children in Church, either morning or afternoons, to hear them recite the catechism and address to them easy questions on the order of salvation. If the sacristan or schoolmaster has no experience in catechising, the minister shall write down for him the questions he must ask, that in this manner, together with their children, the people may be edified and improved in scriptural knowledge.

Tuition fees. In regard to tuition fee, every child, until it can read, shall pay in winter six pennies, after it can read, nine pennies, and when it can write and read, one groschen a week. For the months of summer, however, they shall pay only two-thirds of this fee, so that those who paid six pennies in winter, after his proportion shall pay four; those who paid nine pennies shall pay six; and those who paid one groschen will pay eight pennies. If, in any place the schoolmaster has been paid better, he must continue to receive the customary fees.

Children of the poor. Parents too poor to pay the tuition fee of their children, and orphan children who can not pay, must petition the magistrate, patron, minister or church-council for an allowance from any funds of the church or town at their disposal, that the schoolmaster may get his income, and teach the children of the poor and rich with equal diligence and fidelity.

[*Annual school sermon and collection.* Provides for the general delivery of an annual sermon, on Saint Michael's Sunday, on the subject of Christian education and edification of youth. After the sermon, the collection to provide textbooks for the children of the poor.]

Compulsory attendance. Having made good and sufficient provision for the instruction of the young, all parents, guardians, and others, having children to educate, who act contrary to this ordinance, by withholding them from school, shall still be obliged to pay the common school-fee for the term; and guardians shall not be permitted to charge the money thus paid to the account of their wards. And if, after earnest exhortation of the minister, they do not send their children regularly to school, then the magistrate of the town, in the last resort, shall direct execution against them. It is made the duty of the school-visitors to impose on such parents as have not made their children attend school regularly, a fine of sixteen groschen, to be paid into the school-treasury.

We therefore command all officers and magistrates to ascertain without delay, after receiving notice from the schoolmaster, of the non-attendance of any child, from the parent or guardian of the same the cause of such absence, and if it is for other reason than sickness, they shall employ proper legal means to secure that child's attendance.

School census. To this end, and to enable him the better to control the matter, the schoolmaster shall receive, from the register of the church or the town in which they are engaged, a list of all children of school age, that they may know who are due to the school; and the teacher shall also keep a monthly register, in which the children are enrolled as follows: (1) By their name and surname; (2) their age; (3) the names of their parents; (4) their residence; (5) the date when they enter school; (6) the lessons they study; (7) the degree of their diligence or negligence; (8) their abilities of mind; (9) their morals and conduct; (10) the day when they leave school.

This register, which no child should be suffered to read, is sent to the school-visitor before his annual inspection, and inspected by the minister during his weekly visits that he may know the delinquent children, and exhort them to greater diligence, and speak with their parents in this regard.

Requisites for a teacher. Since the chief requisite in a good school is a competent and faithful teacher, it is our gracious and earnest will that one and all, who have the right of appointment, shall take heed to bring only well-qualified persons into office as teachers and sacristans. A schoolmaster should not only possess the necessary attainments and skill in instruction, but should be an example to the children, and not tear down by his daily life what he builds up by his teaching. He should therefore strive after godliness, and guard against everything which might give offence or temptation to parents or children. Above all things, he should endeavor to obtain a correct knowledge of God and of Christ, thereby laying a foundation to honest life and true Christianity, and feeling that they are entursted with their office from God, as followers of the Saviour, and in it have an opportunity, by diligence and good example, not only to render the children happy in the present life, but also to prepare them for eternal blessedness.

Teacher's habits. Though we intend to leave undiminished the privileges of the nobility and other patrons to select and appoint their sacristans and teachers, yet our superintendents, inspectors, and the clergy must see that no incompetent, unsuitable, nor reckless and wicked person is employed or continued in office. . . . All teachers are forbidden to keep tavern, to sell beer or wine, to engage in any other occupation by which their labor may be hindered or the children lured by their example into habits of idleness and dissipation, such as the hanging around taverns or making music at dinners and balls, which is prohibited under high fine and punishment.

Examination of teachers. No sacristan or teacher can be installed into office before his qualifications, ascertained by actual examination, are certified to by the Inspector. No clergyman can admit any person to such position in church or school who does not produce said certificate of a successful examination. . . .

License to teach. No person shall assume to teach in any school of the country, village, or town, who has not regularly obtained a license to teach; and all schools, whether kept by man or woman, not duly authorized, are entirely prohibited. But parents of wealth may, as heretofore, engage private teachers for their children, provided that the children of others who cannot yet be taught the higher branches, are not induced to withdraw from the regular school in order to share the private elementary instruction.

Attendance to duty. As a schoolmaster is not permitted to employ his pupils for his own work during school hours, neither shall he attend to his trade or other business during such hours, or entrust his wife with the duties of the school-room; though he may employ her or another person to assist when the school is too large for his personal instruction. If for any cause he neglects to teach the prescribed hours, the clergyman shall remind him of his duty; and, in case of persistent neglect, notice must be sent to the inspector that such irregularities may be corrected or punished.

[*School to open with prayer.* Nature of.]

[*School hours.* Eight to eleven, and one to four, unless ordered otherwise.]

[*Course of study.* Rather detailed provision made as to each hour of instruction. Summarized, it is as follows:

Morning.

    1st Hour—Singing of a hymn, a different hymn to be learned each month. This followed by a prayer, and this in turn by instruction in the Catechism. Luther's "Smaller Catechism" for younger children; the larger for the older. Saturday lesson to be preparatory for Sunday, the Epistle for that day being read and written.

    2d Hour—A B C class; reading from Old and New Testament; spelling; finding passages in the Scriptures; and memorizing verses from the Bible and learning Biblical names.

    3d Hour—Reading, writing, spelling; writing in copybooks; rules of reading. School closes with prayer, and reading of psalm. On Saturday children exhorted to behave well on Sunday; to be quiet in church; and to treasure up the word of God for their salvation.

Afternoon.

    4th Hour—Pupils sing verses, read a psalm, and are taught Biblical history from Rochow's "Manual for the Instruction of Children in Country Schools."

    5th Hour—Catechism, after method given in the "Berlin Reader." Pupils commit to memory, reading it with the teacher. Interpretations for the larger children. Children to learn a Bible verse weekly. During second half of hour, larger children to learn to read; middle class to spell; and lower class to learn their letters, as in second hour.

    6th Hour—Upper class write and cipher; middle class spell; and lower class study their A B C.

In cities, where schools had more than one class, the local consistory could regulate the order of the lessons, and the method of instruction.]

Uniform textbooks. As the country has hitherto been deluged with all sorts of school-books, especially with interpretations of the Catechism, and so-called "orders of salvation," because every preacher selects the books after his own pleasure, or writes some himself and has them printed, by which children, especially if parents change their residence, are much confused, it is our will, that henceforth no other books, than such as have been approved by our consistory, shall be used in any country-schools over which we have the right of patron. These books include, according to the wants of the country, the New Testament, the book called "Exercise in Prayer," in which not only are the contents of each book in the Bible, but the main subject of each chapter is framed into a prayer, to assist the young in expressing their invocations in the words of divine truths. Also the Halle or Berlin Bible, both of which agree in their divisions into paragraphs and pages; next the small and large Catechism of Luther; the Index of the books of the Bible; the Christian Doctrines in their connection; the Berlin Spelling-book and Reader; the General Attributes of God, of the world and man; and the Little Book for children in the country, on all sorts of necessary and useful things.

Each pupil to have a book. Each class must not only have the same books, but the clergyman and teacher must see that every child has his own book, so that two pupils need not look over the same book. Children, whose books are furnished from the funds of the church or the commune, are not allowed to take them home, but will deliver them to the master, at the close of the lessons, who will take charge of them as the property of the school.

[*Discipline.* Lays down rules for.]

[*Church attendance.* Parents on Sunday to send children to schoolmaster, who shall escort them to church and note conduct and absences, and on Monday question them on the sermon.]

Relations of schoolmaster and clergyman. In all other affairs of the school, the teacher must avail himself of the advice and suggestions of the clergyman, as his superior officer, and by his school-regulation the teachers are so directed. Of all that regards their office they must, on demand, give an account, and accept directions in reference to the prescribed method and discipline, because we have confidence in our ministers and bind it upon their consciences that in their towns they will earnestly endeavor to abolish all abuses and defects, and improve the condition of the schools. In case however, one or the other of the schoolmasters should neglect the duties of his office, after he is engaged, and be found unreliable, the pastor's duty will be, earnestly to remind him of his duty, with kindness once or twice, and if he still continues in his negligence, to apply for a remedy to the nearest justice; at the same time to inform the Superintendent or Inspector, and if their warning is not heeded, make a report to the consistory, that, according to the circumstances, they may decree a suspension or removal.

Clerical supervision. Especially is it our pleasure, that clergymen in villages and towns shall visit the schools of their place, generally twice a week, sometimes in the morning and sometimes in the afternoon, and shall not only take the information of the sacristans or school-master, but themselves examine the children in the Catechism and question them after other schoolbooks. They shall hold a monthly conference with the schoolteachers *in matre,* and designate to them the portion of the Catechism, the hymn, the psalm and Bible-verses which the children shall learn during the next month. Then he instructs them how to observe the principal divisions of the sermon and how to examine the children; he also points out the defects of their instruction in school, their method, discipline, and gives them other information, that the schoolteachers may fulfil their duties. If a clergyman, against our expectation, should be careless in his visits to the schools, or in the performance of other duties enjoined upon him in these regulations, and not labor earnestly to effect an exact observance of this law on the part of custos and teachers, he shall if convicted of the non-fulfilment of these instructions, be suspended *cum effectu*, for a time, or, as the case may be, removed from office: because the care for the instruction of the young and the supervision thereof, belong to the most important duties of the ministry, as we always desire them to be considered.

Annual inspection. The Superintendents and Inspectors of every district are hereby commanded, in the most expressive manner, annually to inspect every country-school in their jurisdiction, and with due attention to inquire into the condition of the schools, and examine whether parents and school authorities have held their children to regular attendance at school or have been negligent; whether the clergymen have done their duty in the observance of these regulations, by visiting the schools and superintending the teacher; especially whether the schoolmaster has the ability required or is not competent, and whatever else is in need of improvement. About all this the said Superintendents and Inspectors shall remit a dutiful report, every year, to our High Consistory in this city, for further examination and disposition. . . .

Conclusion. In general we here confirm and renew all wholesome laws, published in former times, especially, that no clergyman shall admit to confirmation and the sacrament, any children not of his commune, nor those unable to read, or who are ignorant of the fundamental principles of evangelical religion.

67. ROBERT RAIKES AND THE SUNDAY SCHOOL*

Robert Raikes

Robert Raikes (1735-1811), known as the founder of the Sunday school, was an English philanthropist. In 1800, he organized a Sunday school for children of the poor, hoping to provide instruction sufficient for them to be able to read the Bible. Raikes' school, widely copied, was important in the development of philanthropic schools in the eastern part of the United States. The selection below, in the form of a letter from Raikes, gives information about his school and describes the deplorable living conditions of the poor during this period.

Gloucester, *November 25th,* 1783.

SIR,—My friend, the Mayor (Mr. Colborne) has just communicated to me the letter which you have honoured him with, enquiring into the nature of Sunday Schools. The beginning of this scheme was entirely owing to accident. Some business leading me one morning into the suburbs of the city, where the lowest of the people (who are principally employed in the pin manufactory) chiefly reside, I was struck with concern at seeing a group of children, wretchedly ragged, at play in the streets. I asked an inhabitant whether those children belonged to that part of town, and lamented their misery and idleness. "Ah! sir," said the woman to whom I was speaking, "could you take a view of this part of the town on a Sunday, you would be shocked indeed; for then the street is filled with multitudes of these wretches, who, released on that day from employment spend their time in noise and riot, playing at 'chuck,' and cursing and swearing in a manner so horrid as to convey to any serious mind an idea of hell rather than

*From a letter by Robert Raikes in *Gloucester Journal,* May 24, 1784 and *Gentleman's Magazine,* June, 1784.

any other place. We have a worthy clergyman (said she), curate of our parish, who has put some of them to school; but on the Sabbath day they are all given up to follow their own inclinations without restraint, as their parents, totally abandoned themselves, have no idea of instilling into the minds of their children principles to which they themselves are entire strangers."

This conversation suggested to me that it would be at least a harmless attempt, if it were productive of no good, should some little plan be formed to check the deplorable profanation of the Sabbath. I then enquired of the woman, if there were any decent well-disposed women in the neighbourhood who kept schools for teaching to read. I presently was directed to four: to these I applied, and made an agreement with them to receive as many children as I should send upon the Sunday, whom they were to instruct in reading and in the Church Catechism. For this I engaged to pay them each a shilling for their day's employment. The women seemed pleased with the proposal. I then waited on the clergyman before mentioned, and imparted to him my plan; he was so much satisfied with the idea, that he engaged to lend his assistance, by going round to the schools on a Sunday afternoon, to examine the progress that was made, and to enforce order and decorum among such a set of little heathens.

This, sir, was the commencement of the plan. It is now about three years since we began, and I could wish you were here to make enquiry into the effect. A woman who lives in a lane where I had fixed a school told me, some time ago, that the place was quite a heaven on Sundays, compared to what it used to be. The numbers who have learned to read and say their Catechism are so great that I am astonished at it. Upon the Sunday afternoon the mistresses take their scholars to church, a place into which neither they nor their ancestors had ever before entered, with a view to the glory of God. But what is yet more extraordinary, within this month these little ragamuffins have in great numbers taken it into their heads to frequent the early morning prayers, which are held every morning at the Cathedral at seven o'clock. I believe there were nearly fifty this morning. They assemble at the house of one of the mistresses, and walk before her to church, two and two, in as much order as a company of soldiers. I am generally at church, and after service they all come around me to make their bow; and, if any animosities have arisen, to make their complaints. The great principle I inculcate is, to be kind and good natured to each other; not to provoke one another; to be dutiful to their parents; not to offend God by cursing and swearing; and such little plain precepts as all may comprehend. As my profession is that of a printer, I have printed a little book, which I gave amongst them; and some friends of mine, subscribers to the Society for Promoting Christian Knowledge, sometimes make me a present of a parcel of Bibles, Testaments, &c., which I distribute as rewards to the deserving. The success that has attended this scheme has induced one or two of my friends to adopt the plan, and set up Sunday Schools in other parts of the city, and now a whole parish has taken up the object; so that I flatter myself in time the good effects will appear so conspicuous as to become generally adopted. The number of children at present thus engaged on the Sabbath are between two and three hundred, and they are increasing every week, as the benefit is universally seen. I have endeavoured to engage the clergy of my acquaintance that reside in their parishes; one has entered into the scheme with great fervour, and it was in order to excite others to follow the example that I inserted in my paper the paragraph which I suppose you saw copied into the London papers.

... With regard to the rules adopted, I only require that they may come to the school on Sunday as clean as possible. Many were at first deterred because they wanted decent clothing, but I could not undertake to supply this defect. I argue, therefore, if you can loiter about without shoes, and in a ragged coat, you may as well come to school and learn what may tend to your good in that garb. I reject none on that footing. All that I require are clean hands, clean face, and their hair combed; if you have no clean shirt, come in what you have on.

The want of decent apparel at first kept great numbers at a distance, but they now begin to grow wiser, and all pressing to learn. I have had the good luck to procure places for some that were deserving, which has been of great use. You will understand that these children are from six years old to twelve or fourteen. Boys and girls above this age, who have been totally undisciplined, are generally too refractory for this government. A reformation in society seems to me to be only practicable by establishing notions of duty, and practical habits of order and decorum, at an early age. . . .

I have the honour to be, Sir, yours, &c.,

R. RAIKES.

68. LANCASTER'S MONITORIAL SYSTEM*

Sidney Smith

The monitorial school was developed in England by Joseph Lancaster (1778-1838). It later became the most popular type of philanthropic school in the United States, since, because of the use of monitors, it could be operated at very low cost. The Lancasterian schools eventually developed into public schools. The account below describes the monitorial system in action.

The first or lower class of children are taught to write the printed alphabet, and to name the letters when they see them. The same with the figures used in arithmetic. One day the boy traces the form of a letter, or figure; the next he tells the name, when he sees the letter. These two methods assist each other. When he is required to write H, for example, the shape of the letter which he saw yesterday assists his manual execution—when he is required to say how that letter is named, the shape of the letter reminds him of his manual execution; and the manual execution has associated itself with the name. In the same manner he learns syllables and words; writing them one day—reading them the next. The same process for writing the common epistolary character, and for reading it.

This progress made, the class go up to the master to read—a class consisting perhaps of 30. While one boy is reading, the word, e.g. Ab-so-lu-ti-on, is given out with a loud voice by the monitor, and written down by all the other 29 boys, who are provided with slates for the purpose; which writing is looked over by monitors, and then another word called, and so on; whoever writes a word, spells it of course at the same time, and spells it with much more attention than in the common way. So that there is always one boy reading, and twenty-nine writing and spelling at the same time; whereas, in the ancient method, the other twenty-nine did nothing.

The first and second classes write in sand; the middle classes on slates; only a few of the upper boys on paper with ink. This is a great saving point of expense,—in books the saving is still greater. Twenty or thirty boys stand around

*From *Edinburgh Review,* an article by Sidney Smith, Vol. XI.

a card suspended on a nail, making a semi-circle. On this card are printed the letters in very large characters;—these letters the boys are to name, at the request of the monitor. When one spelling class have said their lessons in this manner, they are despatched off to some other occupation, and another spelling class succeeds. In this way one book or card may serve for two hundred boys, who would, according to the common method, have had a book each. In the same manner, syllables and reading lessons are printed on cards and used with the same beneficial economy.

In arithmetic, the monitor dictates a sum, ex. gr. in addition, which all the boys write down on their slates, for example,

$$724$$
$$378$$
$$946$$

He then tells them, aloud, how to add the sum. First column—6 and 8 are 14, and 4 are 18; set down 8 and carry 1 to the next column; and so on. In this manner, the class acquire facility of writing figures, and placing them; and, by practicing what the monitor dictates, insensibly acquire facility in adding. Again they are placed around arithmetical cards, in the same manner as in paragraph (B), and required to add up the columns. This method evinces what progress they have made from the preceding method of dictating; and the two methods are always used alternately.

It is obvious that a school like this of Mr. Lancaster's, consisting of from 700 to 800 boys, would soon fall into decay, without very close attention to order and method. In this part of his system, Mr. Lancaster has been as eminently successful as in any other; contriving to make the method and arrangement, so necessary to his institution, a source of amusement to the children. In coming into school, in going out, and in moving in their classes from one part of the school to another, the children move in a kind of a measured pace, and in known places, according to their number, of which every boy has one. Upon the first institution of the school, there was great loss and confusion of hats. After every boy has taken his place there, they all stand up expecting the word of command, "Sling your hats!" upon which they immediately suspend their hats round their necks by a string provided for that purpose. When the young children write in sand, they all look attentively to their monitor, waiting for the word, and instantly fall to work, with military precision, upon receiving it. All these little inventions keep children in a constant state of activity, prevent the listlessness so observable in all other institutions for education, and evince (trifling as they appear to be) a very original and observing mind in him who invented them.

The boys assembled round their reading or arithmetical cards take places as in common schools. The boy who is at the head of the class wears a ticket, with some suitable inscription, and has a prize of a little picture. The ticket-bearer yields his badge of honour to whoever can excel him; and the desire of obtaining and the fear of losing the mark of distinction, create, as may easily be conceived, no common degree of enterprize and exertion. Boys have a prize when they are moved from one class to another, as the monitor has also from whose class they are removed. Mr. Lancaster has established a sort of paper currency of tickets. These tickets are given for merit—two tickets are worth a paper kite; three worth a ball; four worth a wooden horse, etc.

It is no unusual thing for me to deliver one or two hundred prizes at the same time. And at such times the countenances of the whole school exhibit a most pleasing scene of delight; as the boys who obtain prizes commonly walk around the school in procession, holding the prizes in their hands, with a herald proclaiming before them, "These good boys have obtained prizes for going into another class." The honour of this has an effect as powerful, if not more so, than the prizes themselves.

A large collection of toys, bats, balls, pictures, kites, is suspended above the master's head beaming glory and pleasure upon the school beneath. Mr. Lancaster has also, as another incentive, an order of merit. No boys are admitted to this order but those who distinguish themselves by attention to their studies, and by their endeavours to check vice. The distinguishing badge is a silver medal and plated chain hanging from the neck. The superior class has a fixed place in the school; any class that can excel it may eject them from this place and occupy it themselves. Every member, both of the attacking and defending classes, feels of course the most lively interest in the issue of the contest.

Mr. Lancaster punishes by shame rather than pain; varying the means of exciting shame, because as he justly observes, any mode of punishment long continued loses its effect.

The boys in the school appointed to teach others are called monitors; they are in the proportion of about one monitor to ten boys. So that, for the whole school of one thousand boys, there is only one master; the rest of the teaching is all done by the boys themselves. Besides the teaching monitors, there are general monitors, such as, inspectors of slates, inspectors of absentees, etc.

69. EDUCATION AND ECONOMIC WELFARE*

Adam Smith

In 1776, Adam Smith (1722-1790) published his An Inquiry into the Nature and Causes of the Wealth of Nations. *While this great work is primarily concerned with problems of labor and economics, parts of it are devoted to education of the common people. In the selection below, Smith advocated state support of elementary education.*

Ought the public, therefore, to give no attention, it may be asked, to the education of the people? Or if it ought to give any, what are the different parts of education which it ought to attend to in the different orders of the people? and in what manner ought it to attend to them?

In some cases the state of the society necessarily places the greater part of individuals in such situations as naturally form in them, without any attention of government, almost all the abilities and virtues which that state requires, or perhaps can admit of. In other cases the state of the society does not place the greater part of individuals in such situations, and some attention of government is necessary in order to prevent the almost entire corruption and degeneracy of the great body of the people.

In the progress of the division of labour, the employment of the far greater part of those who live by labour, that is, of the great body of the people, comes to be confined to a few very simple operations; frequently to one or two. But the understandings of the greater part of men are necessarily formed by their ordinary employments. The man whose whole life is spent in performing a few simple operations, of which the effects are, perhaps, always the same, or very nearly the same, has no occasion to exert his understanding or to exercise his invention in finding out expedients for removing difficulties which never occur. He naturally loses, therefore, the habit of such exertion, and generally becomes

*From *An Inquiry into the Nature and Causes of the Wealth of Nations* by Adam Smith; reprint of Second Edition, Oxford, 1880, Book V.

as stupid and ignorant as it is possible for a human creature to become. The torpor of his mind renders him not only incapable of relishing or bearing a part in any rational conversation, but of conceiving any generous, noble, or tender sentiment, and consequently of forming any just judgment concerning many even of the ordinary duties of private life. Of the great and extensive interests of his country, he is altogether incapable of judging. . . .

The education of the common people requires perhaps, in a civilized and commercial society, the attention of the public more than that of people of some rank and fortune. People of some rank and fortune are generally eighteen or nineteen years of age before they enter upon that particular business, profession, or trade, by which they propose to distinguish themselves in the world. They have before that full time to acquire, or at least to fit themselves for afterwards acquiring, every accomplishment which can recommend them to the public esteem, or render them worthy of it. Their parents or guardians are generally sufficiently anxious that they should be so accomplished, and are, in most cases, willing enough to lay out the expense which is necessary for that purpose. If they are not always properly educated, it is seldom from want of expense laid out upon their education; but from the improper application of that expense. . . .

It is otherwise with the common people. They have little time to spare for education. Their parents can scarce afford to maintain them even in infancy. As soon as they are able to work, they must apply to some trade by which they can earn their subsistence. That trade, too, is generally so simple and uniform as to give little exercise to the understanding; while, at the same time, their labour is both so constant and so severe, that it leaves them little leisure and less inclination to apply to, or even think of anything else.

But though the common people cannot, in any civilised society, be so well instructed as people of some rank and fortune, the most essential parts of education, however, to read, write, and account, can be acquired at so early a period of life, that the greater part even of those who are to be bred to the lowest occupations have time to acquire them before they can be employed in those occupations. For a very small expense the public can facilitate, can encourage, and can even impose upon almost all the whole body of the people, the necessity of acquiring those most essential parts of education.

The public can facilitate this acquisition by establishing in every parish or district a little school, where children may be taught for a reward so moderate, that even a common labourer may afford it; the master being partly, but not wholly paid by the public; because if he was wholly, or even principally paid by it, he would soon learn to neglect his business. In Scotland the establishment of such parish schools has taught almost the whole common people to read, and a very great proportion of them to write and account. In England the establishment of charity-schools has had an effect of the same kind, though not so universally, because the establishment is not so universal. If in those little schools the books, by which the children are taught to read, were a little more instructive than they generally are, and if, instead of a little smattering of Latin, which the children of the common people are sometimes taught there and which can scarce ever be of any use to them, they were instructed in the elementary parts of geometry and mechanics, the literary education of this rank of people would perhaps be as complete as it can be. There is scarce a common trade which does not afford some opportunities of applying to it the principles of geometry and mechanics, and which would not therefore gradually exercise and improve the common people in those principles, the necessary introduction to the most sublime as well as the most useful sciences.

The public can encourage the acquisition of those most essential parts of education by giving small premiums, and little badges of distinction, to the children of the common people who excel in them.

The public can impose upon almost the whole body of the people the necessity of acquiring those most essential parts of education, by obliging every man to undergo an examination or probation in them before he can obtain the freedom in any corporation, or be allowed to be set up in any trade either in a village or town corporate.

. . . Though the state was to derive no advantage from the instruction of the inferior ranks of people, it would still deserve its attention that they should not be altogether uninstructed. The state, however, derives no inconsiderable advantage from their instruction. The more they are instructed, the less liable they are to the delusions of enthusiasm and superstition, which, among ignorant nations, frequently occasion the most dreadful disorders. An instructed and intelligent people besides are always more decent and orderly than an ignorant and stupid one. They feel themselves, each individually, more respectable, and more likely to obtain the respect of their lawful superiors, and they are therefore more disposed to respect those superiors. They are more disposed to examine, and more capable of seeing through, the interested complaints of faction and sedition, and they are, upon that account, less apt to be misled into any wanton or unnecessary opposition to the measures of government. In free countries, where the safety of government depends very much upon the favourable judgment which the people may form of its conduct, it must surely be of the highest importance that they should not be disposed to judge rashly or capriciously concerning it.

EDUCATION IN THE AMERICAN COLONIES
AND THE UNITED STATES

70. DESCRIPTION OF HARVARD COLLEGE*

Richard Mather

In 1636, plans for the establishment of a college were made in Massachusetts Bay Colony. The result was the opening of Harvard College in 1640. The following selection, from a pamphlet published in London in 1643, describes the founding of the new college.

After God had carried us safe to *New England,* and wee had builded our houses, provided necessaries for our liveli-hood, rear'd convenient places for Gods worship, and setled the Civill Government: One of the next things we longed for, and looked after was to advance *Learning,* and perpetuate it to Posterity, dreading to leave an illiterate Ministery to the Churches, when our present Ministers shall lie in the Dust. And as wee were thinking and consulting how to effect this great Work; it pleased God to stir up the heart of one Mr. *Harvard* (a godly Gentleman and a lover of Learning, there living amongst us) to give the one halfe of his Estate (it being in all about 1700. l.) towards the erecting of a Colledge, and all his Library: after him another gave 300. l. others after them cast in more, and the publique hand of the State added the rest: the Colledge was, by common consent, appointed to be at *Cambridge,* a place very pleasant and accommodate and is called (according to the name of the first founder) *Harvard Colledge.*

The Edifice is very faire and comely within and without, having in it a spacious Hall; (where they daily meet at Commons, Lectures, Exercises) and a large Library with some Bookes to it, the gifts of diverse of our friends, their Chambers and studies also fitted for, and possessed by the Students, and all other roomes of Office necessary and convenient, with all needfull Offices thereto belonging: And by the side of the Colledge a faire *Grammar* Schoole, for the training up of young Schollars, and fitting of them for *Academicall Learning,* that still as they are judged ripe, they may be received into the Colledge of this Schoole. Master *Corlet* is the Mr., who hath very well approved himselfe for his abilities, dexterity and painfulnesse in teaching and education of the youth under him.

Over the Colledge is master *Dunster* placed, as President, a learned conscionable and industrious man, who has so trained up his Pupills in the tongues and Arts, and so seasoned them with the principles of Divinity and Christianity that we have to our great comfort, (and in truth) beyond our hopes, beheld their progresse in Learning and godlinesse also; the former of these hath appeared in their publique declamations in *Latine* and *Greeke,* and Disputations Logicall and Philosophicall, which they have been wonted (besides their ordinary Exercises in the Colledge-Hall) in the audience of the Magistrates, Ministers, and other

*From a letter by Richard Mather in *New England's First Fruits,* London, 1643.

Schollars, for the probation of their growth in Learning, upon set dayes, constantly once every moneth to make and uphold: The latter hath been manifested in sundry of them by the savoury breathings of their Spirits in their godly conversation. Insomuch that we are confident, if these early blossomes may be cherished and warmed with the influence of the friends of Learning, and lovers of this pious worke, they will by the help of God, come to happy maturity in a short time.

Over the Colledge are twelve Overseers chosen by the generall Court, six of them are of the Magistrates, the other six of the Ministers, who are to promote the best good of it, and (having a power of influence into all persons in it) are to see that every one be diligent and proficient in his proper place.

71. REGULATIONS AT HARVARD COLLEGE*

Richard Mather

The material below shows the nature of the curriculum and the regulations governing admission at Harvard College in 1643. The outline of studies is similar to those of institutions of higher education during the European Renaissance. Note that the requirements for graduation follow the pattern of the medieval university.

(a) Entrance Requirements

When any Schollar is able to understand *Tully,* or such like classicall Latine Author *extempore,* and make and speake true Latine in Verse and Prose, *suo ut aiunt Marte;* And decline perfectly the Paradigim's of *Nounes* and *Verbes* in the *Greek* tongue: Let him then and not before be capable of admission into the Colledge.

(b) Rules and Precepts

Let every Student be plainly instructed, and earnestly pressed to consider well, the maine end of his life and studies, is *to know God and Jesus Christ which is eternall life, Joh. 17. 3.* and therefore to lay *Christ* in the bottome, as the only foundation of all sound knowledge and Learning.

And seeing the Lord only giveth wisedome, Let every one seriously set himselfe by prayer in secret to seeke it of him, *Prov.* 2, 3.

Every one shall so exercise himselfe in reading the Scriptures twice a day, that he shall be ready to give such an account of his proficiency therein, both in *Theoretticall* observations of the Language, and *Logick,* and in *Practicall* and spirituall truths, as his Tutor shall require, according to his ability; seeing *the entrance of the word giveth light, it giveth understanding to the simple,* Psalm 119. 130.

That they eschewing all profanation of Gods Name, Attributes, Word, Ordinances, and times of Worship, doe studie with good conscience, carefully to retaine God, and the love of his truth in their mindes else let them know, that (notwithstanding their Learning) God may give them up *to strong delusions,* and in the end *to a reprobate minde,* 2. Thes. 2. 11, 12. Rom. 1. 28.

*Richard Mather in *New England's First Fruits,* London, 1643.

That they studiously redeeme the time; observe the generall houres appointed for all the Students, and the special houres for their owne *Classis:* and then dilligently attend the Lectures without any disturbance by word or gesture. And if in any thing they doubt, they shall enquire as of their fellowes, so, (in case of *Non satisfaction*) modestly of their Tutors.

None shall under any pretence whatsoever, frequent the company and society of such men as lead an unfit, and dissolute life.

Nor shall any without his Tutors leave, or (in his absence) the call of Parents or Guardians, goe abroad to other Townes.

Every Schollar shall be present in his Tutors chamber at the 7th. houre in the morning, immediately after the sound of the Bell, at his opening the Scripture and prayer, so also at the 5th. houre at night, and then give account of his owne private reading, as aforesaid in Particular the third, and constantly attend Lectures in the Hall at the houres appointed? But if any (without necessary impediment) shall absent himself from prayer or Lectures, he shall bee lyable to Admonition, if he offend above once a weeke.

If any Schollar shall be found to transgresse any of the Lawes of God, or the Schoole, after twice Admonition, he shall be lyable, if not *adultus,* to correction, if *adultus,* his name shall be given up to the Overseers of the Colledge, that he may bee admonished at the publick monethly Act.

(c) The times and order of their Studies, unlesse experience shall show cause to alter

The second and third day of the weeke, read Lectures, as followeth.

To the first yeare at 8th. of the clock in the morning *Logick,* the first three quarters, *Physicks* the last quarter.

To the second yeare at the 9th houre, *Ethicks* and *Politicks,* at convenient distances of time.

To the third yeare at the 10th. *Arithmetick* and *Geometry,* the three first quarters, *Astronomy* the last.

Afternoone

The first yeare disputes at the second houre.

The 2d. yeare at the 3d. houre.

The 3d. yeare at the 4th. every one in his Art.

The 4th. day reads Greeke

To the first yeare the *Etymologie* and *Syntax* at the eighth houre.

To the 2d. at the 9th. houre, *Prosodia* and *Dialects.*

Afternoone

The first yeare at 2d. houre practice the precepts of *Grammar* in such Authors as have variety of words.

The 2d. yeare at 3d. houre practice in *Poesy, Nonnus, Duport,* or the like.

The 3d. yeare perfect their *Theory* before noone, and exercise *Style, Composition, Imitation, Epitome,* both in Prose and Verse, afternoone.

The fift day reads Hebrew, and the Easterne Tongues

Grammar to the first yeare houre the 8th.

To the 2d. *Chaldee* at the 9th. houre.

To the 3d. *Syriack* at the 10th. houre.

Afternoone

The first yeare practice in the Bible at the 2d. houre.
The 2d. in *Ezra* and *Danel* at the 3d. houre.
The 3d. at the 4th. houre in *Trestius* New Testament.

The 6th. day reads Rhetorick to all at the 8th. houre

Declamations at the 9th. So ordered that every Scholler may declaime once a moneth. The rest of the day *vacat Rhetoricis studiis.*

The 7th. day reads Divinity Catecheticall at the 8th. houre
Common places at the 9th. houre
Afternoone

The first houre reads history in the Winter,
The nature of plants in the Summer.
The summe of every Lecture shall be examined before the new Lecture be read.

(d) Requirements for Degrees

Every Schollar that on proofe is found able to read the Originalls of the *Old* and *New Testament* into the Latine tongue, and to resolve them *Logically;* withall being of godly life and conversation; And at any publick Act hath the Approbation of the Overseers and Master of the Colledge, is fit to be dignified with his first Degree.

Every Schollar that giveth up in writing a *System,* or *Synopsis,* or summe of *Logick,* Naturall and Morall *Phylosophy, Arithmetick, Geometry* and *Astronomy:* and is ready to defend his *Theses* or positions: withall skilled in the Originalls as abovesaid: and of godly life & conversation: and so approved by the Overseers and Master of the Colledge at any publique *Act,* is fit to be dignified with his 2d. Degree.

72. THE FIRST SCHOOL LAW IN THE COLONIES*

The first school law in the American colonies was enacted by the General Court of Massachusetts Bay Colony in 1642. It established no schools, but did affirm the right of the state to establish compulsory education, leaving the method of acquiring the education to the discretion of the parent or master. The law is reproduced below.

This Co^rt, taking into consideration the great neglect of many parents & masters in training up their children in learning, & labo^r, & other implyments which may be proffitable to the common wealth, do hereupon order and decree, that in euery towne ye chosen men appointed for managing the prudentiall affajres of the same shall henceforth stand charged with the care of the redresse of this evill, so as they shalbee sufficiently punished by fines for the neglect thereof, upon presentment of the grand iury, or other information or complaint in any Court within this iurisdiction; and for this end they, or the greater

*From *Records of the Governor and Company of the Massachusetts Bay in New England,* Boston, 1853, Vol. II.

numbe^r of them, shall have power to take account from time to time of all parents and masters, and of their children, concerning their calling and implyment of their children, especially of their ability to read & understand the principles of religion & the capitall lawes of this country, and to impose fines upon such as shall refuse to render such accounts to them when they shall be required; and they shall have power, with consent of any Court or the magistrate, to put forth apprentices the children of such as they shall [find] not to be able & fitt to imploy and bring them up. They shall take . . . that boyes and girles be not suffered to converse together, so as may occasion any wanton, dishonest, or immodest behavio^r; & for their better performance of this trust committed to them, they may divide the towne amongst them, appointing to every of the said townesmen a certaine number of families to have special oversight of. They are also to provide that a sufficient quantity of materialls, as hemp, flaxe, ec^{ra}, may be raised in their severall townes, & tooles & implements provided for working out the same; & for their assistance in this so needfull and beneficiall imploym^t, if they meete wth any difficulty or opposition wch they cannot well master by their own power, they may have reco^{r}se to some of the ma^{trats}, who shall take such course for their help & incuragm^t as the occasion shall require according to iustice; & the said townesmen, at the next Co^{r}t in those limits, after the end of their year, shall give a breife account in writing of their proceedings herein, provided that they have bene so required by some Co^{r}t or magistrate a month at least before; & this order to continew for two yeares, & till the Co^{r}t shall take further order.

73. THE "OLD DELUDER" LAW*

The Massachusetts School Law of 1647 differed from the law of 1642 in that it established a system of schools. It was the first legal statement made in the American colonies asserting that the state had the legal authority to require the establishment of schools. It did not establish compulsory attendance but did require the maintenance of schools. It left to the discretion of the local government the question of how the school was to be supported. However, it gave the power to establish elementary schools which were to be supported by public monies. The law is reproduced below.

It being one cheife proiect of ye ould deluder, Satan, to keepe men from the knowledge of ye Scriptures, as in form^r times by keeping y^m in an unknowne tongue, so in these latt^r times by perswading from ye use of tongues, y^t so at least ye true sence & meaning of ye originall might be clouded by false glosses of saint seeming deceivers, y^t learning may not be buried in ye grave of o^r fath^{rs} in ye church and commonwealth, the Lord assisting o^r endeavo^{r}s,—

It is therefore ord^{r}ed, y^t ev^{r}y towneship in this jurisdiction, aft^r ye Lord hath increased y^m number to 50 houshold^{rs}, shall then forthwth appoint one wthin their towne to teach all such children as shall resort to him to write & reade, whose wages shall be paid eith^r by ye parents or mast^{rs} of such children, or by ye inhabitants in gen^{r}all, by way of supply, as ye maior part of those y^t ord^r ye prudentials of ye towne shall appoint; provided, those y^t send their children be not oppressed by paying much more y^n they can have y^m taught for

*From *Records of the Governor and Company of the Massachusetts Bay in New England,*Boston, 1853, Vol. II.

in oth^r townes; & it is furth^{r}ordered, y^t where any towne shall increase to ye numb^r of 100 families or househould^{rs}, they shall set up a grammer schoole, ye m^r thereof being able to instruct youth so farr as they shall be fited for ye university, provided, y^t if any towne neglect ye performance hereof above one yeare, y^t every such towne shall pay 5 £ to ye next schoole till they shall performe this order.

74. AN EARLY PROPOSAL FOR A STATE EDUCATIONAL SYSTEM*

Thomas Jefferson

In 1779, Thomas Jefferson introduced a bill in the Virginia legislature committing the state to a comprehensive system of public schools. It was too early for the aristocratic Virginians to accept such legislation, and the bill failed to pass. Nevertheless, it demonstrated the direction in which thinking about education was moving and forecast the nature of legislation which was soon to be enacted in all states. In the material below, Jefferson describes the content of the bill.

This bill proposes to lay off every county into small districts of five or six miles squre, called hundreds, and in each of them to establish a school for teaching reading, writing, and arithmetic. The tutor to be supported by the hundred, and every person in it entitled to send their children three years gratis, and as much longer as they please, paying for it. These schools to be under a visitor, who is annually to chuse the boy, of best genius in the school, of those whose parents are too poor to give them further education, and to send him forward to one of the grammar schools, of which twenty are proposed to be erected in different parts of the country, for teaching Greek, Latin, geography, and the higher branches of numerical arithmetic. Of the boys thus sent in any one year, trial is to be made at the grammar schools one or two years, and the best genius of the whole selected, and continued six years, and the residue dismissed. By this means twenty of the best geniuses will be raked from the rubbish annually, and be instructed, at the public expence, so far as the grammar schools go. At the end of six years' instruction, one half are to be discontinued (from among whom the grammar schools will probably be supplied with future masters); and the other half, who are to be chosen for the superiority of their parts and disposition, are to be sent and continued three years in the study of such sciences as they shall chuse, at William and Mary college, the plan of which is proposed to be enlarged, . . . and extended to all the useful sciences. The ultimate result of the whole scheme of education would be the teaching of all the children of the state reading, writing, and common arithmetic: turning out ten annually of superior genius, well taught in Greek, Latin, geography, and the higher branches of arithmetic: turning out ten others annually, of still superior parts, who, to those branches of learning, shall have added such of the sciences as their genius shall have led them to: the furnishing to the wealthier part of the people convenient schools, at which their children may be educated, at their own expense. . . . Of all the view of this law none is more important, none more legitimate, than that of rendering the people safe, as they are the ultimate

*From *Notes of the State of Virginia* by Thomas Jefferson.

guardians of their own liberty. For this purpose the reading in the first stage, where they will receive their whole education, is proposed as has been said, to be chiefly historical. History by apprising them of the past will enable them to judge of the future.

75. A PROPOSAL FOR PUBLIC EDUCATION IN PENNSYLVANIA*

Benjamin Rush

Dr. Benjamin Rush (1745-1813) was a distinguished physician in Philadelphia. He was one of the signers of the Declaration of Independence and a member of the Continental Congress. Convinced that universal education was necessary for the preservation of democracy, he developed, in 1786, a proposal for a complete system of free public schools for Pennsylvania. Note his insistence that schools should be supported by public taxation.

Before I proceed to the subject of this essay, I shall point out, in a few words, the influence and advantages of learning upon mankind.

It is friendly to religion, inasmuch as it assists in removing prejudice, superstition and enthusiasm, in promoting just notions of the Deity, and in enlarging our knowledge of his works.

It is favourable to liberty. Freedom can exist only in the society of knowledge. Without learning, men are incapable of knowing their rights, and where learning is confined to a few people, liberty can be neither equal nor universal.

It promotes just ideas of laws and government. "When the clouds of ignorance are dispelled (says the Marquis of Beccaria) by the radiance of knowledge, power trembles, but the authority of laws remains immovable."

It is friendly to manners. Learning in all countries, promotes civilization, and the pleasures of society and conversation.

It promotes agriculture, the great basis of national wealth and happiness. Agriculture is as much a science as hydraulics, or optics, and has been equally indebted to the experiments and researches of learned men. The highly cultivated state, and the immense profits of the farms in England, are derived wholly from the patronage which agriculture has received in that country, from learned men and learned societies.

Manufactures of all kinds owe their perfection chiefly to learning—hence the nations of Europe advance in manufactures, knowledge, and commerce, only in proportion as they cultivate the arts and sciences.

For the purpose of diffusing knowledge through every part of the state, I beg leave to propose the following simple plan.

Let there be one university in the state, and let this be established in the capital. Let law, physic, divinity, the law of nature and nations, economy, &c. be taught in it by public lectures in the winter season, after the manner of the European universities, and let the professors receive such salaries from the state as will enable them to deliver their lectures at a moderate price.

Let there be four colleges. One in Philadelphia, one at Carlisle, a third, for

*From *Essays, Literary, Moral and Philosophical* by Benjamin Rush, Philadelphia, 1798.

the benefit of our German fellow citizens, at Lancaster, and a fourth, some years hence at Pittsburgh. In these colleges, let young men be instructed in mathematics and in the higher branches of science, in the same manner that they are now taught in our American colleges. After they have received a testimonial from one of these colleges, let them, if they can afford it, complete their studies by spending a season or two in attending the lectures in the university. I prefer four colleges in the state to one or two, for there is a certain size of colleges as there is of towns and armies, that is most favourable to morals and good government. Oxford and Cambridge in England are the seats of dissipation, while the more numerous, and less crowded universities and colleges in Scotland, are remarkable for the order, diligence, and decent behaviour of their students.

Let there be free schools established in every township, or in districts consisting of one hundred families. In these schools let children be taught to read and write the English and German languages, and the use of figures. Such of them as have parents that can afford to send them from home, and are disposed to extend their educations, may remove their children from the free school to one of the colleges.

By this plan the whole state will be tied together by one system of education. The university will in time furnish masters for the colleges, and the colleges will furnish masters for the free schools, while the free schools, in their turns, will supply the colleges and the university with scholars, students and pupils. The same systems of grammar, oratory and philosophy, will be taught in every part of the state, and the literary features of Pennsylvania will thus designate one great, and equally enlightened family.

But, how shall we bear the expense of these literary institutions?—I answer— These institutions will *lessen* our taxes. They will enlighten us in the great business of finance—they will teach us to increase the ability of the state to support government, by increasing the profits of agriculture, and by promoting manufactures. They will teach us all the modern improvements and advantages of inland navigation. They will defend us from hasty and expensive experiments in government, by unfolding to us the experience and folly of past ages, and thus, instead of adding to our taxes and debts, they will furnish us with the true secret of lessening and discharging both of them.

But, shall the estates of orphans, bachelors and persons who have no children, be taxed to pay for the support of schools from which they can derive no benefit? I answer in the affirmative, to the first part of the objection, and I deny the truth of the latter part of it. Every member of the community is interested in the propagation of virtue and knowledge in the state. But I will go further, and add, it will be true economy in individuals to support public schools. The bachelor will in time save his tax for this purpose, by being able to sleep with fewer bolts and locks to his doors—the estates of orphans will in time be benefited, by being protected from the ravages of unprincipled and idle boys, and the children of wealthy parents will be less tempted, by bad company, to extravagance. Fewer pillories and whipping posts, and smaller gaols, with their usual expenses and taxes, will be necessary when our youth are properly educated, than at present; I believe it could be proved, that the expenses of confining, trying and executing criminals, amount every year, in most of the countries, to more money than would be sufficient to maintain all the schools that would be necessary in each county. The confessions of these criminals generally show us, that their vices and punishments are the fatal consequences of the want of a proper education in early life.

I submit these detached hints to the consideration of the legislature and of the citizens of Pennsylvania. The plan for the free schools is taken chiefly from the plans which have long been used with success in Scotland, and in the eastern states of America, where the influence of learning, in promoting religion, morals, manners and good government, has never been exceeded in any country.

The manner in which these schools should be supported and governed—the modes of determining the characters and qualifications of school-masters, and the arrangement of families in each district, so that children of the same religious sect and nation, may be educated as much as possible together, will form a proper part of a law for the establishment of schools, and therefore does not come within the limits of this plan.

76. PROPOSAL FOR NATIONAL SCHOOLS*

George Washington

In 1796, George Washington, then about to leave the presidency, recommended to the Congress the establishment of a national university and a military academy. His dream of a university was not realized, but the United States Military Academy was established in 1802. In the material below, Washington gives his reasons for his proposal.

I have heretofore proposed to the consideration of Congress the expediency of establishing a National University, and also a Military Academy. The desirability of both these institutions has so constantly increased with every new view I have taken of the subject, that I cannot omit the opportunity of one for all recalling your attention to them.

The assembly to which I address myself, is too enlightned not to be fully sensible how much a flourishing state of the arts and sciences contributes to national prosperity and reputation. True it is, that our country, much to its honor, contains many seminaries of learning highly respectable and useful; but the funds upon which they rest are too narrow to command the ablest professors, in the different departments of liberal knowledge, for the institution contemplated, though they would be excellent auxiliaries.

Amongst the motives to such an institution, the assimilation of the principles, opinions, and manners of our countrymen, by the common education of a portion of our youth from every quarter, well deserves attention. The more homogeneous our citizens can be made in these particulars, the greater will be our prospect of permanent union; and a primary object of such a national institution should be, the education of our youth in the science of government. In a republic, what species of knowledge can be equally important, and what duty more pressing on its legislature, than to patronize a plan for communicating it to those, who are to be the future guardians of the liberties of the country?

The institution of a military academy is also recommended by cogent reasons. However pacific the general policy of a nation may be, it ought never to be without an adequate stock of military knowledge for emergencies. The first would impair the energy of its character, and both would hazard its safety, or expose it to greater evils when war could not be avoided. Besides that war might often not depend upon its own choice. In proportion as the observance of pacific maxims might exempt a nation from the necessity of practising the rules of the military art, ought to be its care in preserving and transmitting, by proper

*From *The Writings of George Washington,* Jared Sparks, ed., Little, Brown and Co., 1885.

establishments, the knowledge of that art. Whatever argument may be drawn from particular examples, superficially viewed, a thorough examination of the subject will evince, that the art of war is at once comprehensive and complicated; that it demands much previous study; and that the possession of it, in its most improved and perfect state, is always of great moment to the security of a nation. This, therefore, ought to be a serious care of every government; and for this purpose, an academy, where a regular course of instruction is given, is an obvious expedient, which different nations have successfully employed.

77. EARLY CONSTITUTIONAL PROVISIONS CONCERNING EDUCATION*

In 1791, Vermont became the fourteenth state of the Union. Twelve of the fourteen states, by 1800, had formulated written constitutions, and seven of these constitutions included formal statements concerning the obligation of the state toward education. While the statements made in the various constitutions differ widely, all of them agree that responsibility for education and for the establishment of schools is to be borne by the state.

VERMONT, 1. *Constitution of* 1777

Sec. XL. A school or schools shall be established in every town, by the legislature, for the convenient instruction of youth, with such salaries to the masters, paid by each town; making proper use of school lands in each town, thereby to enable them to instruct youth at low prices. One grammar school in each county, and one university in this State, ought to be established by direction of the General Assembly.

Sec. XLI. Laws for the encouragement of virtue and prevention of vice and immorality, shall be made and constantly kept in force; and provision shall be made for their due execution; and all religious societies or bodies of men, that have or may be hereafter united and incorporated, for the advancement of religion and learning, or for other pious and charitable purposes, shall be encouraged and protected in the enjoyment of the privileges, immunities and estates which they, in justice ought to enjoy, under such regulations, as the General Assembly of this State shall direct.

2. *Constitution of* 1787

Chap. II, Sec. 38. Laws for the encouragement of virtue, and prevention of vice and immorality, ought to be constantly kept in force, and duly executed; and a competent number of schools ought to be maintained in each town for the convenient instruction of youth; and one or more grammar schools be incorporated, and properly supported in each county in this State. And all religious societies, or bodies of men, that may be hereafter united or incorporated, for the advancement of religion and learning, or for other pious and charitable purposes, shall be encouraged and protected in the enjoyment of the privileges, immunities, and estates, which they in justice ought to enjoy under such regulations as the General Assembly of this State shall direct.

MASSACHUSETTS, *Constitution of* 1780
(Part II, chap. V, The University at Cambridge, and
Encouragement of Literature, etc.)

SECTION I. *The university*

ART. 1. Whereas our wise and pious ancestors, so early as the year 1636, laid

*From *Charters and Constitutions*, B. P. Poore, Washington, 1877.

the foundation of Harvard College, in which university many persons of great eminence have, by the blessing of God, been initiated in those arts and sciences which qualified them for public employments, both in church and state; and whereas the encouragement of arts and sciences and all good literature, tends to the honor of God, the advantage of the Christian religion, and the great benefit of this and the other United States of America, it is declared, that the president and fellows of Harvard College, in their corporate capacity, and their successors in their capacity, their officers and servants, shall have, hold, use, exercise, and enjoy all the powers, authorities, rights, liberties, privileges, immunities, and franchises which they now have, or are entitled to have, hold, use, exercise, and enjoy; and the same are hereby ratified and confirmed unto them, the said president and fellows of Harvard College, and to their successors, and to their officers and servants respectively, forever.

ART. 2. And whereas there have been, at sundry times, by divers persons, gifts, grants, devises of houses, lands, tenements, goods, chattels, legacies, and conveyances heretofore made, either to Harvard College, in Cambridge, in New England, or to the president and fellows of Harvard College, or to the said college by some other description, under several charters successively, it is declared that all the said gifts, grants, devises, legacies, and conveyances are hereby forever confirmed unto the president and fellows of Harvard College, and to their successors, in the capacity aforesaid, according to the true intent and meaning of the donor or donors, grantor or grantors, devisor or devisors.

ART. 3. And whereas by an act of the general court of the colony of Massachusetts Bay, passed in the year 1642, the governor and deputy governor, for the time being, and all the magistrates of that jurisdiction, were, with the president, and a number of the clergy, in the said act described, constituted the overseers of Harvard College, and it being necessary, in this new constitution of government, to ascertain who shall be deemed successors to the said governor, deputy governor, and magistrates, it is declared that the governor, lieutenant-governor, council, and senate of this commonwealth, are, and shall be deemed, their successors; who, with the president of Harvard College, for the time being, together with the ministers of the Congregational churches in the towns of Cambridge, Watertown, Charlestown, Boston, Roxbury, and Dorchester, mentioned in the said act, shall be, and hereby are, vested with all the powers and authority belonging or in anyway appertaining to the overseers of Harvard College: *Provided,* That nothing herein shall be construed to prevent the legislature of this Commonwealth from making such alterations in the government of the said university as shall be conducive to its advantage and the interest of the republic of letters, in as full a manner as might have been done by the legislature of the late province of the Massachusetts Bay.

SECTION 2. *The encouragement of literature*

Chap. V, Sec. 2. Wisdom and knowledge, as well as virtue, diffused generally among the body of the people, being necessary for the preservation of their rights and liberties; and as these depend on spreading the opportunities and advantages of education in the various parts of the country, and among the different orders of the people, it shall be the duty of the legislatures and magistrates, in all future periods of this Commonwealth, to cherish the interests of literature and the sciences, and all seminaries of them; especially the university at Cambridge, public schools, and grammar-schools in the towns; to encourage private societies and public institutions, by rewards and immunities, for the promotion of agriculture, arts, sciences, commerce, trades, manufactures, and a natural history of the country; to countenance and inculcate the principles of humanity and general benevolence, public and private charity, industry and frugality, honesty and punctuality in their dealings; sincerity, good humor, and all social affections and generous sentiments among the people.

NEW HAMPSHIRE, *Constitution of* 1784, *and* 1792
(The constitution of 1776 had been silent on the subject)

Sec. 83. Knowledge and learning generally diffused through a community being essential to the preservation of a free government, spreading the opportunities and advantages of education through the various parts of the country being highly conducive to promote this end, it shall be the duty of the legislatures and magistrates, in all future periods of this government, to cherish the interest of literature and the sciences, and all seminaries and public schools; to encourage private and public institutions, rewards and immunities for the promotion of agriculture, arts, sciences, commerce, trade, manufactures, and natural history of the country; to countenance and inculcate the principles of humanity and general benevolence, public and private charity, industry and economy, honesty and punctuality, sincerity, sobriety, and all social affections and generous sentiments among the people.

PENNSYLVANIA, 1. *Constitution of* 1776

Sec. 44. A school or schools shall be established in every county by the legislature, for the convenient instruction of youth, with such salaries to the masters, paid by the public, as may enable them to instruct youth at low prices; and all useful learning shall be duly encouraged and promoted in one or more universities.

Sec. 45. Laws for the encouragement of virtue, and prevention of vice and immorality, shall be made and constantly kept in force, and provision shall be made for their due execution; and all religious societies or bodies of men heretofore united or incorporated for the advancement of religion or learning, or for other pious and charitable purposes, shall be encouraged and protected in the enjoyment of the privileges, immunities, and estates which they were accustomed to enjoy, or could of right have enjoyed, under the laws and former constitution of this State.

2. *Constitutions of* 1790 *and* 1838

Sec. 1. The legislature shall, as soon as conveniently may be, provide, by law, for the establishment of schools throughout the State, in such manner that the poor may be taught *gratis*.

Sec. 2. The arts and sciences shall be promoted in one or more seminaries of learning.

DELAWARE, *Constitution of* 1792
(The constitution of 1776 had been silent on the subject)

ART. VIII, Sec. 12. The Legislature shall, as soon as conveniently may be, provide by law for . . . establishing schools, and promoting arts and sciences. (Continued unchanged in the Constitution of 1831.)

NORTH CAROLINA, *Constitution of* 1776

41. That a school or schools shall be established by the legislature, for the convenient instruction of youth, with such salaries to the masters, paid by the public, as may enable them to instruct at low prices; and all useful learning shall

be duly encouraged, and promoted, in one or more universities. (Continued unchanged in the Constitution of 1835.)

GEORGIA, 1. *Constitution of* 1777

ART. 54. Schools shall be erected in each county, and supported at the general expense of the State, as the Legislature shall hereafter point out.

2. *Constitution of* 1798

ART. IV, Sec. 13. The arts and sciences shall be promoted, in one or more seminaries of learning; and the legislature shall, as soon as conveniently may be, give such further donations and privileges to those already established as may be necessary to secure the objects of their institution; and it shall be the duty of the general assembly, at their next session, to provide effectual measures for the improvement and permanent security of the funds and endowments of such institutions.

78. EDUCATION IN BOSTON AT THE BEGINNING OF THE NINETEENTH CENTURY*

William B. Fowle

Caleb Bingham (1757-1817) was a prominent teacher in Boston at the close of the eighteenth century. After Bingham's death, William Fowle wrote Memoir of Caleb Bingham, *in which he eulogized the educator and, at the same time, described the system of schools operated in Boston during Bingham's tenure. The extract from the* Memoir, *given below, provides an excellent picture of the Boston schools as they existed well into the nineteenth century.*

Schools for girls. The main object of Mr. Bingham in coming to Boston was to establish a school for girls; and the project was of the most promising description, for the town of Boston had even then become eminent for its wealth and intelligence, and, strange to say, was deficient in public and private schools for females. It certainly is a remarkable fact, that, while the girls of every town in the state were allowed and expected to attend the village schools, no public provision seems to have been made for their instruction in the metropolis, and men of talents do not seem to have met with any encouragement to open private schools for this all important class of children. The only schools in the city to which girls were admitted, were kept by the teachers of public schools, between the forenoon and afternoon sessions, and how insufficient this chance for an education was, may be gathered from the fact, that all the public teachers who opened private schools, were uneducated men, selected for their skill in penmanship and the elements of arithmetic. The schools were called writing schools; and, although reading and spelling were also taught in them, this instruction was only incidental, being carried on, we cannot say "attended to," while the teachers were making or mending pens, preparatory to the regular writing lesson.

This had probably been the state of things for more than a century, and at the advent of Mr. Bingham, there were only two such schools, while there were two others devoted exclusively to the study of Latin and Greek, although the pupils of these latter schools hardly numbered one tenth of the others. Of course, the proposal of Mr. Bingham to open a school, in which girls should be taught, not only writing and arithmetic, but, reading, spelling and English

*From *Memoir of Caleb Bingham* by William B. Fowle, in Barnard's *American Journal of Education,* Vol. V.

grammar, met with a hearty reception, and his room, which was in State street, from which schools and dwelling houses had been banished nearly half a century, was soon filled with children of the most respectable families. There does not seem to have been any competition, and Mr. Bingham had the field to himself for at least four years before any movement was made to improve the old public system, or to extend the means of private instruction.

The public writing schools. At that time, and for more than a century and a half, the public schools of Boston, and indeed, those of the state had been under the control and supervision of the selectmen, three to nine citizens, elected annually to manage the financial and other concerns of the several towns, without much, if any, regard to their literary qualifications. The selectmen of Boston were generally merchants, several of whom, at the time under consideration, had daughters or relatives in the school of Mr. Bingham. It was natural that the additional expense thus incurred, for they were taxed to support the public schools, from which their daughters were excluded, should lead them to inquire why such a preference was given to parents with boys; and the idea seemed, for the first time, to be started, that the prevailing system was not only imperfect, but evidently unfair. The simplest and most natural process would have been to open the schools to both sexes, as the spirit of the laws required, but this would have left the instruction in the hands of the incompetent writing masters, when a higher order of teachers was required; or it would have involved the dismission of all the writing masters, a bold step, which the committee dared not to hazard, because many citizens were opposed to any innovation, and the friends of the masters were so influential, that no change was practicable which did not provide for their support. After much consultation, therefore, there being some complaint of the insufficient number of the schools, the school committee proposed the only plan which seemed to secure the triple object—room for the girls, employment for the old masters, and the introduction of others better qualified.

Origin of the reading schools. The new plan was to institute three new schools, to be called READING SCHOOLS, in which reading, spelling, grammar and perhaps geography, should be taught by masters to be appointed; the two old writing schools to be continued, a new one established; and one of the Latin schools to be abolished. As no rooms were prepared, temporary ones were hired, so that the same pupils attended a writing school in one building half the day, and a reading school in a different building, at a considerable distance, and under a different and independent teacher, the other half. Each reading school had its corresponding writing school, and while the boys were in one school, the girls were in the other, alternating forenoon and afternoon, and changing the half day once a month, because, Thursday and Saturday afternoons being vacation, this arrangement was necessary to equalize the lessons taught in the separate schools. This system afterwards acquired the name of the double-headed system, and it was continued, essentially, for more than half a century, in spite of all the defects and abuses to which it was exposed. Even when the town built new schoolhouses, the upper room was devoted to the reading school, and the lower to the writing, the masters never changing rooms, and the boys and girls alternating as before. The points gained, however, were very important, the girls were provided for, better teachers were appointed, and the sexes were separated into different rooms. . . .

The Latin schools. Another evil in the new system also held its ground for many years. Boys had been admitted into the Latin school at the early age of seven years, on the mistaken idea, that the very young are best qualified to learn a dead language, as they undoubtedly are to learn a spoken one. The age was increased to ten years by the new system, but, as before, no provision was made in the Latin school for their instruction in English, in penmanship, or in any of the common branches. To remedy this serious defect, the Latin scholars were *allowed* to attend the writing schools two hours, forenoon or afternoon, and about thirty availed themselves of the privilege, although they were obliged to neglect one school to attend the other, and unpunctuality and disorder, in all the schools, were the natural consequence. . . .

Books used; Methods of instruction. The books used in the reading schools were, the Holy Bible, Webster's Spelling Book, Webster's Third Part, and the Young Lady's Accidence. The Children's Friend and Morse's Geography were allowed, not required; and "Newspapers were to be introduced, occasionally, at the discretion of the masters." . . .

Furthermore, it was ordered that, in the writing schools, the children "should begin to learn arithmetic at eleven years of age; that, at twelve, they should be taught to make pens." Until eleven years old, all the pupils did, in a whole forenoon or afternoon, was to write one page of a copy book, not exceeding ten lines. When they began to cipher, it rarely happened that they performed more than two sums in the simplest rules. These were set in the pupil's manuscript, and the operation was there recorded by him. No printed book was used. Such writing and ciphering, however, were too much for one day, and the boys who ciphered, only did so every other day. If it be asked, how were the three hours of school time occupied? The answer is, in one of three ways,—in mischief; in play; or in idleness. . . .

In the reading schools, the course was for every child to read one verse of the Bible, or a short paragraph of the Third Part. The master heard the first and second, that is, the two highest classes, and the usher heard the two lowest. While one class was reading, the other studied the spelling lesson. The lesson was spelled by the scholars in turn, so that, the classes being large, each boy seldom spelled more than one or two words. In grammar, the custom was to recite six or more lines once a fortnight, and to go through the book three times before any application of it was made to what was called parsing. No geography was prepared for the schools until Mr. Bingham left them. Morse's abridgment began to be a reading book about the year 1800, and soon after, Mr. Bingham prepared his little Catechism, which was probably based upon it. When Mr. B.'s American Preceptor was published, it displaced Webster's Third Part. His Child's Companion superseded Webster's Spelling Book in the lower classes, and the Columbian Orator was the reading book of the upper class, to the displacement of the Bible, which, instead of being read by the children, was read by the reading masters as a religious exercise, at the opening of school in the morning, and at its close in the afternoon. The writing masters were not required to read or pray for fifteen or twenty years after the great reform.

79. PHILANTHROPIC EDUCATION IN NEW YORK*

At the beginning of the nineteenth century, few schools existed except those provided by private agencies and churches. Large numbers of children, especially

*"Address" published in New York City papers of May, 1805 and reproduced in *History of the Public School Society of the City of New York* by William O. Bourne, New York, 1870.

among the poor, had no access to education. Many philanthropic societies were organized to provide free education for these children. In 1805, such a society was organized in New York City, bearing the ponderous title of the "Society for Establishing a Free School in the City of New York for the Education of such Poor Children as do not belong to, or are not Provided for by, any Religious Society." An Address of the organization, soliciting donations, is reproduced below. Many philanthropic schools later developed into public schools. ·

TO THE PUBLIC

Address of the Trustees of the "Society for Establishing a Free School in the City of New York, for the Education of such Poor Children as do not Belong to, or are not Provided for by, any Religious Society."

While the various religious and benevolent societies in this city, with a spirit of charity and zeal which the precepts and example of the Divine Author of our religion could alone inspire, amply provide for the education of such poor children as belong to their respective associations, there still remains a large number living in total neglect of religious and moral instruction, and unacquainted with the common rudiments of learning, essentially requisite for the due management of the ordinary business of life. This neglect may be imputed either to the extreme indigence of the parents of such children, their intemperance and vice, or to a blind indifference to the best interests of their offspring. The consequences must be obvious to the most careless observer. Children thus brought up in ignorance, and amidst the contagion of bad example, are in imminent danger of ruin; and too many of them, it is to be feared, instead of being useful members of the community, will become the burden and pests of society. Early instruction and fixed habits of industry, decency, and order, are the surest safeguards of virtuous conduct; and when parents are either unable or unwilling to bestow the necessary attention on the education of their children, it becomes the duty of the public, and of individuals, who have the power, to assist them in the discharge of this important obligation. It is in vain that laws are made for the punishment of crimes, or that good men attempt to stem the torrent of irreligion and vice, if the evil is not checked at its source; and the means of prevention, by the salutary discipline of early education, seasonably applied. It is certainly in the power of the opulent and charitable, by a timely and judicious interposition of their influence and aid, if not wholly to prevent, at least to diminish, the pernicious effects resulting from the neglected education of the children of the poor.

Influenced by these considerations, and from a sense of the necessity of providing some remedy for an increasing and alarming evil, several individuals, actuated by similar motives, agree to form an association for the purpose of extending the means of education to such poor children as do not belong to, or are not provided for, by any religious society. After meetings, numerously attended, a plan of association was framed, and a Memorial prepared and addressed to the legislature, soliciting an Act of Incorporation, the better to enable them to carry into effect their benevolent design. Such a law the Legislature, at their last session, was pleased to pass; and at a meeting of the Society, under the Act of Incorporation, on the sixth instant, thirteen Trustees were elected for the ensuing year.

The particular plan of the school, and the rules for its discipline and management, will be made known previous to its commencement. Care will be exercised in the selection of teachers, and, besides the elements of learning usually taught in schools, strict attention will be bestowed on the morals of the children, and all suitable means be used to counteract the disadvantages resulting from the situation of their parents. It is proposed, also, to establish, on the first day of the week, a school, called a Sunday School, more particularly for such children as, from peculiar circumstances, are unable to attend on the other days of the week. In this, as in the Common School, it will be a primary object, without observing the peculiar forms of any religious Society, to inculcate the sublime truths of religion and morality contained in the Holy Scriptures.

This Society, as will appear from its name, interferes with no existing institution, since children already provided with the means of education, or attached to any other Society, will not come under its care. Humble gleaners in the wide field of benevolence, the members of this Association seek such objects only as are left by those who have gone before, or are fellow-laborers with them in the great work of charity. They, therefore, look with confidence for the encouragement and support of the affluent and charitable of every denomination of Christians; and when they consider that in no community is to be found a greater spirit of liberal and active benevolence than among the citizens of New York, they feel assured that adequate means for the prosecution of their plan will be easily obtained. In addition to the respectable list of original subscriptions, considerable funds will be requisite for the purchase or hire of a piece of ground, and the erection of a suitable building for the school, to pay the teachers, and to defray other charges incident to the establishment. To accomplish this design, and to place the Institution on a solid and respectable foundation, the Society depend on the voluntary bounty of those who may be charitably disposed to contribute their aid in the promotion of an object of great and universal concern.

DE WITT CLINTON, *President.*
JOHN MURRAY, JR., *Vice-President.*
LEONARD BLEEKER, *Treasurer.*
B. D. PERKINS, *Secretary.*

New York, May (5th Month) 18, 1805.

80. THE FIRST AMERICAN HIGH SCHOOL*

By 1818, a complete system of free, public elementary education had been established in Boston. The Latin Grammar School, a college preparatory school, was also operated. In 1821, the city government established the English Classical School, retitled in 1824 as the English High School. This institution, to provide advanced education for boys not preparing for college, was the first American high school. The material below, taken from the Report of the School Committee, justifies the need for the school and outlines its curriculum.

Though the present system of public education, and the munificence with which it is supported, are highly beneficial and honorable to the town; yet, in the opinion of the Committee, it is susceptible of a greater degree of perfection and usefulness, without materially augmenting the weight of the public burdens. Till recently, our system occupied a middle station: it neither commenced with the rudiments of Education, nor extended to the higher branches of knowledge.

*Report of the School Committee to the Town Meeting of Boston, January, 1821.

This system was supported by the Town at a very great expense, and to be admitted to its advantages, certain preliminary qualifications were required at individual cost, which have the effect of excluding many children of the poor and unfortunate classes of the community from the benefits of a public education. The Town saw and felt this inconsistency in the plan, and have removed the defect by providing Schools (Primary) in which the children of the poor can be fitted for admission into the public seminaries.

The present system, in the opinion of the Committee, requires still further amendment. The studies that are pursued at the English grammar schools are merely elementary, and more time than is necessary is devoted to their acquisition. A scholar is admitted at seven, and is dismissed at fourteen years of age; thus, seven years are expended in the acquisition of a degree of knowledge, which with ordinary diligence and a common capacity, may be easily and perfectly acquired in five. If then, a boy remain the usual term, a large portion of the time will have been idly or uselessly expended, as he may have learned all that he may have been taught long before its expiration. This loss of time occurs at that interesting and critical period of life, when the habits and inclinations are forming by which the future character will be fixed and determined. This evil, therefore, should be removed, by enlarging the present system, not merely that the time now lost may be saved, but that those early habits of industry and application may be acquired, which are so essential in leading to a future life of virtue and usefulness.

Nor are these the only existing evils. The mode of education now adopted, and the branches of knowledge that are taught at our English grammar schools, are not sufficiently extensive nor otherwise calculated to bring the powers of the mind into operation nor to qualify a youth to fill usefully and respectably many of those stations, both public and private, in which he may be placed. A parent who wishes to give a child an education that shall fit him for active life, and shall serve as a foundation for eminence in his profession, whether Mercantile or Mechanical, is under the necessity of giving him a different education from any which our public schools can now furnish. Hence, many children are separated from their parents and sent to private academies in this vicinity, to acquire that instruction which cannot be obtained at the public seminaries. Thus, many parents, who contribute largely to the support of these institutions, are subjected to heavy expense for the same object, in other towns.

The Committee, for these and many other weighty considerations that might be offered, and in order to render the present system of public education more nearly perfect, are of the opinion that an additional School is required. They therefore recommend the founding of a seminary which shall be called the English Classical School, and submit the following as a general outline of a plan for its organization and of the course of studies to be pursued.

1st. That the term of time for pursuing the course of studies proposed, be three years.

2ndly. That the School be divided into three classes, and one year be assigned to the studies of each class.

3rdly. That the age of admission be not less than twelve years.

4thly. That the School be for Boys exclusively.

5thly. That candidates for admission be proposed on a given day annually; but scholars with suitable qualifications may be admitted at any intermediate time to an advanced standing.

6thly. That candidates for admission shall be subject to a strict examination, in such manner as the School Committee may direct, to ascertain their qualifications according to these rules.

7thly. That it be required of every candidate, to qualify him for admission, that he be well acquainted with reading, writing, English grammar in all its branches, and arithmetic as far as simple proportion.

8thly. That it be required of the Masters and Ushers, as a necessary qualification, that they shall have been regularly educated at some University.

First Class: Composition; reading from the most approved authors; exercises in criticism, comprising critical analyses of the language, grammar, and style of the best English authors, their errors and beauties; Declamation; Geography; Arithmetic continued.

Second Class: Composition, Reading, Exercises in Criticism, Declamation; Algebra; Ancient and Modern History and Chronology; Logic; Geometry; Plane Trigonometry, and its application to mensuration of heights and distances; Navigation; Surveying; Mensuration of Surfaces and Solids; Forensic Discussions.

Third Class: Composition; Exercises in Criticism; Declamation; Mathematics; Logic; History, particularly that of the United States; Natural Philosophy, including Astronomy; Moral and Political Philosophy.

81. HIGH SCHOOLS REQUIRED BY LAW*

In 1827, legislation was passed in Massachusetts making mandatory the establishment of public high schools. This is the first law in the United States setting such a requirement. Note that the curriculum includes the basic subjects taught in the Latin Grammar School. This fact led eventually to the decline of the Latin Grammar School as a public institution. The law is reproduced below.

Be it enacted by the Senate and House of Representatives in General Court assembled and by the authority of the same. That each town or district within this Commonwealth, containing fifty families, or householders, shall be provided with a teacher or teachers, of good morals, to instruct children in orthography, reading, writing, English grammar, geography, arithmetic, and good behavior, for such term of time as shall be equivalent to six months for one school in each year; and every town or district containing one hundred families or householders, shall be provided with such teacher or teachers, for such term of time as shall be equivalent to eighteen months, for one school in each year. And every city, town, or district, containing five hundred families, or householders, shall be provided with such teacher or teachers for such term of time as shall be equivalent to twenty-four months, for one school in each year, and shall also be provided with a master of good morals, competent to instruct, in addition to the branches of learning aforesaid, the history of the United States, bookkeeping by single entry, geometry, surveying, algebra; and shall employ such master to instruct a school, in such city, town, or district, for the benefit of all the inhabitants thereof, at least ten months in each year, exclusive of vacations, in such convenient place, or alternately at such places in such city, town, or district, as the said inhabitants, at their meeting in March, or April, annually, shall determine; and in every city, or town, containing four thousand inhabitants, such master shall be competent in addition to all the foregoing branches, to instruct the Latin and Greek languages, history, rhetoric, and logic.

*Laws of Massachusetts, January Session, 1827.

82. THE DEMAND FOR FREE SCHOOLS*

Horace Mann

Horace Mann (1796-1859), more than any other person, was responsible for the development of free public schools in the United States. As the first secretary to the Massachusetts State Board of Education, he campaigned for free schools by means of widespread speaking tours and voluminous writing. He published twelve Annual Reports to the State Board of Education. These reports, disseminated throughout the country, greatly increased the progress toward free schools. The material below, from the Annual Report for 1846, is typical of his arguments for free public education.

The Pilgrim Fathers, amid all their privations and dangers, conceived the magnificent idea, not only of a universal, but of a free education for the whole people. To find the time and the means to reduce this grand conception to practice, they stinted themselves, amid all their poverty, to a still scantier pittance; amid all their toils, they imposed upon themselves still more burdensom labors; and, amid all their perils, they braved still greater dangers. Two divine ideas filled their great hearts—their duty to God and to posterity. For the one they built the church, for the other they opened the school. Religion and knowledge—two attributes of the same glorious and eternal truth, and that truth the only one on which immortal or mortal happiness can be securely founded!

It is impossible for us adequately to conceive the boldness of the measure which aimed at universal education through the establishment of free schools. As a fact, it had no precedent in the world's history; and, as a theory, it could have been refuted and silenced by a more formidable array of argument and experience than was ever marshalled against any other institution of human origin. But time has ratified its soundness. Two centuries of successful operation now proclaim it to be as wise as it was courageous, and as beneficent as it was disinterested. Every community in the civilized world awards it the meed of praise; and states at home and nations abroad, in the order of their intelligence, are copying the bright example. What we call the enlightened nations of Christendom are approaching, by slow degrees, to the moral elevation which our ancestors reached at a single bound. . . .

In later times, and since the achievement of American independence, the universal and ever-repeated argument in favor of free schools has been that the general intelligence which they are capable of diffusing, and which can be imparted by no other human instrumentality, is indispensable to the continuance of a republican government. This argument, it is obvious, assumes, as a *postulatum*, the superiority of a republican over all other forms of government; and, as a people, we religiously believe in the soundness both of the assumption and of the argument founded upon it. But, if this be all, then a sincere monarchist, or a defender of arbitrary power, or a believer in the divine right of kings, would oppose free schools for the identical reasons we offer in their behalf. . . .

Again, the expediency of free schools is sometimes advocated on grounds of

*From *Tenth Annual Report* to the Massachusetts State Board of Education by Horace Mann, Boston, 1846.

political economy. An educated people is always a more industrious and productive people. Intelligence is a primary ingredient in the wealth of nations. . . . The moralist, too, takes up the argument of the economist. He demonstrates that vice and crime are not only prodigals and spendthrifts of their own, but defrauders and plunderers of the means of others, that they would seize upon all the gains of honest industry and exhaust the bounties of Heaven itself without satiating their rapacity; and that often in the history of the world whole generations might have been trained to industry and virtue by the wealth which one enemy to his race has destroyed.

And yet, notwithstanding these views have been presented a thousand times with irrefutable logic, and with a divine eloquence of truth which it would seem that nothing but combined stolidity and depravity could resist, there is not at the present time [1846], with the exception of the States of New England and a few small communities elsewhere, a country or a state in Christendom which maintains a system of free schools for the education of its children. . . .

I believe that this amazing dereliction from duty, especially in our own country, originates more in the false notions which men entertain *respecting the nature of their right to property* than in anything else. In the district school meeting, in the town meeting, in legislative halls, everywhere, the advocates for a more generous education could carry their respective audiences with them in behalf of increased privileges for our children, were it not instinctively foreseen that increased privileges must be followed by increased taxation. Against this obstacle, argument falls dead. The rich man who has no children declares that the exaction of a contribution from him to educate the children of his neighbor is an invasion of his rights of property. The man who has reared and educated a family of children denounces it as a double tax when he is called upon to assist in educating the children of others also; or, if he has reared his own children without educating them, he thinks it peculiarly oppressive to be obliged to do for others what he refrained from doing even for himself. Another, having children, but disdaining to educate them with the common mass, withdraws them from the public school, puts them under what he calls "selecter influences," and then thinks it a grievance to be obliged to support a school which he contemns. Or, if these different parties so far yield to the force of traditionary sentiment and usage, and to the public opinion around them, as to consent to do something for the cause, they soon reach the limit of expense at which their admitted obligation or their alleged charity terminates.

It seems not irrelevant, therefore, in this connection, and for the purpose of strengthening the foundation on which our free-school system reposes, to inquire into the nature of a man's right to the property he possesses, and to satisfy ourselves respecting the question whether any man has such an indefeasible title to his estates or such an absolute ownership of them as renders it unjust in the government to assess upon him his share of the expenses of educating the children of the community up to such a point as the nature of the institutions under which he lives, and the well-being of society, require.

I bring my argument on this point, then, to a close; and I present a test of its validity, which, as it seems to me, defies denial or evasion.

In obedience to the laws of God and to the laws of all civilized communities, society is bound to protect the natural life of children; and this natural life cannot be protected without the appropriation and use of a portion of the property which society possesses. We prohibit infanticide under penalty of death. We practice a refinement in this particular. The life of an infant is inviolable, even before he is born; and he who feloniously takes it, even before birth, is as subject to the extreme penalty of the law as though he had struck down manhood in its vigor, or taken away a mother by violence from the sanctuary of home where she blesses her offspring. But why preserve the natural life of a child, why preserve unborn embryos of life, if we do not intend to watch over and to protect them, and to expand their subsequent existence into usefulness and happiness? As individuals, or as an organized community, we have no natural right, we can derive no authority or countenance from reason, we can cite no attribute or purpose of the divine nature, for giving birth to any human being, and then inflicting upon that being the curse of ignorance, of poverty, and of vice, with all their attendant calamities. We are brought, then, to this startling but inevitable alternative,—the natural life of an infant should be extinguished as soon as it is born, or the means should be provided to save that life from being a curse to its possessor; and, therefore, every State is morally bound to enact a code of laws legalizing and enforcing infanticide or a code of laws establishing free schools.

The three following propositions, then, describe the broad and ever-during foundation on which the common-school system of Massachusetts reposes:

The successive generations of men, taken collectively, constitute one great commonwealth.

The property of this commonwealth is pledged for the education of all its youth, up to such a point as will save them from poverty and vice, and prepare them for the adequate performance of their social and civil duties.

The successive holders of this property are trustees, bound to the faithful execution of their trust by the most sacred obligations; and embezzlement and pillage from children and descendants have not less of criminality, and have more of meanness, than the same offences when perpetrated against contemporaries.

83. RELIGION AND THE PUBLIC SCHOOLS*

Horace Mann

The arguments concerning religion in the public schools of the nineteenth century are amazingly similar to arguments heard today. In 1846, in a sermon called "The Ark of God on a New Cart," the Reverend W. H. Smith attacked Horace Mann and the Massachusetts State Board of Education, claiming that crime and immorality had been increased as the result of the "Godless schools." Smith later published the sermon, along with some correspondence with Mann. Mann responded by publishing a reply, some of which is reproduced below. Note his position concerning the treatment of religion in public schools.

It is easy to see that the experiment would not stop with having half a dozen conflicting creeds taught by authority of law in the different schools of the same town or vicinity. Majorities will change in the same place. One sect may have the ascendency to-day; another tomorrow. This year there will be three Persons in the Godhead; next year but one; and the third year the Trinity will be restored to hold its precarious sovereignty until it shall be again dethroned by the worms of the dust it has made. This year, the everlasting fires of hell will burn to terrify

*Sequel to the So-Called Correspondence Between the Rev. M. H. Smith and Horace Mann, Horace Mann, Boston, 1847.

the impenitent; next year, and without any repentance, its eternal flames will be extinguished, to be rekindled forever, or to be quenched forever as it may be decided at annual town meetings. This year, under Congregational rule, the Rev. Mr. So and So and the Rev. Dr. So and So will be on the committee; but next year these reverends and reverend doctors will be plain misters, never having had apostolic consecration from the bishop. This year the ordinance of baptism is inefficacious without immersion; next year one drop of water will be as good as forty fathoms. Children attending the district school will be taught one way; going from the district school to the high school they will be taught another way. In controversies involving such momentous interests, the fiercest party spirit will rage, and all the contemplations of heaven be poisoned by the passions of earth. Will not town lines and school district lines be altered, to restore an unsuccessful or to defeat a successful party? Will not fiery zealots move from place to place, to turn the theological scale, as it is said is sometimes now done to turn a political one? And will not the godless make a merchandise of religion by being bribed to do the same thing? Can aught be conceived more deplorable, more fatal to the interests of the young than this? Such strifes and persecutions on the question of total depravity as to make all men depraved at any rate; and such contests about the nature and the number of persons in the Godhead in heaven, as to make little children atheists on earth.

If the question, "What theology shall be taught in school?" is to be decided by districts or towns, then all the prudential and the superintending school committees must be chosen with express reference to their faith; the creed of every candidate for teaching must be investigated; and when litigations arise—and such a system will breed them in swarms—an ecclesiastical tribunal, some star chamber, or high commission court must be created to decide them. If the governor is to have power to appoint the judges of this spiritual tribunal, he also must be chosen with reference to the appointments he will make, and so, too, must the legislators who are to define their power, and to give them the purse and sword of the State, to execute their authority. Call such officers by the name of judge and governor, or cardinal and pope, the thing will be the same. The establishment of the true faith will not stop with the schoolroom. Its grasping jurisdiction will extend over all schools, over all private faith and public worship, until at last, after all our centuries of struggle and of suffering, it will come back to the inquisition, the faggot, and the rack.

Let me ask here, too, where is the consistency of those who advocate the right of a town or a district to determine, by a majority, what theology shall be taught in the schools, but deny the same right to the State? Does not this inconsistency blaze out into the faces of such advocates so as to make them feel, if they are too blind to see? This would be true, even if the State had written out the theology it would enforce. But ours has not. It has only said that no one sect shall obtain any advantage over other sects by means of the school system, which, for purposes of self-preservation, it has established.

84. THE KALAMAZOO DECISION*

The power of the state to support elementary education through taxation had been established in the seventeenth century. In addition, the city of Boston

*Charles E. Stuart *et. al. vs.* School District No. 1 of the Village of Kalamazoo, 30 *Michigan*, p. 69.

*had, in 1821, established a high school to be supported by public money. In
1827, the state of Massachusetts had established a similar school. With the
development of the Middle West, tax-supported high schools began to appear, but
their legality was questioned. Finally, a group of citizens brought suit against the
school board of Kalamazoo, Michigan, seeking to prevent the operation of a high
school at public expense. In 1874, a decision was handed down by the Michigan
supreme court, affirming the right of the state to provide money for high
schools. The decision led to the rapid growth of the public high school.*

The bill in this case is filed to restrain the collection of such portion of the
school taxes assessed against complainants for the year 1872, as have been voted
for the support of the high school in that village, and for the payment of the
salary of the superintendent. While, nominally, this is the end sought to be
attained by the bill, the real purpose of the bill is wider and vastly more
comprehensive than this brief statement would indicate, inasmuch as it seeks a
judicial determination of the right of school authorities, in what are called union
school districts of the state, to levy taxes upon the general public for the support
of what in this state are known as high schools, and to make free by such
taxation the instruction of children in other languages than the English.

The more general question which the record presents we shall endeavor to
state in our own language, but so as to make it stand out distinctly as a naked
question of law, disconnected from all considerations of policy or expediency, in
which light alone we are at liberty to consider it. It is, as we understand it, that
there is no authority in this state to make the high schools free by taxation
levied on the people at large. The argument is that while there may be no
constitutional provision expressly prohibiting such taxation, the general course of
legislation in the state and the general understanding of the people have been
such as to require us to regard the instruction in the classics and in the living
modern languages in these schools as in the nature not of practical and therefore
necessary instruction for the benefit of the people at large, but rather as
accomplishments for the few, to be sought after in the main by those best able
to pay for them, and to be paid for by those who seek them, and not by general
tax. And not only has this been the general state policy, but this higher learning
of itself, when supplied by the state, is so far a matter of private concern to
those who receive it that the courts ought to declare it incompetent to supply it
wholly at the public expense. This is in substance, as we understand it, the
position of the complainants in this suit.

When this doctrine was broached to us, we must confess to no little surprise
that the legislation and policy of our state were appealed to against the right of
the state to furnish a liberal education to the youth of the state in schools
brought within the reach of all classes. We supposed it had always been
understood in this state that education, not merely in the rudiments, but in an
enlarged sense, was regarded as an important practical advantage to be supplied
at their option to rich and poor alike, and not as something pertaining merely to
culture and accomplishment to be brought as such within the reach of those
whose accumulated wealth enabled them to pay for it. As this, however, is now
so seriously disputed, it may be necessary, perhaps, to take a brief survey of the
legislation and general course, not only of the state, but of the antecedent
territory, on the subject.

(The court reviews the history of education in Michigan, including educational provisions in the constitution of 1850. It then speaks of these provisions.)

The instrument submitted by the convention to the people and adopted by them provided for the establishment of free schools in every school district for at least three months in each year, and for the university. By the aid of these we have every reason to believe the people expected a complete collegiate education might be obtained. . . . The inference seems irresistible that the people expected the tendency towards the establishment of high schools in the primary-school districts would continue until every locality capable of supporting one was supplied. And this inference is strengthened by the fact that a considerable number of our union schools date their establishment from the year 1850 and the two or three years following.

If these facts do not demonstrate clearly and conclusively a general state policy, beginning in 1817 and continuing until after the adoption of the present constitution, in the direction of free schools in which education, and at their option the elements of classical education, might be brought within the reach of all the children of the state, then, as it seems to us, nothing can demonstrate it. We might follow the subject further and show that the subsequent legislation has all concurred with this policy, but it would be a waste of time and labor. We content ourselves with the statement that neither in our state policy, in our constitution, or in our laws, do we find the primary-school districts restricted in the branches of knowledge which their officers may cause to be taught, or the grade of instruction that may be given, if their voters consent in regular form to bear the expense and raise the taxes for the purpose.

85. A TYPICAL EARLY HIGH SCHOOL*

By 1860, public high schools had become a relatively common phenomenon. The curriculum varied from school to school. However, it tended to be a combination of the curriculum of the American Academy and the Latin Grammar School, which was college preparatory in nature. The material below shows the curriculum of Woodward High School, established in Cincinnati in 1856.

FIRST YEAR

First Session	Second Session
English Grammar, Brown or Pinneo, completed	Weld's Latin Lessons, to Part II.
English History, Goodrich or Markham, completed	Fitch's Physical Geography
Ray's Algebra, to Sec. 172	Andrews' and Stoddard's Latin Grammar
	Ray's Algebra, to Sec. 305
	Physical Geography (3 lessons)
	Reading (2 lessons)

(Five lessons in each of the above weekly)

*From *American Journal of Education*, 1858, Vol. IV.

Once a Week During the Year

Lectures, by the Principal, on Morals and Manners
Aids to Composition, completed
Composition and Declamation, by sections, each once in three weeks
Reading and Vocal Music
Penmanship, if needed

SECOND YEAR

First Session	*Second Session*
Weld's Latin Lessons, to History	Weld's Latin Lessons, completed
Andrews' and Stoddard's Latin Grammar	Andrews and Stoddard, completed
Geometry, Davies' Legendre, to Book V	Geometry, Davies' Legendre, to Book IX
Gray's Natural Philosophy, to Pneumatics	Gray's Natural Philosophy, completed

(Five lessons in each of the above weekly)

Once a Week During the Year

Reading, Elemental Sounds
Rhetoric and Vocal Music
Composition and Declamation, by sections

THIRD YEAR

First Session	*Second Session*
Silliman's Chemistry, to Sec. 282	Silliman's Chemistry, to Vegetable Chemistry
Algebra and Spherics, Ray's and Davies' Legendre completed	Davies' Trigonometry, completed
Andrews' Caesar or Sallust, 50 Sections (3d)	Cooper's Virgil's Aeneid, 3 books (3d)
German or French (3 days)	German or French (3 days)

Once a Week Throughout the Year

Constitution of the United States
Hedge's Logic
Reading, Rhetoric, and Vocal Music
Composition and Declamation, by sections

FOURTH YEAR

First Session	*Second Session*
Cutter's Physiology & Hygiene	Davies' Navigation and Surveying
McIntire's Astronomy	Weber's General History
Gray and Adams' Geology	Wayland's Mental Philosophy
Folsom's Cicero, 3 Orations (3 days)	Evidences of Christianity (1 day)
Moral Philosophy (1 day)	German or French (3 days)
German or French (3 days)	

Once a Week Throughout the Year

Critical Readings, Vocal Music
Compositions, by sections
Original Addresses, by sections

COLLEGE CLASS

For those preparing to enter college, the following may be substituted for the regular studies of the fourth year,

> Virgil's Aeneid, six books
> Caesar or Sallust, completed
> Cicero's Orations, six
> Crosby's Greek Grammar
> Felton's Greek Reader

86. THE NEW METHODS AT OSWEGO*

C. T. Richardson

Edward A. Sheldon (1823-1897), like Francis W. Parker, popularized the use of Pestalozzian methods. Working with Margaret E. M. Jones, an English disciple of Pestalozzi, he introduced the new methods in the schools of Oswego, New York. His success is evident in the remarks below, made by the president of the Oswego Board of Education in 1861. The selection also provides a clear statement of the bases of the new methods.

From a partial trial during the past year in the Primary Schools, which has been very satisfactory, and from information obtained from various sources, the Board has decided to introduce as far as practicable the system of teaching known as Pestalozzian, the basis of which is Object Lessons.

It will be necessary to make a brief explanation of the system.

The name originated with Pestalozzi, a Swiss philanthropist of Italian extraction, who first, about one hundred years ago, among the children of Switzerland introduced its distinctive characteristics. Since his time it has been modified and improved, and his ideas have been established and developed, until under one name or another they form the basis of all truly philosophical mental culture. The central ideas of the system are as follows:

First. That all education should be according to the natural order of development of the human faculties.

Second. That all knowledge is derived in the first instance from the perceptions of the senses, and therefore that all instruction should be based upon the observation of real objects and occurrences.

Third. That the object of primary education is to give a harmonious cultivation to the faculties of the mind, and not to communicate technical knowledge.

The development of the faculties of the mind in the natural order is in this wise,—first the power to receive impressions; after that the power to conceive thoughts; after that the power to reason. In other words, the Sense, the Understanding and the Reason.

The proper method, then, consists in presenting to the child's mind the quality of knowledge suited to its state of development. The ordinary method disregards this principle and is frequently just the reverse of this practice. In arithmetic, for example, the children are taught to repeat rules. Now a rule is a

*Remarks by C. T. Richardson in *Eighth Annual Report of the Board of Education, of the City of Oswego, for the Year Ending March 31, 1861.*

generalization from many simple facts, and to a child ignorant of those facts conveys no idea whatever, although it may repeat it by an effort of memory.

By the new method the idea of number is made familiar to the child by appealing to the faculties that are already developed; that is, by showing them objects, marbles, pebbles, &c. When the idea of concrete number is attained, they are led to dispense with the objects and deal with figures which are symbols and rules which are abstract.

How many children can repeat the ordinary tables of weight and measure, but how few have any real conception of what constitutes an inch or a pound?

Usually a child is taught as a vessel is laden at the wharf, in bulk, facts are thrown in loose without any regard to the fitness of the child's faculties to receive them, and when a certain amount has been committed to memory the child is considered educated. The true course is to present no other facts, and those no faster, than can be assimilated and organized into the mind. By this method, education answers its definition; it is to *lead out* the faculties. It is organic—it is growth from within, not an addition from without. It is just the difference between knowledge chemically combined with the child's mind, and knowledge mechanically held in solution.

Take the growing plant putting forth in all directions its roots and fibres seeking food. But put the right elements in its way and the plant will organize them into its growth, varying its demands according to its different stages, obstinately refusing at a later period what it obstinately demanded at an earlier, and *vice versa,* till we have first the blade, then the full corn in the ear. So with a child's mind. If when it requires simple impressions on the senses you feed it with complex abstractions, it pines and withers, or at best attains but the development of one faculty at the expense of the rest. But if you place before it the right elements, it absorbs them, organizes them, each faculty taking what it needs, till the simple elements reappear, in the leaf, the flower, the ripe fruit, of vigorous healthy mental growth.

It is simply placing in the child's way the knowledge suited to its natural requirements that the art of Teaching consists. The teacher must furnish the material at the right time. The child must educate itself.

87. INTEREST IN METHODOLOGY*

Francis W. Parker

In the second half of the nineteenth century, the attention of American educators was centered on methodology. The new methods were adopted from European schools, particularly from those of Pestalozzi. Francis Wayland Parker (1837-1902), superintendent of schools in Quincy, Massachusetts, was a leader in the use of Pestalozzian techniques. In a report of the Quincy School Committee, Parker called attention to the success of the new methods.

The first step in the direction of better teaching has been the introduction of improved methods for those hitherto used.

The utter impracticability of the methods in common use has been clearly shown by great thinkers and educators, from Pestalozzi down. The commonly used A B C method has been condemned by every *prominent* educator in the United States, for the last twenty years; and, with very few exceptions, the same can be said in regard to the prevailing methods of teaching Grammar, Arithmetic, and Geography. Doubt about the matter on the part of thoughtful persons is no

*Francis W. Parker in *Report of the School Committee of the Town of Quincy, for the School Year 1875-76.*

longer possible. Their use is a great extravagance of money and time. Proofs of the meagre results produced by them are to be seen on every hand. It costs the town of Quincy, at the least calculation, $25,000 to prepare a class for the High School. Now take the large pile of examination papers of candidates for that school, in this office, and look them over; there is not a single good business handwriting among them all. The language, punctuation, and capitalization are exceedingly poor; much of the spelling is worthy the invention of a Josh Billings. The results in other branches can be better imagined than described. I wish that the taxpayers of Quincy would examine these papers for themselves.

These, then, are the results of the investment of $25,000, and the time and toil of the children for nine years,—and the best results too,—for they are the work of the few who remain in school the entire course. This state of things is not the fault of the teachers, but of the methods and the system,—or, rather, the lack of a system. The methods that are now being introduced into the schools of Quincy are by no means experiments. They have been tested for thirty years in Germany, and for several years in parts of our own country. Their application have produced as great a change in teaching, as Harvey's great discovery did in medicine. Although derived from a careful study of mental laws, they have been, in many respects, intuitively known and practiced in real life; by the mother in the nursery, the mechanic in the shop, the farmer in the field, and the chemist in his laboratory, the essence of them all is the *teaching of things,* and not *words* alone.

The special basis is the thing. What carpenter would attempt to teach an apprentice to build a house, by rules and definitions alone? What farmer would instruct his son in the science of agriculture before he had mastered its elementary processes, and with the active aid of the hoe, plow, and scythe? How long would it take a boy to make a good boot in a shop where the foreman taught, from a textbook, the rules and definitions of cutting, pegging, and stitching? How would children learn to talk, if the same abominable system of mnemonics were practiced in the nursery as in the primary schools? Fortunately, the child has five or six years of wholesome instruction to prepare for the terrible ordeal.

In short, it is proposed to use the common sense of real life in the schoolroom. . . .

Hegel, the great German philosopher, says that a child learns more in the first six years of its life, than it ever afterwards can learn.

After these five or six years of active object teaching and healthful play, the child enters the schoolroom. Imagination, curiosity, love for mental and physical activity are in a state of vigorous development. It is very evident that Nature's great methods, object teaching, and play, should not be abruptly changed to dull, wearisome hours of listless inactivity upon hard benches, interspersed with occasional glimpses into a mysterious volume crowded with black, ugly-looking hieroglyphics, as meaningless to the innocent little one as Chinese or Sanscrit signs are to most of us. And, to add to its misery, these black objects are given names far uglier than themselves, and these names must be laboriously learned before the poor child can obtain one glimpse of the bright objects that lie beyond.

No wonder that the love for school, and all that pertains to it, is so often crushed out of the little innocents.

Every good element that has entered into the child's life should be used,—in a word a primary school should have all the attributes of a pleasant, cheerful home. Home, playground, school, should be the golden pathways to a higher culture.

I am happy to report that the work in the lowest primary schools has been entirely and radically changed. The old A B C method has been abolished (I hope forever), and a far better one established. The little folks play, sing, read, count objects, write, draw, and are happy under the direction of very faithful and efficient teachers. At a comparatively small expense, many of the best features of the Kindergarten could be very profitably introduced into this grade.

88. THE QUINCY METHODS*

Lelia A. Patridge

The "Quincy Methods," as the Pestalozzian adaptations came to be called, quickly developed great popularity in the United States. In 1885, a teacher named Lelia A. Patridge, who was a proponent of the new methodology, summarized the atmosphere of the Quincy classroom as well as the new methods in use there.

...I found that there were multitudes of teachers who were disappointed with the results of their hard but unsatisfactory labors, and were anxious to know of better ways.

To them I presented the distinguishing features of the Quincy work:

1. The joyous life of the schools and the comradeship of teacher and pupils.

2. By grouping their pupils (in the lower grades) they obtained many of the benefits of individual teaching.

3. The skillful use of a great amount and variety of "Busy-Work."

4. Lessons in subjects not usually taught—Drawing, Modeling, Form, Color, Natural History, etc.

5. The constant use of Drawing as a means of expression.

6. Use of text-books as repositories of knowledge.

7. Amount and variety of Supplementary Reading.

8. Substitution of the expression of original thought on the part of the pupils for the old-fashioned memoriter recitation.

9. Carefully varied programme, *whose order was known only to the teacher.*

10. The atmosphere of happy work which encompassed teachers and pupils.

11. Disorder not worrying the teacher and wasting her time.

12. The confidence, courtesy, and respect characterizing the attitude not only of pupils to teacher, but teacher to pupils.

13. The absence of scolding, snubbing, or spying.

14. The dignity, self-possession, and lack of self-consciousness of pupils.

15. The making of the child the objective point, and not Courses of Study, examinations, or promotions.

16. The great economy, naturalness, and practicability of the devices employed.

17. The marked attention paid to the so-called dull pupils.

18. The evident growth of moral power.

19. The remarkable skill of the teachers evidencing their comprehension of underlying principles.

The "Quincy Methods" Illustrated by Lelia A. Patridge, New York, 1885.

20. The wonderful originality and individuality of the teachers—none being imitators; the devices used varying from day to day.

21. The high ideal set before the teachers by the Superintendent, and their hearty co-operation with him in striving to attain it.

22. The absence of machinery, and the absolute freedom from any fixed or prescribed mode of work, each teacher being encouraged to invent and try any device not violating fundamental laws.

23. Examinations aimed to test the teacher's power to teach.

24. Examinations such as to test the children's power to do, not their power to memorize.

89. THE SEVEN CARDINAL PRINCIPLES*

In the early years of the twentieth century, the attitude of the American people toward secondary education changed. The old pattern of a high school which was chiefly college preparatory no longer seemed appropriate. Secondary education, it was believed, should become in reality a part of universal education. Further, it was believed that secondary education should enable the citizens to live a fuller, nobler life. One of the clearest statements of this philosophy is found in the report of the Commission on the Reorganization of Secondary Education (1918). The famous "Seven Cardinal Principles of Secondary Education" was a part of the report.

Secondary education should be determined by the needs of the society to be served, the character of the individuals to be educated, and the knowledge of educational theory and practice available. These factors are by no means static. Society is always in process of development; and the sciences on which educational theory and practice depend constantly furnish new information. Secondary education, however, like any other established agency of society, is conservative and tends to resist modification. Failure to make adjustments when the need arises leads to the necessity for extensive reorganization at irregular intervals. The evidence is strong that such a comprehensive reorganization of secondary education is imperative at the present time.

1. *Changes in society.*—Within the past few decades changes have taken place in American life profoundly affecting the activities of the individual. As a citizen, he must to a greater extent and in a more direct way cope with problems of community life, State and National Governments, and international relationships. As a worker, he must adjust himself to a more complex economic order. As a relatively independent personality, he has more leisure. The problems arising from these three dominant phases of life are closely interrelated and call for a degree of intelligence and efficiency on the part of every citizen that can not be

*From *Cardinal Principles of Secondary Education* (Washington, Government Printing Office, 1918), Bulletin No. 35, 1918, Department of the Interior, Bureau of Education. A report of the Commission on the Reorganization of Secondary Education, pp. 7-11.

secured through elementary education alone, or even through secondary education unless the scope of that education is broadened.

The responsibility of the secondary school is still further increased because many social agencies other than the school afford less stimulus for education than heretofore. In many vocations there have come such significant changes as the substitution of the factory system for the domestic system of industry; the use of machinery in place of manual labor; the high specialization of processes with a corresponding subdivision of labor; and the break-down of the apprentice system. In connection with home and family life have frequently come lessened responsibility on the part of the children; the withdrawal of the father and sometimes the mother from home occupations to the factory or store; and increased urbanization, resulting in less unified family life. Similarly, many important changes have taken place in community life, in the church, in the State, and in other institutions. These changes in American life call for extensive modifications in secondary education.

2. *Changes in the secondary-school population.* – In the past 25 years there have been marked changes in the secondary school population of the United States. The number of pupils has increased, according to Federal returns, from one for every 210 of the total population in 1889-90, to one for every 121 in 1899-1900, to one for every 89 in 1909-10, and to one for every 73 of the estimated total population in 1914-15. The character of the secondary-school population has been modified by the entrance of large numbers of pupils of widely varying capacities, aptitudes, social heredity, and destinies in life. Further, the broadening of the scope of secondary education has brought to the school many pupils who do not complete the full course but leave at various stages of advancement. The needs of these pupils can not be neglected, nor can we expect in the near future that all pupils will be able to complete the secondary school as full-time students.

At present only about one-third of the pupils who enter the first year of the elementary school reach the four-year high school, and only about one in nine is graduated. Of those who enter the seventh school year, only one-half to two-thirds reach the first year of the four-year high school. Of those who enter the four-year high school about one-third leave before the beginning of the second year, about one-half are gone before the beginning of the third year, and fewer than one-third are graduated. These facts can no longer be safely ignored.

3. *Changes in educational theory.* – The sciences on which educational theory depends have within recent years made significant contributions. In particular, educational psychology emphasizes the following factors:

(a) Individual differences in capacities and aptitudes among secondary-school pupils. Already recognized to some extent, this factor merits fuller attention.

(b) The reexamination and reinterpretation of subject values and the teaching methods with reference to "general discipline." – While the final verdict of modern psychology has not as yet been rendered, it is clear that former conceptions of "general values" must be thoroughly revised.

(c) Importance of applying knowledge. – Subject values and teaching methods must be tested in terms of the laws of learning and the application of knowledge to the activities of life, rather than primarily in terms of the demands of any subject as a logically organized science.

(d) Continuity in the development of children. – It has long been held that psychological changes at certain stages are so pronounced as to overshadow the continuity of development. On this basis secondary education has been sharply separated from elementary education. Modern psychology, however, goes to show

that the development of the individual is in most respects a continuous process and that, therefore, any sudden or abrupt break between the elementary and the secondary school or between any two successive stages of education is undesirable.

The foregoing changes in society, in the character of the secondary-school population, and in educational theory, together with many other considerations, call for extensive modifications of secondary education. Such modifications have already begun in part. The present need is for the formulation of a comprehensive program of reorganization, and its adoption, with suitable adjustments, in all the secondary schools in the Nation. Hence it is appropriate for a representative body like the National Education Association to outline such a program. This is the task entrusted by that association to the Commission on the Reorganization of Secondary Education.

Education in the United States should be guided by a clear conception of the meaning of democracy. It is the ideal of democracy that the individual and society may find fulfillment each in the other. Democracy sanctions neither the exploitation of the individual by society, nor the disregard of the interests of society by the individual. More explicitly—

The purpose of democracy is so to organize society that each member may develop his personality primarily through activities designed for the well-being of his fellow members and of society as a whole.

This ideal demands that human activities be placed upon a high level of efficiency; that to this efficiency be added an appreciation of the significance of these activities and loyalty to the best ideals involved; and that the individual choose that vocation and those forms of social service in which his personality may develop and become most effective. For the achievement of these ends democracy must place chief reliance upon education.

Consequently, education in a democracy, both within and without the school, should develop in each individual the knowledge, interests, ideals, habits, and powers whereby he will find his place and use that place to shape both himself and society toward ever nobler ends.

In order to determine the main objectives that should guide education in a democracy it is necessary to analyze the activities of the individual. Normally he is a member of a family, of a vocational group, and of various civic groups, and by virtue of these relationships he is called upon to engage in activities that enrich the family life, to render important vocational services to his fellows, and to promote the common welfare. It follows, therefore, that worthy home-membership, vocation, and citizenship, demand attention as three of the leading objectives.

Aside from the immediate discharge of these specific duties, every individual should have a margin of time for the cultivation of personal and social interests. This leisure, if worthily used, will recreate his powers and enlarge and enrich life, thereby making him better able to meet his responsibilities. The unworthy use of leisure impairs health, disrupts home life, lessens vocational efficiency, and destroys civic-mindedness. The tendency in industrial life, aided by legislation, is to decrease the working hours of large groups of people. While shortened hours tend to lessen the harmful reactions that arise from prolonged strain, they increase, if possible, the importance of preparation for leisure. In view of these considerations, education for the worthy use of leisure is of increasing importance as an objective.

To discharge the duties of life and to benefit from leisure, one must have good health. The health of the individual is essential also to the vitality of the race and to the defense of the Nation. Health education is, therefore, fundamental.

There are various processes, such as reading, writing, arithmetical computations, and oral and written expression, that are needed as tools in the affairs of life. Consequently, command of these fundamental processes, while not an end in itself, is nevertheless an indispensable objective.

And, finally, the realization of the objectives already named is dependent upon ethical character, that is, upon conduct founded upon right principles, clearly preceived and loyally adhered to. Good citizenship, vocational excellence, and the worthy use of leisure go hand in hand with ethical character; they are at once the fruits of sterling character and the channels through which such character is developed and made manifest. On the one hand, character is meaningless apart from the will to discharge the duties of life, and, on the other hand, there is no guarantee that these duties will be rightly discharged unless principles are substituted for impulses, however well-intentioned such impulses may be. Consequently ethical character is at once involved in all the other objectives and at the same time requires specific consideration in any program of national education.

This commission, therefore, regards the following as the main objectives of education: 1. Health. 2. Command of fundamental processes. 3. Worthy home-membership. 4. Vocation. 5. Citizenship. 6. Worthy use of leisure. 7. Ethical character.

The naming of the above objectives is not intended to imply that the process of education can be divided into separated fields. This can not be, since the pupil is indivisible. Nor is the analysis all-inclusive. Nevertheless, we believe that distinguishing and naming these objectives will aid in directing efforts; and we hold that they should constitute the principal aims in education.

90. JOHN DEWEY ON EDUCATION*

The educational philosophy of John Dewey (1859-1952), more than that of any other man, has shaped the nature of modern American education. Early in his career (1897), he published "My Pedagogic Creed," which clearly stated his philosophy and which also provided a basis for the child-centered movement in American education.

ARTICLE I. WHAT EDUCATION IS.

I believe that all education proceeds by the participation of the individual in the social consciousness of the race. This process begins unconsciously almost at birth, and is continually shaping the individual's powers, saturating his consciousness, forming his habits, training his ideas, and arousing his feelings and emotions. Through this unconscious education the individual gradually comes to share in the intellectual and moral resources which humanity has succeeded in getting together. He becomes an inheritor of the funded capital of civilization. The most formal and technical education in the world cannot safely depart from this general process. It can only organize it; or differentiate it in some particular direction.

I believe that the only true education comes through the stimulation of the child's powers by the demands of the social situations in which he finds himself. Through these demands he is stimulated to act as a member of a unity, to emerge from his original narrowness of action and feeling and to conceive of himself from the standpoint of the welfare of the group to which he belongs.

*From "My Pedagogic Creed," by John Dewey in *The School Journal,* Volume LIV, Number 3, January 16, 1897.

Through the responses which others make to his own activities he comes to know what these mean in social terms. The value which they have is reflected back into them. For instance, through the response which is made to the child's instinctive babblings the child comes to know what those babblings mean; they are transformed into articulate language and thus the child is introduced into the consolidated wealth of ideas and emotions which are now summed up in language.

I believe that this educational process has two sides—one psychological and one sociological; and that neither can be subordinated to the other or neglected without evil results following. Of these two dies, the psychological is the basis. The child's own instincts and powers furnish the material and give the starting point for all education. Save as the efforts of the educator connect with some activity which the child is carrying on of his own initiative independent of the educator, education becomes reduced to a pressure from without. It may, indeed, give certain external results but cannot truly be called educative. Without insight into the psychological structure and activities of the individual, the educative process will, therefore, be haphazard and arbitrary. If it chances to coincide with the child's activity it will get a leverage; if it does not, it will result in friction, or disintegration, or arrest of the child nature.

I believe that knowledge of social conditions, of the present state of civilization, is necessary in order properly to interpret the child's powers. The child has his own instincts and tendencies, but we do not know what these mean until we can translate them into their social equivalents. We must be able to carry them back into a social past and see them as the inheritance of previous race activities. We must also be able to project them into the future to see what their outcome and end will be. In the illustration just used, it is the ability to see in the child's babblings the promise and potency of a future social intercourse and conversation which enables one to deal in the proper way with that instinct.

I believe that the psychological and social sides are organically related and that education cannot be regarded as a compromise between the two, or a superimposition of one upon the other. We are told that the psychological definition of education is barren and formal—that it gives us only the idea of a development of all the mental powers without giving us any idea of the use to which these powers are put. On the other hand, it is urged that the social definition of education, as getting adjusted to civilization, makes of it a forced and external process, and results in subordinating the freedom of the individual to a preconceived social and political status.

I believe each of these objections is true when urged against one side isolated from the other. In order to know what a power really is we must know what its end, use, or function is; and this we cannot know save as we conceive the individual as active in social relationships. But, on the other hand, the only possible adjustment which we can give to the child under existing conditions, is that which arises through putting him in complete possession of all his powers. With the advent of democracy and modern industrial conditions, it is impossible to foretell definitely just what civilization will be twenty years from now. Hence it is impossible to prepare the child for any precise set of conditions. To prepare him for the future life means to give him command of himself; it means so to train him that he will have the full and ready use of all his capacities; that his eye and ear and hand may be tools ready to command, that his judgment may be capable of grasping the conditions under which it has to work, and the executive forces be trained to act economically and efficiently. It is impossible to reach this sort of adjustment save as constant regard is had to the individuals' own powers, tastes, and interests—says, that is, as education is continually converted into psychological terms.

In sum, I believe that the individual who is to be educated is a social individual and that society is an organic union of individuals. If we eliminate the social factor from the child we are left only with an abstraction; if we eliminate the individual factor from society, we are left only with an inert and lifeless mass. Education, therefore, must begin with a psychological insight into the child's capacities, interests, and habits. It must be controlled at every point by reference to these same considerations. These powers, interests, and habits must be continually interpreted—we must know what they mean. They must be translated into terms of their social equivalents—into terms of what they are capable of in the way of social service.

ARTICLE II. WHAT THE SCHOOL IS.

I believe that the school is primarily a social institution. Education being a social process, the school is simply that form of community life in which all those agencies are concentrated that will be most effective in bringing the child to share in the inherited resources of the race, and to use his own powers for social ends.

I believe that education, therefore, is a process of living and not a preparation for future living.

I believe that the school must represent present life—life as real and vital to the child as that which he carries on in the home, in the neighborhood, or on the play-ground.

I believe that education which does not occur through forms of life, or that are worth living for their own sake, is always a poor substitute for the genuine reality and tends to cramp and to deaden.

I believe that the school, as an institution, should simplify existing social life; should reduce it, as it were, to an embryonic form. Existing life is so complex that the child cannot be brought into contact with it without either confusion or distraction; he is either overwhelmed by the multiplicty of activities which are going on, so that he loses his own power of orderly reaction, or he is so stimulated by these various activities that his powers are prematurely called into play and he becomes either unduly specialized or else disintegrated.

I believe that, as such simplified social life, the school life should grow gradually out of the home life; that it should take up and continue the activities with which the child is already familiar in the home.

I believe that it should exhibit these activities to the child, and reproduce them in such ways that the child will gradually learn the meaning of them, and be capable of playing his own part in relation to them.

I believe that this is a psychological necessity, because it is the only way of securing continuity in the child's growth, the only way of giving a background of past experience to the new ideas given in school.

I believe it is also a social necessity because the home is the form of social life in which the child has been nurtured and in connection with which he has had his moral training. It is the business of the school to deepen and extend his sense of the values bound up in his home life.

I believe that much of present education fails because it neglects this fundamental principle of the school as a form of community life. It conceives the school as a place where certain information is to be given, where certain lessons are to be learned, or where certain habits are to be formed. The value of these is conceived as lying largely in the remote future; the child must do these things for the sake of something else he is to do; they are mere preparation. As a result they do not become a part of the life experience of the child and so are not truly educative.

I believe that the moral education centers about this conception of the school as a mode of social life, that the best and deepest moral training is precisely that which one gets through having to enter into proper relations with others in a unity of work and thought. The present educational systems, so far as they destroy or neglect this unity, render it difficult or impossible to get any genuine, regular moral training.

I believe that the child should be stimulated and controlled in his work through the life of the community.

I believe that under existing conditions far too much of the stimulus and control proceeds from the teacher, because of neglect of the idea of the school as a form of social life.

I believe that the teacher's place and work in the school is to be interpreted from this same basis. The teacher is not in the school to impose certain ideas or to form certain habits in the child, but is there as a member of the community to select the influences which shall affect the child and to assist him in properly responding to these influences.

I believe that the discipline of the school should proceed from the life of the school as a whole and not directly from the teacher.

I believe that the teacher's business is simply to determine on the basis of larger experience and riper wisdom, how the discipline of life shall come to the child.

I believe that all questions of the grading of the child and his promotion should be determined by reference to the same standard. Examinations are of use only so far as they test the child's fitness for social life and reveal the place in which he can be of the most service and where he can receive the most help.

ARTICLE III. THE SUBJECT-MATTER OF EDUCATION.

I believe that the social life of the child is the basis of concentration, or correlation, in all his training or growth. The social life gives the unconscious unity and the background of all his efforts and of all his attainments.

I believe that the subject-matter of the school curriculum should mark a gradual differentiation out of the primitive unconscious unity of social life.

I believe that we violate the child's nature and render difficult the best ethical results, by introducing the child too abruptly to a number of special studies, of reading, writing, geography, etc., out of relation to this social life.

I believe, therefore, that the true center of correlation on the school subjects is not science, nor literature, nor history, nor geography, but the child's own social activities.

I believe that education cannot be unified in the study of science, or so called nature study, because apart from human activity, nature itself is not a unity; nature in itself is a number of diverse objects in space and time, and to attempt to make it the center of work by itself, is to introduce a principle of radiation rather than one of concentration.

I believe that literature is the reflex expression and interpretation of social experience; that hence it must follow upon and not precede such experience. It, therefore, cannot be made the basis, although it may be made the summary of unification.

I believe once more that history is of educative value in so far as it presents phases of social life and growth. It must be controlled by reference to social life. When taken simply as history it is thrown into the distant past and becomes dead and inert. Taken as the record of man's social life and progress it becomes full of meaning. I believe, however, that it cannot be so taken excepting as the child is also introduced directly into social life.

I believe accordingly that the primary basis of education is in the child's powers at work along the same general constructive lines as those which have brought civilization into being.

I believe that the only way to make the child conscious of his social heritage is to enable him to perform those fundamental types of activity which make civilization what it is.

I believe, therefore, in the so-called expressive or constructive activities as the center of correlation.

I believe that this gives the standard for the place of cooking, sewing, manual training, etc., in the school.

I believe that they are not special studies which are to be introduced over and above a lot of others in the way of relaxation or relief, or as additional accomplishments. I believe rather that they represent, as types, fundamental forms of social activity; and that it is possible and desirable that the child's introduction into the more formal subjects of the curriculum be through the medium of these activities.

I believe that the study of science is educational in so far as it brings out the materials and processes which make social life what it is.

I believe that one of the greatest difficulties in the present teaching of science is that the material is presented in purely objective form, or is treated as a new peculiar kind of experience which the child can add to that which he has already had. In reality, science is of value because it gives the ability to interpret and control the experience already had. It should be introduced, not as so much new subject-matter, but as showing the factors already involved in previous experience and as furnishing tools by which that experience can be more easily and effectively regulated.

I believe that at present we lose much of the value of literature and language studies because of our elimination of the social element. Language is almost always treated in the books of pedagogy simply as the expression of thought. It is true that language is a logical instrument, but it is fundamentally and primarily a social instrument. Language is the device for communication; it is the tool through which one individual comes to share the ideas and feelings of others. When treated simply as a way of getting individual information, or as a means of showing off what one has learned, it loses its social motive and end.

I believe that there is, therefore, no succession of studies in the ideal school curriculum. If education is life, all life has, from the outset, a scientific aspect; an aspect of art and culture and an aspect of communication. It cannot, therefore, be true that the proper studies for one grade are mere reading and writing, and that at a later grade, reading, or literature, or science, may be introduced. The progress is not in the succession of studies but in the development of new attitudes towards, and new interests in, experience.

I believe finally, that education must be conceived as a continuing reconstruction of experience; that the process and the goal of education are one and the same thing.

I believe that to set up any end outside of education, as furnishing its goal and standard, is to deprive the educational process of much of its meaning and tends to make us rely upon false and external stimuli in dealing with the child.

ARTICLE IV. THE NATURE OF METHOD.

I believe that the question of method is ultimately reducible to the question of the order of development of the child's powers and interests. The law for presenting and treating material is the law implicit within the child's own nature. Because this is so I believe the following statements are of supreme importance as determining the spirit in which education is carried on:

1. I believe that the active side precedes the passive in the development of the child nature; that expression comes before conscious impression; that the muscular development precedes the sensory; that movements come before conscious sensations. I believe that consciousness is essentially motor or impulsive; that conscious states tend to project themselves in action.

I believe that the neglect of this principle is the cause of a large part of the waste of time and strength in school work. The child is thrown into a passive, receptive or absorbing attitude. The conditions are such that he is not permitted to follow the law of his nature; the result is friction and waste.

I believe that ideas (intellectual and rational processes) also result from action and devolve for the sake of the better control of action. What we term reason is primarily the law of orderly or effective action. To attempt to develop the reasoning powers, the power of judgment, without reference to the selection and arrangement of means in action, is the fundamental fallacy in our present methods of dealing with this matter. As a result we present the child with arbitrary symbols. Symbols are a necessity in mental development, but they have their place as tools for economizing effort; presented by themselves they are a mass of meaningless and arbitrary ideas imposed from without.

2. I believe that the image is the great instrument of instruction. What a child gets out of any subject presented to him is simply the images which he himself forms with regard to it.

I believe that if nine tenths of the energy at present directed towards making the child learn certain things, were spent in seeing to it that the child was forming proper images, the work of instruction would be indefinitely facilitated.

I believe that much of the time and attention now given to the preparation and presentation of lessons might be more wisely and profitably expended in training the child's power of imagery and in seeing to it that he was continually forming definite, vivid, and growing images of the various subjects with which he comes in contact in his experience.

3. I believe that interests are the signs and symptoms of growing power. I believe that they represent dawning capacities. Accordingly the constant and careful observation of interests is of the utmost importance for the educator.

I believe that these interests are to be observed as showing the state of development which the child has reached.

I believe that they prophesy the stage upon which he is about to enter.

I believe that only through the continual and sympathetic observation of childhood's interests can the adult enter into the child's life and see what it is ready for, and upon what material it could work most readily and fruitfully.

I believe that these interests are neither to be humored nor repressed. To repress interest is to substitute the adult for the child, and so to weaken intellectual curiosity and alertness, to suppress initiative, and to deaden interest. To humor the interests is to substitute the transient for the permanent. The interest is always the sign of some power below; the important thing is to discover this power. To humor the interest is to fail to penetrate below the surface and its sure result is to substitute caprice and whim for genuine interest.

4. I believe that the emotions are the reflex of actions.

I believe that to endeavor to stimulate or arouse the emotions apart from their corresponding activities, is to introduce an unhealthy and morbid state of mind.

I believe that if we can only secure right habits of action and thought, with reference to the good, the true, and the beautiful, the emotions will for the most part take care of themselves.

I believe that next to deadness and dullness, formalism and routine, our education is threatened with no greater evil than sentimentalism.

I believe that this sentimentalism is the necessary result of the attempt to divorce feeling from action.

ARTICLE V. THE SCHOOL AND SOCIAL PROGRESS.

I believe that education is the fundamental method of social progress and reform.

I believe that all reforms which rest simply upon the enactment of law, or the threatening of certain penalties, or upon changes in mechanical or outward arrangements, are transitory and futile.

I believe that education is a regulation of the process of coming to share in the social consciousness; and that the adjustment of individual activity on the basis of this social consciousness is the only sure method of social reconstruction.

I believe that this conception has due regard for both the individualistic and socialistic ideals. It is duly individual because it recognizes the formation of a certain character as the only genuine basis of right living. It is socialistic because it recognizes that this right character is not to be formed by merely individual precept, example, or exhortation, but rather by the influence of a certain form of institutional or community life upon the individual, and that the social organism through the school, as its organ, may determine ethical results.

I believe that in the ideal school we have the reconciliation of the individualistic and the institutional ideals.

I believe that the community's duty to education is, therefore, its paramount moral duty. By law and punishment, by social agitation and discussion, society can regulate and form itself in a more or less haphazard and chance way. But through education society can formulate its own purposes, can organize its own means and resources, and thus shape itself with definiteness and economy in the direction in which it wishes to move.

I believe that when society once recognizes the possibilities in this direction, and the obligations which these possibilities impose, it is impossible to conceive of the resources of time, attention, and money which will be put at the disposal of the educator.

I believe it is the business of every one interested in education to insist upon the school as the primary and most effective interest of social progress and reform in order that society may be awakened to realize what the school stands for, and aroused to the necessity of endowing the educator with sufficient equipment properly to perform his task.

I believe that education thus conceived marks the most perfect and intimate union of science and art conceivable in human experience.

I believe that the art of thus giving shape to human powers and adapting them to social service, is the supreme art; one calling into its service the best of artists; that no insight, sympathy, tact, executive power is too great for such service.

I believe that with the growth of psychological service, giving added insight into individual structure and laws of growth; and with growth of social science, adding to our knowledge of the right organization of individuals, all scientific resources can be utilized for the purposes of education.

I believe that when science and art thus join hands the most commanding motive for human action will be reached; the most genuine springs of human conduct aroused and the best service that human nature is capable of guaranteed.

I believe, finally, that the teacher is engaged, not simply in the training of individuals, but in the formation of the proper social life.

I believe that every teacher should realize the dignity of his calling; that he is a social servant set apart for the maintenance of proper social order and the securing of the right social growth.

I believe that in this way the teacher always is the prophet of the true God and the usherer in of the true kingdom of God.

91. A CRITIC OF CURRENT EDUCATION*

Max Rafferty

The period from 1950 to the present has been a time of great controversy in American education. Many people have felt that the American schools, following the precepts of the child-centered movement, have become too "soft" and unscholarly. One outspoken critic has been Max Rafferty, California's State Superintendent of Public Instruction. Rafferty believes that the schools should return to what he calls "education in depth." The following selection, from Rafferty's What They Are Doing to Your Children, states his position, as well as that of other strong critics of modern education.

What is the real nature of this revolution? What is the new philosophy that we in the west are recommending to the nation in the place of out-worn, exploded progressive education?

Californians are calling it "education in depth." And as is usual in such matters, it's easier to tell what it isn't than what it is.

It is not, for instance, a return to the dear, dead past. It believes in the "three R's," right enough, but only as a springboard for vastly more complex subject matter. It doesn't want a curriculum that harks back to the turn of the century, when a reading and speaking knowledge of Greek and Latin was required to get into Harvard and when a sterile and stereotyped classicism was the major goal of the learning process. It doesn't approve, either, of the often brutal "hickory-stick" discipline of the old days.

Education in depth does not believe that the children belong to the schools, but rather that they belong to the parents. These parents pay the teachers to provide expert information, to teach the skills that a child must learn if he is to become a well-rounded, successful adult, and above all to open the multiplicity of doors to which only education has the key. It is not the job of the school to amuse the child, to condition him psychologically, to feed and clothe him, or indeed to do anything except teach him. This, heaven knows, is a big enough task in itself to preclude virtually everything else.

Education in depth calls a spade a spade. History is taught as history, geography as geography, and civics as civics. It is not all caught up together, and blended, and watered down, and broadened, and pre-chewed until it comes out as something labeled "social studies," or worse yet, "social living." The theory behind this is simple: while it is perfectly true that a knowledge of geography will help in the study of history, it does not follow that therefore the two should be combined and taught as a single subject. This would be just as ridiculous as to claim that because a knowledge of algebra will help in the study of physics, the two should be combined and taught as a single subject labeled "quantitative studies" or "quantitative living."

Education in depth holds that there is a tremendous accumulation of knowledge added to each generation by the thinkers and doers of that period and that one of the principal functions of the schools is to transmit this cultural heritage to the citizens of tomorrow. This means that a reasonable amount of material must be committed to memory and that there is nothing wrong with this. In addition, memorizing phrases and lines from famous works of poetry and prose should be encouraged as a means of perpetuating our literary birthright.

A new philosophy means a new curriculum. Subjects like "ninth-grade orientation" and "student leadership" and "senior problems" should come out. Subjects like "world geography" and "modern economics" should go in. On the elementary level, the units on "the home and the community" can safely be turned out to pasture in favor of some on "great American heroes" and "the Bill of Rights." In junior high school, the repetitive, boring courses in "general math" and "general science" could well be telescoped into single seventh-grade subjects, with specific foreign languages, biology, and algebra taught in the eighth grade for those fitted to tackle them. The new mathematics, geared to the Space Age, is already appearing on the scene. It should be welcomed, its weaknesses analyzed and eliminated, and its strengths acknowledged.

Education in depth stands for the equal dignity and status of each subject, whether it be art or auto mechanics, history or homemaking, mathematics or metal shop. If it is in the school curriculum, placed there by the people through their own locally elected representatives, then it deserves to be accorded exactly the same respect as any other subject. Furthermore, it deserves to be taught by a teacher who is prepared to teach it, who honors its importance in the overall picture—yes, and who loves it for its own sake. If a subject is not worth this kind of treatment, take it out of the school altogether. But don't set up first- and second-class citizens among our teachers, based on the imagined superiority of one subject or group of subjects over another.

The same advice, however, does not apply to reading materials. Here a very definite priority listing should be made. Children today do not have nearly the time for reading that their parents did, especially at home. A dozen stimuli, unknown to an older generation of Americans, compete for the attention of the boys and girls. Therefore it behooves the schools to assign literary materials carefully chosen from the great children's classics and to see that this basic food of the mind is carefully ingested and digested before the less tried and tested items of current and popular taste are placed before the pupil. After the child has trudged the Scottish hills with David Balfour and plumbed the ocean's depths with Captain Nemo, there will be ample time for him to explore the space lanes with Flash Gordon. First things first.

Education in depth demands from the teacher a knowledge of subject matter in excess of what has been demanded during the past twenty years or more. The English teacher is going to be expected to know English grammar backwards and forwards, and no nonsense about teaching "toastmastership" or "how to be popular in a mixed group." The history instructor will be expected to be able to distinguish between the Guelfs and the Ghibellines on the one hand, and between Benjamin Harrison and William Henry Harrison on the other. The physical-education teacher is seeing the time rapidly drawing to a close when he can toss a few basketballs or volleyballs to a swarm of boys and tell them to choose up sides and get some games going. The elementary instructor is going to have to tighten up and bear down. No more pupil papers handed back with grades of *A* but containing misspelled words and faulty constructions that haven't even been circled.

Education in depth stresses the value and importance of competition in the schools. Such competition should not be excessive or unreasonable, but it should exist. Life itself is competition, and the sooner the child learns to compete, the better for him and for his country. Within the range of the child's own ability potential, good work should be praised and rewarded, bad work criticized and labeled unacceptable. Subject-matter report cards graded *A-B-C-D-F* or a reasonable facsimile thereof are a must. Parent-teacher conferences are fine, but they cannot and should not take the place of report cards. The latter constitute a sort of semiannual day of reckoning, a summing up of assets and liabilities that is invaluable training for later life.

Speaking of a day of reckoning, we are going to have to have one for the elementary reading and "social-studies" books, and in the near future. The new philosophy cannot coexist with Dick and Jane, and Tom and Susan, and their ilk. The namby-pamby, nonexistent plots; the one-dimensional and insipid characters; the painfully successful attempts to remove anything exciting or adventurous or *glamorous* from the contents—all these things will have to be changed. Before the great publishing houses can expect to sell their wares in California at least, they are going to have to get us some books with real meat in them, books with sparkle and zing, books that are worth reading. After all, children don't learn to read in order to please the teacher or gratify their parents. They learn to read because they become sufficiently interested in what they are reading to want to tackle page two because of what happened on page one. I submit that for far too long we haven't supplied them with books that would cause anyone to want to turn the pages.

There is another fault to find with the school books, however, other than general lack of interest. There are downright inaccuracies and misrepresentations in all too many cases. For instance, one complaint against publishers lies in the way they treat our racial minorities, picturing the Negro either as a barefooted plantation hand or an Olympic athlete, and our Mexican neighbors invariably wearing sandals and serapes. If there is one vital area of weakness in our entire educational structure that deserves to be singled out and taken vigorously in hand, it is the textbook situation.

Let us sum up the differences between progressive education and education in depth, always remembering that we do not intend to throw the baby out along with the bath water. Progressivism had some good points. Few things are all black or all white. The problem-solving approach fathered by Dewey was sound. It should be retained. So should the willingness on the part of the instructor to give reasons to the children for the many things he must ask them to do every day. Basically, however, the differences are these:

1. Progressive education teaches that there are no positive and eternal values. Education in depth maintains that there are and that the main purpose of education is to seek out these lasting truths, to identify them, and to explore them to the greater benefit of the individual and the nation.

2. Progressive education stresses "life adjustment" and "group acceptance" as the primary goals of the instructional program. Education in depth holds that the teaching of organized, disciplined, and systematic subject matter is the principal objective of the schools.

3. Progressive education downgrades the role of the individual and glorifies the importance of the group. Education in depth intends to regard the individual as the be-all and the end-all of the educative process.

4. Progressive education feels that the curriculum should depend upon the interests and needs of the group. Education in depth wants a curriculum to provide for the individual the tools and skills he needs to be a cultured, productive, patriotic American citizen.

5. Progressive education believes that memorization is stultifying and a waste of time. Education in depth teaches that committing important names, places, events, dates, and passages of poetry and prose to memory is a necessary part of instruction.

6. Progressive education advocates "experiencing" learning through as many sense avenues as practicable. Education in depth thinks this is a pronounced waste of time and regards reading and recitative discussion as still the most effective and economical method of instruction.

7. Progressive education holds that the pupil should be encouraged to compete only with himself, or rather with his own previous best efforts. Education in depth believes that the very survival of our country and the success of the individual in later life depends upon how well he is taught to hold his own in a highly competitive world.

8. Progressive education, as interpreted by several of its high priests, has doubts about the American free-enterprise system and has advocated various form of collectivism. Education in depth teaches the facts about our country's phenomenal growth and development and reminds its pupils that our economic system has made us the envy and the wonder of the whole world.

The issue is clearly drawn. The difference is as great as that between day and night. Public opinion all over the United States is lining up on one side or the other. No greater or more significant decision will be made by our people in this century.

In California, the determination has already been reached. But we have no monopoly on truth; there is room in education in depth for all.

92. RELEASED TIME FOR RELIGIOUS INSTRUCTION*

The development of education in America in the twentieth century has been greatly influenced by court decisions. The relation between religion and public education has caused much controversy. A frequently used method to provide some religious instruction without legal involvement was to provide "released time" for such instruction. Eventually, plans for released time became the subject of legal procedures. The two most important cases heard by the United States Supreme Court were the McCollum case (1945) and the Zorach case (1952).

*From *People of State of Illinois Ex Rel. McCollum v. Board of Education of School Dist. No. 71, Champaign County, Ill. Supreme Court of the United States, 1948. 333 U. S. 203, 68 S. Ct. 461.*

Basing its decisions primarily on the amount of involvement by the schools, the Supreme Court ruled that the use of released time as described in the McCollum case was unconstitutional but that the use of released time as described in the Zorach case was constitutional.

PEOPLE OF STATE OF ILLINOIS EX REL. McCOLLUM v. BOARD OF EDUCATION OF SCHOOL DIST. NO. 71, CHAMPAIGN COUNTY, ILL., Supreme Court of the United States, 1948. 333 U.S. 203, 68 S.Ct. 461.

JUSTICE BLACK delivered the opinion of the Court.

This case relates to the power of a state to utilize its tax-supported public school system in aid of religious instruction insofar as that power may be restricted by the First and Fourteenth Amendments to the Federal Constitution. . . .

Appellant's petition for mandamus alleged that religious teachers, employed by private religious groups, were permitted to come weekly into the school buildings during the regular hours set apart for secular teaching, and then and there for a period of thirty minutes substitute their religious teaching for the secular education provided under the compulsory education law. The petitioner charged that this joint public-school religious-group program violated the First and Fourteenth Amendments to the United States Constitution. The prayer of her petition was that the Board of Education be ordered to "adopt and enforce rules and regulations prohibiting all instruction in and teaching of religious education in all public schools in Champaign School District Number 71, . . . and in all public school houses and buildings in said district when occupied by public schools." . . .

Although there are disputes between the parties as to various inferences that may or may not properly be drawn from the evidence concerning the religious program, the following facts are shown by the record without dispute. In 1940 interested members of the Jewish, Roman Catholic, and a few of the Protestant faiths formed a voluntary association called the Champaign Counsel on Religious Education. They obtained permission from the Board of Education to offer classes in religious instruction to public school pupils in grades four to nine inclusive. Classes were made up of pupils whose parents signed printed cards requesting that their children be permitted to attend; they were held weekly, thirty minutes for the lower grades, forty-five minutes for the higher. The council employed the religious teachers at no expense to the school authorities, but the instructors were subject to the approval and supervision of the superintendent of schools. The classes were taught in three separate religious groups by Protestant teachers, Catholic priests, and a Jewish rabbi, although for the past several years there have apparently been no classes instructed in the Jewish religion. Classes were conducted in the regular classrooms of the school building. Students who did not choose to take the religious instruction were not released from public school duties; they were required to leave their classrooms and go to some other place in the school building for pursuit of their secular studies. On the other hand, students who were released from secular study for the religious instructions were required to be present at the religious classes. Reports of their presence or absence were to be made to their secular teachers.

The foregoing facts, without reference to others that appear in the record, show the use of tax-supported property for religious instruction and the close cooperation between the school authorities and the religious council in promoting religious education. The operation of the State's compulsory education system thus assists and is integrated with the program of religious instruction carried on by separate religious sects. Pupils compelled by law to go to school for secular education are released in part from their legal duty upon the condition that they attend the religious classes. This is beyond all question a utilization of the tax-established and tax-supported public school system to aid religious groups to spread their faith. And it falls squarely under the ban of the First Amendment (made applicable to the States by the Fourteenth) as we interpreted it in Everson v. Board of Education, 330 U.S. 1. . . .

To hold that a state cannot consistently with the First and Fourteenth Amendments utilize its public school system to aid any or all religious faiths or sects in the dissemination of their doctrines and ideals does not, as counsel urge, manifest a governmental hostility to religion or religious teachings. A manifestation of such hostility would be at war with our national tradition as embodied in the First Amendment's guaranty of the free exercise of religion. For the First Amendment rests upon the premise that both religion and government can best work to achieve their lofty aims if each is left free from the other within its respective sphere. Or, as we said in the Everson case, the First Amendment has erected a wall between Church and State which must be kept high and impregnable.

Here not only are the State's tax-supported public school buildings used for the dissemination of religious doctrines. The State also affords sectarian groups an invaluable aid in that it helps to provide pupils for their religious classes through use of the State's compulsory public school machinery. This is not separation of Church and State.

The cause is reversed and remanded to the State Supreme Court for proceedings not inconsistent with this opinion. Reversed and Remanded.

ZORACH v. CLAUSON, Supreme Court of the United States, 1952. 343 U.S. 306, 72 S.Ct. 679.

MR. JUSTICE DOUGLAS delivered the opinion of the Court.

New York City has a program which permits its public schools to release students during the school day so that they may leave the school buildings and school grounds and go to religious centers for religious instruction or devotional exercises. A student is released on written request of his parents. Those not released stay in the classrooms. The churches make weekly reports to the schools, sending a list of children who have been released from public school but who have not reported for religious instruction.

This "released time" program involves neither religious instruction in public school classrooms nor the expenditure of public funds. All costs, including the application blanks, are paid by the religious organizations. The case is therefore unlike McCollum v. Board of Education, 333 U.S. 203, 68 S.Ct. 461, which involved a "released time" program from Illinois. In that case the classrooms were turned over to religious instructors. We accordingly held that the program violated the First Amendment which (by reason of the Fourteenth Amendment)[1] prohibits the states from establishing religion or prohibiting its free exercise.

Appellants, who are taxpayers and residents of New York City and whose children attend its public schools,[2] challenge the present law, contending it is in essence not different from the one involved in the McCollum case. Their argument, stated elaborately in various ways, reduces itself to this: the weight and influence of the school is put behind a program for religious instruction; public school teachers police it, keeping tab on students who are released; the classroom activities come to a halt while the students who are released for religious instruction are on leave; the school is a crutch on which the churches are leaning for support in their religious training; without the cooperation of the schools this "released time" program, like the one in the *McCollum* case, would be futile and ineffective. The New York Court of Appeals sustained the law against this claim of unconstitutionality. 303 N.Y. 161, 100 N.E.2d 463. The case is here on appeal. 28 U.S.C. § 1257 (2), 28 U.S.C.A. 1257(2).

It takes obtuse reasoning to inject any issue of the "free exercise" of religion into the present case. No one is forced to go to the religious classroom and no religious exercise or instruction is brought to the classrooms of the public schools. A student need not take religious instruction. He is left to his own desires as to the manner or time of his religious devotions, if any.

There is a suggestion that the system involves the use of coercion to get public school students into religious classrooms. There is no evidence in the record before us that supports that conclusion. The present record indeed tells us that the school authorities are neutral in this regard and do no more than release students whose parents so request. If in fact coercion were used, if it were established that any one or more teachers were using their office to persuade or force students to take the religious instruction, a wholly different case would be presented. Hence we put aside that claim of coercion both as respects the "free exercise" of religion and "an establishment of religion" within the meaning of the First Amendment. . . .

We would have to press the concept of separation of Church and State to these extremes to condemn the present law on constitutional grounds. . . .

We are a religious people whose institutions presuppose a Supreme Being. We guarantee the freedom to worship as one chooses. We make room for as wide a variety of beliefs and creeds as the spiritual needs of man deem necessary. We sponsor an attitude on the part of government that shows no partiality to any one group and that lets each flourish according to the zeal of its adherents and the appeal of its dogma. When the state encourages religious instruction or cooperates with religious authorities by adjusting the schedule of public events to sectarian needs, it follows the best of our traditions. For it then respects the religious nature of our people and accommodates the public service to their spiritual needs. To hold that it may not would be to find in the Constitution a requirement that the government show a callous indifference to religious groups. That would be preferring those who believe in no religion over those who do believe. Government may not finance religious groups nor undertake religious instruction nor blend secular and sectarian education nor use secular institutions to force one or some religion on any person. But we find no constitutional requirement which makes it necessary for government to be hostile to religion and to throw its weight against efforts to widen the effective scope of religious influence. The government must be neutral when it comes to competition between sects. It may not thrust any sect on any person. It may not make a religious observance compulsory. It may not coerce anyone to attend church, to observe a religious holiday, or to take religious instruction. But it can close its doors or suspend its operations as to those who want to repair to their religious sanctuary for worship or instruction. No more than that is undertaken here. . . .

In the *McCollum* case the classrooms were used for religious instruction and the force of the public school was used to promote that instruction. Here, as we have said, the public schools do no more than accommodate their schedules to a program of outside religious instruction. We follow the *McCollum* case. But we cannot expand it to cover the present released time program unless separation of

Church and State means that public institutions can make no adjustments of
their schedules to accommodate the religious needs of the people. We cannot
read into the Bill of Rights such a philosophy of hostility to religion.
Affirmed.

FOOTNOTES

[1]See Stromberg v. California, 283 U.S. 359, 51 S.Ct. 532; Cantwell v. Connecticut, 310
U.S. 296, 60 S.Ct. 900; Murdock v Pennsylvania, 319 U.S. 105, 63 S.Ct. 870.

[2]No problem of this Court's jurisdiction is posed in this case since, unlike the appellants
in Doremus v. Board of Education, 342 U.S. 429, 72 S.Ct. 394, appellants here are parents
of children currently attending schools subject to the released time program.

93. PRAYER AND BIBLE READING
IN PUBLIC SCHOOLS*

*Another problem involving the relationship between the public school and
religion is the legality of prayer and Bible reading in the school. Within recent
years, three important rulings on this matter have been made by the United
States Supreme Court. These are typically known as the Engel case, the Schempp
case, and the Murray case. The last two cases were combined by the Court. The
two decisions are reproduced below.*

ENGEL v. VITALE, Supreme Court of the United States, 1962. 370 U.S. 421,
82 S.Ct. 1261.

MR. JUSTICE BLACK delivered the opinion of the Court.
The respondent Board of Education of Union Free School District No. 9,
New Hyde Park, New York, acting in its official capacity under state law,
directed the School District's principal to cause the following prayer to be said
aloud by each class in the presence of a teacher at the beginning of each school
day:

"Almighty God, we acknowledge our dependence upon Thee, and we
beg Thy blessings upon us, our parents, our teachers and our
Country."

This daily procedure was adopted on the recommendation of the State Board of
Regents, a governmental agency created by the State Constitution to which the
New York Legislature has granted broad supervisory, executive, and legislative
powers over the State's public school system.[1] These state officials composed the
prayer which they recommended and published as a part of their "Statement on
Moral and Spiritual Training in the Schools," saying: "We believe that this
Statement will be subscribed to by all men and women of good will, and we call
upon all of them to aid in giving life to our program." . . .
     We think that by using its public school system to encourage recitation of
the Regents' prayer, the State of New York has adopted a practice wholly
inconsistent with the Establishment Clause. There can, of course, be no doubt
that New York's program of daily classroom invocation of God's blessings as
prescribed in the Regents' prayer is a religious activity. It is a solemn avowal of

*Zorach v. Clauson, Supreme Court of the United States, 1952. 343 U. S. 306,
72 S. Ct. 679.

divine faith and supplication for the blessings of the Almighty. The nature of such a prayer has always been religious, . . .

The petitioners contend among other things that the state laws requiring or permitting use of the Regents' prayer must be struck down as a violation of the Establishment Clause because that prayer was composed by governmental officials as a part of a governmental program to further religious beliefs. For this reason, petitioners argue, the State's use of the Regents' prayer in its public school system breaches the constitutional wall of separation between Church and State. We agree with that contention since we think that the constitutional prohibition against laws respecting an establishment of religion must at least mean that in this country it is no part of the business of government to compose official prayers for any group of the American people to recite as a part of a religious program carried on by government. . . .

There can be no doubt that New York's state prayer program officially establishes the religious beliefs embodied in the Regents' prayer. The respondents' argument to the contrary, which is largely based upon the contention that the Regents' prayer is "non-denominational" and the fact that the program, as modified and approved by state courts, does not require all pupils to recite the prayer but permits those who wish to do so to remain silent or be excused from the room, ignores the essential nature of the program's constitutional defects. Neither the fact that the prayer may be denominationally neutral nor the fact that its observance on the part of the students is voluntary can serve to free it from the limitations of the Establishment Clause, as it might from the Free Exercise Clause, of the First Amendment, both of which are operative against the States by virtue of the Fourteenth Amendment. Although these two clauses may in certain instances overlap, they forbid two quite different kinds of governmental encroachment upon religious freedom. The Establishment Clause, unlike the Free Exercise Clause, does not depend upon any showing of direct governmental compulsion and is violated by the enactment of laws which establish an official religion whether those laws operate directly to coerce nonobserving individuals or not. This is not to say, of course, that laws officially prescribing a particular form of religious worship do not involve coercion of such individuals. When the power, prestige and financial support of government is placed behind a particular religious belief, the indirect coercive pressure upon religious minorities to conform to the prevailing officially approved religion is plain. But the purposes underlying the Establishment Clause go much further than that. Its first and most immediate purpose rested on the belief that a union of government and religion tends to destroy government and to degrade religion. The history of governmentally established religion, both in England and in this country, showed that whenever government had allied itself with one particular form of religion, the inevitable result had been that it had incurred the hatred, disrespect and even contempt of those who held contrary beliefs. That same history showed that many people had lost their respect for any religion that had relied upon the support of government to spread its faith. The Establishment Clause thus stands as an expression of principle on the part of the Founders of our Constitution that religion is too personal, too sacred, too holy, to permit its "unhallowed perversion" by a civil magistrate. . . . The New York laws officially prescribing the Regents' prayer are inconsistent both with the purposes of the Establishment Clause and with the Establishment Clause itself.

It has been argued that to apply the Constitution in such a way as to prohibit state laws respecting an establishment of religious services in public schools is to indicate a hostility toward religion or toward prayer. Nothing, of course, could be more wrong. . . . It is neither sacrilegious nor antireligious to say that each separate government in this country should stay out of the business of writing or sanctioning official prayers and leave that purely religious function to the people themselves and to those the people choose to look to for religious guidance.

It is true that New York's establishment of its Regents' prayer as an officially approved religious doctrine of that State does not amount to a total establishment of one particular religious sect to the exclusion of all others—that, indeed, the governmental endorsement of that prayer seems relatively insignificant when compared to the governmental encroachments upon religion which were commonplace 200 years ago. To those who may subscribe to the view that because the Regents' official prayer is so brief and general there can be no danger to religious freedom in its governmental establishment, however, it may be appropriate to say in the words of James Madison, the author of the First Amendment:

> "[I]t is proper to take alarm at the first experiment on our liberties. . . . Who does not see that the same authority which can establish Christianity, in exclusion of all other Religions, may establish with the same ease any particular sect of Christians, in exclusion of all other Sects? That the same authority which can force a citizen to contribute three pence only of his property for the support of any one establishment, may force him to conform to any other establishment in all cases whatsoever?"[2]

The judgment of the Court of Appeals of New York is reversed and the cause remanded for further proceedings not inconsistent with this opinion.

Reversed and remanded.

FOOTNOTES

[1]See New York Constitution, Art. V,   4; New York Education Law,   101, 120 et seq., 202, 214-219, 224, 245 et seq., 704, and 801 et seq.

[2]Memorial and Remonstrance Against Religious Assessments, II Writings of Madison 183, at 185-186.

SCHOOL DISTRICT OF ABINGTON TOWNSHIP v. SCHEMPP and MURRAY v. CURLETT, Supreme Court of the United States, 1963. 374 U.S. 203, 83 S.Ct. 1560.

MR. JUSTICE CLARK delivered the opinion of the Court.

Once again we are called upon to consider the scope of the provision of the First Amendment to the United States Constitution which declares that "Congress shall make no law respecting an establishment of religion, or prohibiting the free exercise thereof . . . ." These companion cases present the issues in the context of state action requiring that schools begin each day with readings from the Bible. While raising the basic questions under slightly different factual situations, the cases permit of joint treatment. In light of the history of the First Amendment and of our cases interpreting and applying its requirements, we hold that the practices at issue and the laws requiring them are unconstitutional under the Establishment Clause, as applied to the States through the Fourteenth Amendment.

The Facts in Each Case: No. 142. The Commonwealth of Pennsylvania by law, 24 Pa.Stat. § 15-1516, as amended, Pub.Law 1928 (Supp.1960) Dec. 17, 1959, requires that "At least ten verses from the Holy Bible shall be read, without comment, at the opening of each public school on each school day. Any child shall be excused from such Bible reading, or attending such Bible reading, upon the written request of his parent or guardian." The Schempp family, husband and wife and two of their three children, brought suit to enjoin enforcement of the statute, contending that their rights under the Fourteenth Amendment to the Constitution of the United States are, have been, and will continue to be violated unless this statute be declared unconstitutional as violative of these provisions of the First Amendment. They sought to enjoin the appellant school district, wherein the Schempp children attend school, and its officers and the Superintendent of Public Instruction of the Commonwealth from continuing to conduct such readings and recitation of the Lord's Prayer in the public schools of the district pursuant to the statute. . . .

No. 119. In 1905 the Board of School Commissioners of Baltimore City adopted a rule pursuant to Art. 77, § 202 of the Annotated Code of Maryland. The rule provided for the holding of opening exercises in the schools of the city, consisting primarily of the "reading, without comment, of a chapter in the Holy Bible and/or the use of the Lord's Prayer." The petitioners, Mrs. Madalyn Murray and her son, William J. Murray III, are both professed atheists. Following unsuccessful attempts to have the respondent school board rescind the rule, this suit was filed for mandamus to compel its rescission and cancellation. It was alleged that William was a student in a public school of the city and Mrs. Murray, his mother, was a taxpayer therein; that it was the practice under the rule to have a reading on each school morning from the King James version of the Bible; that at petitioners' insistence the rule was amended[1] to permit children to be excused from the exercise on request of the parent and that William had been excused pursuant thereto; that nevertheless the rule as amended was in violation of the petitioners' rights "to freedom of religion under the First and Fourteenth Amendments" and in violation of "the principle of separation between church and state, contained therein. . . ." . . .

Applying the Establishment Clause principles to the cases at bar we find that the States are requiring the selection and reading at the opening of the school day of verses from the Holy Bible and the recitation of the Lord's Prayer by the students in unison. These exercises are prescribed as part of the curricular activities of students who are required by law to attend school. They are held in the school buildings under the supervision and with the participation of teachers employed in those schools. None of these factors, other than compulsory school attendance, was present in the program upheld in Zorach v. Clauson. The trial court in No. 142 has found that such an opening exercise is a religious ceremony and was intended by the State to be so. We agree with the trial court's finding as to the religious character of the exercises. Given that finding, the exercises and the law requiring them are in violation of the Establishment Clause.

There is no such specific finding as to the religious character of the exercises in No. 119, and the State contends (as does the State in No. 142) that the program is an effort to extend its benefits to all public school children without regard to their religious belief. Included within its secular purposes, it says, are the promotion of moral values, the contradiction to the materialistic trends of our times, the perpetuation of our institutions and the teaching of literature. The case came up on demurrer, of course, to a petition which alleged that the uniform practice under the rule had been to read from the King James version of the Bible and that the exercise was sectarian. The short answer, therefore, is that the religious character of the exercise was admitted by the State. But even if its purpose is not strictly religious, it is sought to be accomplished through readings, without comment, from the Bible. Surely the place of the Bible as an instrument of religion cannot be gainsaid, and the State's recognition of the pervading religious character of the ceremony is evident from the rule's specific permission of the alternative use of the Catholic Douay version as well as the recent amendment permitting nonattendance at the exercises. None of these factors is consistent with the contention that the Bible is here used either as an instrument for nonreligious moral inspiration or as a reference for the teaching of secular subjects.

The conclusion follows that in both cases the laws require religious exercises and such exercises are being conducted in direct violation of the rights of the appellees and petitioners. Nor are these required exercises mitigated by the fact that individual students may absent themselves upon parental request, for that fact furnishes no defense to a claim of unconstitutionality under the Establishment Clause. See Engel v. Vitale, supra, 370 U.S., at 430, 82 S.Ct., at 1266-1267, 8 L.Ed.2d 601. Further, it is no defense to urge that the religious practices here may be relatively minor encroachments on the First Amendment. The breach of neutrality that is today a trickling stream may all too soon become a raging torrent and, in the words of Madison, "it is proper to take alarm at the first experiment on our liberties." Memorial and Remonstrance Against Religious Assessments . . . .

It is insisted that unless these religious exercises are permitted a "religion of secularism" is established in the schools. We agree of course that the State may not establish a "religion of secularism" in the sense of affirmatively opposing or showing hostility to religion, thus "preferring those who believe in no religion over those who do believe." Zorach v. Clauson, supra, 343 U.S., at 314, 72 S.Ct., at 684, 96 L.Ed. 954. We do not agree, however, that this decision in any sense has that effect. In addition, it might well be said that one's education is not complete without a study of comparative religion or the history of religion and its relationship to the advancement of civilization. It certainly may be said that the Bible is worthy of study for its literary and historic qualities. Nothing we have said here indicates that such study of the Bible or of religion, when presented objectively as part of a secular program of education, may not be effected consistently with the First Amendment. But the exercises here do not fall into those categories. They are religious exercises, required by the States in violation of the command of the First Amendment that the Government maintain strict neutrality, neither aiding nor opposing religion.

Finally, we cannot accept that the concept of neutrality, which does not permit a State to require a religious exercise even with the consent of the majority of those affected, collides with the majority's right to free exercise of religion. While the Free Exercise Clause clearly prohibits the use of state action to deny the rights of free exercise to *anyone*, it has never meant that a majority could use the machinery of the State to practice its beliefs. Such a contention was effectively answered by Mr. Justice Jackson for the Court in West Virginia Board of Education v. Barnette, 319 U.S. 624, 638, 63 S.Ct. 1178, 1185, 87 L.Ed. 1628 (1943):

> "The very purpose of a Bill of Rights was to withdraw certain subjects from the vicissitudes of political controversy, to place them beyond the reach of majorities and officials to establish them as legal principles to be applied by the courts. One's right . . . freedom of

worship . . . and other fundamental rights may not be submitted to vote; they depend on the outcome of no elections."

The place of religion in our society is an exalted one, achieved through a long tradition of reliance on the home, the church and the inviolable citadel of the individual heart and mind. We have come to recognize through bitter experience that it is not within the power of government to invade that citadel, whether its purpose or effect be to aid or oppose, to advance or retard. In the relationship between man and religion, the State is firmly committed to a position of neutrality. Though the application of that rule requires interpretation of a delicate sort, the rule itself is clearly and concisely stated in the words of the First Amendment. Applying that rule to the facts of these cases, we affirm the judgment in No. 142. In No. 119, the judgment is reversed and the cause remanded to the Maryland Court of Appeals for further proceedings consistent with this opinion.

It is so ordered.

Judgment in No. 142 affirmed; judgment in No. 119 reversed and cause remanded with directions.

FOOTNOTES

[1]The rule as amended provides as follows "Opening Exercises. Each school, either collectively or in classes, shall be opened by the reading, without comment, of a chapter in the Holy Bible and/or the use of the Lord's Prayer. The Douay version may be used by those pupils who prefer it. Appropriate patriotic exercises should be held as a part of the general opening exercise of the school or class. Any child shall be excused from participating in the opening exercises or from attending the opening exercises upon the written request of his parent or guardian."

94. RACIAL INTEGRATION OF PUBLIC SCHOOLS*

Of numerous recent rulings by the Supreme Court concerning problems of racial integration of public schools, the landmark decision is probably the one referred to as the Brown case. Other more recent rulings of the Supreme Court have, in general, dealt with the implementation of this decision. The decision is reproduced below.

BROWN v. BOARD OF EDUCATION OF TOPEKA, Supreme Court of the United States, 1954. 347 U.S. 483, 74 S.Ct. 686.

MR. CHIEF JUSTICE WARREN delivered the opinion of the Court.

These cases come to us from the States of Kansas, South Carolina, Virginia, and Delaware. They are premised on different facts and different local conditions, but a common legal question justifies their consideration together in this consolidated opinion.

In each of the cases, minors of the Negro race, through their legal representatives, seek the aid of the courts in obtaining admission to the public schools of their community on a nonsegregated basis. In each instance, they have been denied admission to schools attended by white children under laws requiring or permitting segregation according to race. This segregation was alleged to deprive the plaintiffs of the equal protection of the laws under the Fourteenth Amendment. In each of the cases other than the Delaware case, a three-judge

*Engel v. Vitale, Supreme Court of the United States, 1962. 370 U. S. 421, 82 S. Ct. 1261.

federal district court denied relief to the plaintiffs on the so-called "separate but equal" doctrine announced by this Court in Plessy v. Ferguson, 163 U.S. 537, 16 S.Ct. 1138, 41 L.Ed. 256. Under that doctrine, equality of treatment is accorded when the races are provided substantially equal facilities, even though these facilities be separate. In the Delaware case, the Supreme Court of Delaware adhered to that doctrine, but ordered that the plaintiffs be admitted to the white schools because of their superiority to the Negro schools.

The plaintiffs contend that segregated public schools are not "equal" and cannot be made "equal," and that hence they are deprived of the equal protection of the laws. Because of the obvious importance of the question presented, the Court took jurisdiction. Argument was heard in the 1952 Term, and reargument was heard this Term on certain questions propounded by the Court. . . .

In the first cases in this Court constructing the Fourteenth Amendment, decided shortly after its adoption, the Court interpreted it as proscribing all state-imposed discriminations against the Negro race. The doctrine of "separate but equal" did not make its appearance in this Court until 1896 in the case of Plessy v. Ferguson, supra, involving not education but transportation. American courts have since labored with the doctrine for over half a century. In this Court, there have been six cases involving the "separate but equal" doctrine in the field of public education. In Cumming v. Board of Education of Richmond County, 175 U.S. 528, 20 S.Ct. 197, 44 L.Ed. 262, and Gong Lum v. Rice, 275 U.S. 78, 48 S.Ct. 91, 72 L.Ed. 172, the validity of the doctrine itself was not challenged. In more recent cases, all on the graduate school level, inequality was found in that specific benefits enjoyed by white students were denied to Negro students of the same educational qualifications. State of Missouri ex rel. Gaines v. Canada, 305 U.S. 337, 59 S.Ct. 232, 83 L.Ed. 208; Sipuel v. Board of Regents of University of Oklahoma, 332 U.S. 631, 68 S.Ct. 299, 92 L.Ed. 247; Sweatt v. Painter, 339 U.S. 629, 70 S.Ct. 848, 94 L.Ed. 1114; McLaurin v. Oklahoma State Regents, 339 U.S. 637, 70 S.Ct. 851, 94 L.Ed. 1149. In none of these cases was it necessary to re-examine the doctrine to grant relief to the Negro plaintiff. And in Sweatt v. Painter, supra, the Court expressly reserved decision on the question whether Plessy v. Ferguson should be held inapplicable to public education.

In the instant cases, that question is directly presented. Here, unlike Sweatt v. Painter, there are findings below that the Negro and white schools involved have been equalized, or are being equalized, with respect to buildings, curricula, qualifications and salaries of teachers, and other "tangible" factors. Our decision, therefore, cannot turn on merely a comparison of these tangible factors in the Negro and white schools involved in each of the cases. We must look instead to the effect of segregation itself on public education.

In approaching this problem, we cannot turn the clock back to 1868 when the Amendment was adopted, or even to 1896 when Plessy v. Ferguson was written. We must consider public education in the light of its full development and its present place in American life throughout the Nation. Only in this way can it be determined if segregation in public schools deprives these plaintiffs of the equal protection of the laws.

Today, education is perhaps the most important function of state and local governments. Compulsory school attendance laws and the great expenditures for education both demonstrate our recognition of the importance of education to our democratic society. It is required in the performance of our most basic public responsibilities, even service in the armed forces. It is the very foundation of good citizenship. Today it is a principal instrument in awakening the child to cultural values, in preparing him for later professional training, and in helping him to adjust normally to his environment. In these days, it is doubtful that any child may reasonably be expected to succeed in life if he is denied the opportunity of an education. Such an opportunity, where the state has undertaken to provide it, is a right which must be made available to all on equal terms.

We come then to the question presented: Does segregation of children in public schools solely on the basis of race, even though the physical facilities and other "tangible" factors may be equal, deprive the children of the minority group of equal educational opportunities? We believe that it does.

In Sweatt v. Painter, supra [339 U.S. 629, 70 S.Ct. 850], in finding that a segregated law school for Negroes could not provide them equal educational opportunities, this Court relied in large part on "those qualities which are incapable of objective measurement but which make for greatness in a law school." In McLaurin v. Oklahoma State Regents, supra [339 U.S. 638, 70 S.Ct. 853]. the Court, in requiring that a Negro admitted to a white graduate school be treated like all other students, again resorted to intangible considerations: ". . . his ability to study, to engage in discussions and exchange views with other students, and, in general, to learn his profession." Such considerations apply with added force to children in grade and high schools. To separate them from others of similar age and qualifications solely because of their race generates a feeling of inferiority as to their status in the community that may affect their hearts and minds in a way unlikely ever to be undone. The effect of this separation on their educational opportunities was well stated by a finding in the Kansas case by a court which nevertheless felt compelled to rule against the Negro plaintiffs:

> "Segregation of white and colored children in public schools has a detrimental effect upon the colored children. The impact is greater when it has the sanction of the law; for the policy of separating the races is usually interpreted as denoting the inferiority of the Negro group. A sense of inferiority affects the motivation of a child to learn. Segregation with the sanction of law, therefore, has a tendency to [retard] the educational and mental development of Negro children and to deprive them of some of the benefits they would receive in a racial[ly] integrated school system."

Whatever may have been the extent of psychological knowledge at the time of Plessy v Ferguson, this finding is amply supported by modern authority. Any language in Plessy v Ferguson contrary to this finding is rejected.

We conclude that in the field of public education the doctrine of "separate but equal" has no place. Separate educational facilities are inherently unequal. Therefore, we hold that the plaintiffs and others similarly situated for whom the actions have been brought are, by reason of the segregation complained of, deprived of the equal protection of the laws guaranteed by the Fourteenth Amendment. This disposition makes unnecessary any discussion whether such segregation also violates the Due Process Clause of the Fourteenth Amendment.

Because these are class actions, because of the wide applicability of this decision, and because of the great variety of local conditions, the formulation of decrees in these cases presents problems of considerable complexity. On reargument, the consideration of appropriate relief was necessarily subordinated to the primary question—the constitutionality of segregation in public education. We have now announced that such segregation is a denial of the equal protection of the laws. In order that we may have the full assistance of the parties in formulating decrees, the cases will be restored to the docket, and the parties are requested to present further argument on Questions 4 and 5 previously propounded by the Court for the reargument this Term. The Attorney General of the United States is again invited to participate. The Attorneys General of the states requiring or permitting segregation in public education will also be permitted to appear as *amici curiae* upon request to do so by September 15, 1954, and submission of briefs by October 1, 1954.

It is so ordered.